Sons of Feminism

Men Have Their Say

INTRODUCED AND EDITED BY JANICE FIAMENGO

Little Nightingale Press, Ottawa, Ontario, Canada

LITTLE NIGHTINGALE
PRESS

Published by Little Nightingale Press, Ottawa, Ontario, Canada.

ISBN: 978-1-7750813-0-2 First edition paperback
ISBN: 978-1-7750813-2-6 Second edition paperback
ISBN: 978-1-7750813-1-9 First edition hardcover

Sons of Feminism is intended as part of a series, with *Daughters of Feminism*, edited by David Shackleton, as the second part to be issued in the winter of 2018. A second volume of men's stories is also in preparation.

For all the innocent men who have suffered as a result of feminist policies and the general misandry of our age

Table of Contents

by Frank Farmer. *The author explores how his generation of New Men were destined to fail as husbands and fathers, and how the Deadbeat Dad is the ultimate creation of Cultural Marxist Feminism.*

by John Savage. *The author presents his school experiences, from his earliest years to his graduate training, to show how even an unscathed life can be shadowed by experience of cultural bias.*

by Anonymous. *The author describes how his mother's mental disorder and abuse, and the unwillingness of those around her to see it, have permanently damaged him and his sister.*

by Angelica Perduta. *A transgender woman explains why she rejects the feminist narrative of male privilege.*

by Argentarii. *A father outlines his fears that feminism will sabotage his son and alienate his daughter.*

by David Shackleton. *The author analyzes how he came to recognize women's unconscious power to shame men.*

by David. *The author analyzes the series of baseless allegations that led to his firing.*

by Matt Ryan. *The author outlines the effects of second-wave feminist assumptions and policies in the workplace and in intimate relationships, with a particular focus on sexual harassment versus sexual exploitation.*

by Mal Maguire. *The author explains how, as a man who was abused by his partner, his attempts to set up counselling and other support services for male victims of domestic violence were deliberately thwarted.*

by a Military Officer. *The author explains his concerns about the weakening of the armed forces by the perceived need to showcase women's achievements and welcome significant numbers of women into the military.*

Acknowledgements

Many people encouraged me and offered useful advice along the way to producing this book. Special thanks are due to Steve Brulé, of Studio Brulé, for first offering to create the *Fiamengo File* video series, for producing it brilliantly, and for being a font of ideas, creative energy, technical assistance, and moral support. Without him, none of this would have got off the ground.

David Shackleton has been a constant intellectual support and friend. He copy-edited the manuscript and prepared it for publication, saving me many mistakes and headaches. His influence on my thinking through his writing and videos has been significant, and I have greatly appreciated many stimulating intellectual exchanges. We may not always agree, but I always come away wiser from our debates.

Over the course of preparing this book, I have benefitted from hundreds of email messages offering special insights, sharing personal experiences, and confirming the importance of telling men's stories. Thank you to all of those who have taken the time to write, and especially to those with whom I have had long-term exchanges. In addition to those who contributed essays to this project, I am grateful to Anthony Maradin, Andrew Balog, Christine Malcolm, Davy, Dean Hedges, Diana Sitek, James Morris, Jenny Achuthan, Jeremy Swanson, Kevin Flanagan, Pete Saueracker, Stephen Doyle, Tina Russell, and Tim Murray.

I have made many valuable friends in the men's rights movement. I am especially grateful to Paul Elam, founder of *A Voice For Men*, for his stalwart encouragement across the miles, and to Mike Buchanan, founder of the political party Justice 4 Men and Boys, for organizing the 2016

International Conference on Men's Issues, where I first envisioned this book whole.

My father, Vince Fiamengo, and husband, David Solway— neither of whom has ever given a thought to men's rights— are two of the best men in the world, living proof that feminism has it all wrong.

Introduction – Being Male in a Feminist Culture

Janice Fiamengo

There's no easier way to get yourself labeled a kook or a hater than to say that you're an advocate for men's rights (or "men's issues," as some like to say in an attempt to lower the derision level).[1] Empathy for male suffering is one of our society's biggest taboos, and those who break it are often rebuked by being told that, whatever men might suffer, women suffer far more, as if human empathy were a zero-sum game.[2] If men are so powerful, one wonders, how come it is so difficult to speak about men's problems? [3]

Some advocates for men bend over backwards to try to pre-empt the usual dismissals and rebuttals, emphasizing that they recognize that women still have many challenges in our society and that they support women wholeheartedly in their efforts to achieve equality. Such professions, no matter how sincere (and in my experience, they are almost *always* sincere), don't seem to help: on the contrary, often they make detractors even more angry, leading them to charge men's advocates with duplicity and dishonesty as well as woman-hatred, that most damning of accusations.[4]

Even the acronym MRA (Men's Rights Activist) has now become a slur, as in "MRA! Go away!" chanted by protesters at men's events. For years, whenever the men's advocacy group I belong to has tried to host a speaker at my university campus—including such gentle souls as scholar Paul Nathanson or equity feminist journalist Cathy Young—

students calling themselves the Revolutionary Student Movement or the Proletarian Feminist Front put up posters calling on the university community to "Join the Fight Against MRA Reactionaries!" [5] Note the assumption that caring about men's issues makes one a "reactionary." Our group's desire to talk sympathetically about men's lives outside of a feminist framework caused these students such outrage that they regularly tore down our posters, blocked the entranceways to rooms where talks were being held, and pulled the fire alarm to disrupt the speaker.

It is generally accepted in our society that men have it easy. According to our dominant cultural narrative, men are "privileged." They hold power, including power over women, and they have used that power throughout history to oppress women.[6] They are the decision makers in our societies, and they make decisions that benefit men and disadvantage women.[7] Men's voices carry the weight of centuries of authority, and they use that authority to objectify and dehumanize women. Many men hate women, perhaps because they envy them, and the proof of their hatred is etched in our cultural history.[8] That's the story.

It doesn't matter how much evidence shows that it isn't true. It doesn't matter how many examples of male suffering and sacrifice are brought forward—or conversely, how many examples of male admiration, respect, and love for women are cited.[9] The story of male advantage and female disadvantage is a cultural narrative of such undisputed legitimacy that it seems impervious to contrary evidence.

For this introduction, I originally attempted to sum up the situation of men today in western societies: with data on such issues as male suicide, depression, homelessness, joblessness, declining numbers at post-secondary institutions, unequal treatment in family court, disproportionate criminal sentences, and experience of discrimination in hiring practices. I sought to show that the narrative of male privilege simply did not correspond to men's actual experience of falling behind in employment and education, of blatant job discrimination, of being deprived of the right to parent their children, and so on. I documented the taken-for-granted misandry that passes for informed opinion in the mainstream news, the regularity with which men (alone of all socially identifiable groups) are negatively stereotyped, the ease with which pundits dismiss and deride their issues. I sought to head off objections, shore up the men's rights position, make a watertight case that men are not merely whining about the loss of their much-vaunted privilege, but rather that men and boys have always suffered and sacrificed, have always been disposable, have always given, often out of love, a great deal of their blood, sweat, and tears.

I scrapped that introduction because it was turning into a ponderous dissertation, statistics-heavy and pedantic, and moreover one that said nothing that had not been said before by researchers who know the subject far better than I, and whom I invite you to consult to investigate the reality behind the stories in this book (please see the Appendix on Recommended Reading).

If it were a matter of presenting compelling, fact-based arguments, the myth of male privilege (and female powerlessness) would have been decisively demolished long ago, in books such as Warren Farrell's *The Myth of Male Power: Why Men are the Disposable Sex* (1993). If it were a matter of showing the dishonesty and inaccuracy of feminist statistics about rape or domestic violence or employment discrimination, Christina Hoff Sommers' *Who Stole Feminism: How Women Have Betrayed Women* (1994) and her subsequent Factual Feminist video series would have conclusively delegitimized feminism as a social scientific theory. If it were a matter of showing with abundant examples and rigorous analysis the damage done by feminist policies in the workplace, then Daphne Patai's *Heterophobia: Sexual Harassment and the Future of Feminism* (1998) would have reversed the direction of contemporary HR interventions in corporations, businesses, university classrooms, and government offices. If it were a matter of showing feminism's glaring illogic and irrational animus towards men, the smash-hit videos of anti-feminists such as Karen Straughan and Paul Elam (and many others) would have brought the whole house of cards down.[10] Yet the policies, the statistics, and the beliefs remain powerful, perhaps more powerful than ever.

Statistics can tell us only so much. Men's own accounts provide another perspective about how it feels to believe, with justification, that one is unwelcome—even despised—in one's own society.[11] We can keep telling men that they're privileged, that they have power, but the number of men able to believe that comforting myth is fast dwindling. We can keep telling men that when they articulate experiences of powerlessness and injustice, they're really just bitter about sharing power with women, but the sting of the injustice will not thereby diminish.[12] We can keep showing men that if they object to the feminist story, a massive arsenal of blame will be unleashed upon them, but that will only increase men's anger and withdrawal.[13]

I first started to wonder about men's experiences when I became a full-time university teacher in 1999. It was hard not to notice, as a Professor of English, that male numbers in the Humanities were in rapid decline and that nobody seemed to care (certainly the fact was never mentioned by anyone at the university as a concern). Men now make up only about one quarter of students who study English at my university, and they are a clear minority at universities overall (about 40% of the student body at universities across North America).[14] There are complex reasons for the male decline, but it seems indisputable that one of those reasons is a demonstrably anti-male environment in the university classroom and in the larger society.

Feminist and other sociological approaches to the study of western culture associate masculinity with violence, oppression, and unjust hierarchy; femininity, in contrast, is associated with life, love, and healing. The message in nearly every literature classroom in the country is some variation of this: women's literature should be respectfully studied as evidence of the positive contribution made by women to culture; men's literature should be critiqued as evidence of how men have oppressed women and have been responsible for the social ills of war, poverty, violence, and environmental degradation.

I began to wonder what it must be like listening to that, in all its versions, day after day, month after month, year after year—learning that women are vulnerable, courageous, and admirable while men are dangerous and despicable, being told that your sex has had it too good for too long, and that you need to apologize for that and be ashamed of it for your whole life. In campus culture as a whole, men are told that they contribute to a rape culture in which women are terrorized by male sexual violence and by men's failure to take it seriously or to act to change their "toxic masculinity."[15]

I began to speak publicly about my perception of the bias against men in academia. My lectures were often protested by feminist and social justice groups, who said that my criticisms of feminism denied the reality of rape and encouraged men to be violent.[16] When I was prevented from speaking at my own university, feminist activists were pleased that my hateful message had been silenced.[17]

I didn't (and don't) accept their account of who I am or what I know. I am neither a "rape apologist" nor a brave heroine. I merely seek to tell the truth as I understand it and to shed light on what seems to me the greatest and most under-recognized injustice of our time. To see men cruelly treated, misrepresented, and unjustly blamed in our society with no public outcry violates the commitment to fairness that my parents taught me as a child. As someone who grew up in the 1970s, in the immediate wake of the women's movement, I was the beneficiary of male willingness to end sexist discrimination and to support women in pursuing their career aspirations. I encountered nothing from my many male teachers, mentors, friends, and colleagues but decency, generosity, and commitment to excellence. I grew up in a culture in which I always knew that the men in my life cared about me and listened to me; why shouldn't women also care about and listen to men? This book is an attempt to repay a debt of gratitude to men.

When my first public talk in 2013 was posted on YouTube, my inbox was flooded with emails from men young and old who told me of their experiences. They told how they'd been falsely accused of sexual assault or harassment at their university or workplace.[18] One young man was expelled from an American university after two women complained about him; apparently, as he was told by the harassment officer, his "gaze was too intense." Another man lost his job due to the complaints of several women on his shop floor: one woman had complained because he "[stood] too close" (though he studiously avoided her from the moment he learned of the complaint) and another because he had called and spoken to her on the phone at her house (thinking they were friends) and then called again because he couldn't believe she had actually reported him to the police for that. Many young men were investigated and humiliated merely for asking girls out on dates or trying to strike up a romantic friendship, not realizing that what seemed like shy encouragement was actually an inability to say no. One man told about being publicly shamed for objecting to a teacher's assertion that all men need to be taught not to rape. One man related his experience of sexual assault by a gang of older girls when he was twelve years old.

I heard about a feminist vigilante group that drove a man out of his job and destroyed his reputation, accusing him of murder after a mentally ill woman who had been in love with him committed suicide. One man showed me irrefutable evidence of the near impossibility of advancing in his academic job while women with far fewer credentials regularly received plum positions at top-tier universities because of the push to hire women into STEM fields. Yet this man still had to attend gender and race sensitivity workshops in which he was compelled to confess his privilege as a white man.

One man told me about being beaten by the police and left permanently disabled because of a woman's false allegation; he has endured a lengthy, financially debilitating court case on trumped-up charges of resisting arrest and assaulting a police officer; it is still ongoing. Another man was accused of raping his estranged teenage daughter, who made up the story so that she wouldn't have to live at home anymore. With no evidence other than her testimony, the man was sentenced to seven years in prison.

Many men experienced terrible divorces in which they were threatened that if they objected to any of their wives' financial demands they would lose access to their children. Many never saw their children again anyway, even though they paid out hundreds of thousands of dollars in alimony and child support over the years.

I heard from young men who said that from day one in public school, they were told, explicitly and implicitly, that the lives of girls mattered more, that girls needed to be respected and treated well and supported and encouraged, and that boys didn't need or deserve that. They learned that boys needed to be reformed through lectures about the dangers of their masculinity; they had to learn that they could hurt girls, sometimes just by looking at them.

I heard from young men about what it was like to be raised by a mother who didn't like men, and who made them terrified of their own sexuality. I heard from men whose experience of abuse or neglect at the hands of a feminist mother was so extreme that it left them permanently skeptical about our culture's tendency to see women as innocent victims.

I heard from men about their anguish at being told that they were a danger to women and a blight on society, when all they had ever wanted was to love and cherish a wife and family. I heard from many young men about the difficulty of knowing how to behave around a young woman, whether *any* behavior was not harassment that might get them in serious trouble.

The messages I received totally contradicted the feminist narrative of how relatively easy it is to be male in our culture, how men have a sense of entitlement with regard to women, how men have power and women don't, and how when men are angry about feminism it's because they don't like the idea of sharing their privilege with women.

Over the years, after receiving hundreds of such emails, I came to realize that their stories weren't just for me. The idea for this book was born.

***

I received over 60 submissions in response to my question, "How has feminism affected you?" Sent from contributors in the United States, Canada, the United Kingdom, Australia, New Zealand, Thailand, Germany, the Netherlands, France, and South Africa, the stories ranged from a few paragraphs to 18,000 words, and told of loneliness, injustice, and a deep sense of alienation. For readers who believe that feminism is about gender equality, these stories offer a powerful corrective. A number of the contributors chose anonymity because of the risks associated with speaking against our cultural orthodoxy.

I couldn't include all of the submissions: the book would have been too long and probably overwhelming. It was difficult to select among the compelling, often heartbreaking stories of personal pain and insight. In the end, I chose essays that represent a cross-section of experiences and perspectives, some focusing on specific injustices and others commenting generally on the blame, ridicule, and lack of empathy directed men's way simply because they are male. And because I received so many powerful essays, a second volume is in the planning stage.

I don't expect that ideologues will change their minds upon reading these stories, but I am hopeful that some non-ideologues will hear what these men are saying and may be moved to listen more carefully to the men in their own lives when they talk about their experiences and problems.

A few general observations can be made about the contributions I received, even those I was not able to include.

First, not one of the contributors expressed any hatred of women as a sex. Most were not even particularly angry at the specific women or feminist authorities whose actions harmed them. On the contrary, most expressed love for women and the desire to protect them, which many believe to be an innate part of who they are as men. Their reaction to feminism is a profound sense of bafflement and a visceral rejection of its characterization of them as sexually violent or entitled. Many of these men declare that their deepest longing—sadly unfulfilled for a large number—is to experience a tender intimacy with a woman.

Likewise, not a single one of the contributors expressed any discomfort with the principle or practice of equality before the law. Many welcomed aspects of the feminist revolution of the 1960s, specifically concerning the liberation of both men and women from restrictive gender roles. Many were more than happy to take a more active role in parenting and devastated when they were denied the right to be a parent. Many were happy with the idea of women taking a more active role in initiating sexual relations, and frustrated to discover that most women would not do so.

Not one contributor expressed any skepticism about women's ability to compete with men intellectually or to assume leadership roles in business and government. What did cause objection was the consistent undermining of claims of equality by feminist practices of overt discrimination against men and unfair advantages for women, which many men could not help but observe at school, in the workplace, in law, and in social attitudes. For many men, these inequities have become so egregious and so long-lived as to be intolerable.

A number of the contributors to this book have been victims of violence, in some cases by female loved ones, especially mothers or girlfriends/wives. For these men, the feminist emphasis on *male violence against women*—with the corollary assumptions that males are rarely victims of violence and females almost never the perpetrators—is both a soul-searing denial of their experience and a factor in their inability to receive the help they need or even to have their suffering believed. To be a victim of violence is always terrible, but to have that experienced belittled, denied or ignored is even worse. Services for male victims are shockingly scarce in our ostensibly victim-conscious culture, and public sympathy or recognition is just as rare.

As a number of the contributors to this book note, feminism is not the sole cause of the often painful experiences related here, and in some cases it is perhaps not even the determining cause. The issue may well be more general: a culture that has always prioritized women's safety and well-being over men's. But the fact that feminist leaders and activists have not shown themselves to be actively interested in the kinds of experiences recounted here has, in my opinion, entirely undermined their claims to represent an equality movement.

It is also true, of course, that if I had sought from men accounts of positive experiences of feminism, I would have been able to find some. There are male feminists, some quite famous, who are enthusiastic about condemning male perfidy,[19] enumerating the benefits to men of joining the feminist revolution, and analyzing "Guyland" in a patronizing, negative manner.[20] The stories in this book represent the voices that are rarely heard or validated in our politically correct culture. Naysayers will claim that these stories are examples of "cherry-picking," but on the contrary they are fully representative of all that I have heard from men and observed with my own eyes over the past years. I affirm that they will resonate with many, and that there is nothing peculiar or idiosyncratic about them. On that basis, those who claim to care about equality and justice should pay them heed.

Men have always known that, under certain circumstances like war, dangerous work, or threats to family, their lives are expendable. Most men, for physiological and psychological reasons, have been willing to accept that reality in exchange for the basic social recognition that once came with it. To be told, now, that not only are their lives still expendable but that their very existence is often unwanted, and that they must constantly apologize for and unlearn their toxic masculinity, is an assault on male dignity that has become unendurable for more and more men.

What happens to men when their sense of worth and purpose are actively denied and undermined by the culture at large? These accounts tell that story.

We ignore such accounts at our grave peril, for a society cannot flourish if it tells men that they do not matter. It makes pragmatic sense to listen to men's concerns—but I hope that readers of this book will listen for other reasons as well, out of empathy and love.

—April 2017

Notes

[1] For a representative if particularly unsympathetic feminist response to men's rights activism, see Amanda Marcotte, "The solution to MRA problems? More feminism." *The Daily Dot* 19 January 2015. https ://www.dailydot.com/via/mra-problems-feminism/. Referring to men's rights activists as "a loose coalition of men embittered that they're not getting as much tail as they believe they're due and men embittered after having their wives up and leave against their wishes," Marcotte could not find a single issue on which men's rights activists had anything legitimate to say: "They're so wrong about everything," she quipped, "they're wrong even when they're right."

[2] In "Why I hate men," feminist Julie Bindel, after alluding to the "millions" of incidents of male violence and sexual abuse against women as the reason for her hatred, pre-empted reasoned response: "Before the misogynists start ranting on about how many men are abused by women, how many women kill their children, etc, etc, don't bother. Every piece of credible research produced in every country in the world where this work has been done shows that sexual and domestic violence is committed overwhelmingly by men against females." Only a misogynist, according to Bindel, would seek to exonerate men from their collective characterization as the killers and abusers of women. She didn't cite the "credible research" because she couldn't. Sober statistics demonstrate that men and women are both capable of violence, and that indeed women are more likely than men to kill their children. See Julie Bindel, "Why I hate men." *The Guardian* 2 November 2006. https://www.theguardian.com/commentisfree/2006/nov/02/whyihatem en.
For a factual article decisively rebutting Bindel's claims, see Cathy Young, "Hope Solo and the Surprising Truth about Women and Violence," *Time* 25 June 2014. http://time.com/2921491/hope-solo-women-violence/

Citing national surveys of domestic violence, Young notes that researchers have consistently found that "women were just as likely as men to report hitting a spouse and men were just as likely as women to report getting hit." Moreover, Young points out, studies show that women are "at least as likely as men to kill their children—more so if one counts killings of newborns—and account for more than half of child maltreatment perpetrators." This article has many useful references for those wishing to delve more deeply into the reality of male and female violence.

[3] For an excellent discussion of what he calls an "empathy gap" in western culture, see Glen Poole, "Nine out of ten victims of police-related deaths are male. Who cares?" *InsideMan* 24 July 2015. http://www.inside-man.co.uk/2015/07/24/nine-out-of-ten-victims-of-police-related-deaths-are-male-who-cares/ Poole highlights the gendered nature of news reporting by showing how when men or boys are killed or injured, they are referred to as "people," while when women or girls are killed or injured, their sex is specified. The only time men and boys are singled out by sex in media reports is when they have committed a crime or perpetrated an atrocity. Thus empathy for male people is consistently minimized while animus against them is heightened. Empathy for women and girls is taken for granted.

[4] For a typical example of feminist rage at men's attempts to declare solidarity with women while articulating discomfort at being held personally responsible for the evil that some men do, see Andrea Dworkin, "I Want a 24 Hour Truce During Which There is No Rape." Vancouver Rape Relief and Women's Shelter. http://www.rapereliefshelter.bc.ca/learn/resources/i-want-24hour-truce-during-which-there-no-rape. For Dworkin, the only acceptable stance for a non-violent man is to embrace the harshest of feminist judgments on male perfidy.

[5] See "Join the Fight Against MRA Reactionaries! CAFE Has No Place in Our Communities." 15 March 2016. http://mer-rsm.ca/join-the-fight-against-mra-reactionaries-cafe-has-no-place-in-our-communities/

[6] For a pithy articulation of the commonly held view, see Thomas Tudor, "Rabble Rouser: Men have made a mess of society." *Courier-Post* 25 March 2015. http://www.courierpostonline.com/story/opinion/readers/2015/03/25/rabble-rouser-men-made-mess-society/70455508/

---

[7] For an articulation of the view that men are powerful and women powerless (and that therefore hatred of men is both justifiable and harmless), one could read nearly any article by feminist columnist Jessica Valenti, but one good example is her "Feminists Don't Hate Men, But It Wouldn't Matter if We Did." *The Guardian US* 13 March 2015. https://www.theguardian.com/commentisfree/2015/mar/13/feminists-do-not-hate-men

[8] For perhaps the most comprehensive expression of this viewpoint, see Andrea Dworkin's brilliant and deranged *Woman Hating: A Radical Look at Sexuality*. E. P. Dutton Publishers, 1974.

[9] A number of male authors have made the case that the history of humanity, perhaps particularly of western societies, demonstrates the male imperative to protect women and children through male sacrifice. Tim Goldich makes a strong case for male sacrifice as a cultural norm in his *Loving Men, Respecting Women: The Future of Gender Politics* (2011). Herbert Purdy has argued in *Their Angry Creed: The Shocking History of Feminism and How it is Destroying Our Way of Life* (2016) that "Social leadership by men was a tacit, natural development, born of aeons of natural selection for survival that morphed into men becoming the law-making, law-enforcing agents within developing nations, which not only had to be protected from outside attack, but often from power struggles within" (92). The protection of women and children was a key objective, and traditional patriarchal societies, far from being woman-hating, were (and remain) focused on the well-being and safety of women. David Shackleton argues in *The Hand that Rocks the World: An Inquiry into Truth, Power, and Gender* (2015) that men's physical power has been consistently balanced by women's significant moral power, the power to shame and influence men.

[10] There are many excellent YouTube video series on men's issues. In addition to the aforementioned, my thinking about masculinity and culture has been shaped and deepened by the work of Diana Davison, John the Other, Janet Bloomfield, Lucian Valsan, and Tim Goldich, among others.

[11] A startling example of feminist indifference to male troubles is exemplified in feminist Jane Caro's dismissal of recent concerns about boys falling behind in school (fully documented in Christina Hoff Sommers' must-read *The War on Boys*). According to Caro, boys don't bother to work hard in school because they know they don't need to; the world outside the classroom is biased in their favor. See "How to help

boys do better at school. Stop giving them a leg-up in the outside world." *Life & Style* 15 August 2016. http://www.stuff.co.nz/life-style/life/83181546/How-to-help-boys-do-better-at-school-Stop-giving-them-a-leg-up-in-the-outside-world

[12] Journalist Rose Hackman, who was surprised that every time she wrote about gender issues, men wrote to say that they felt "wronged—silenced, even," devoted an (astoundingly under-researched) article to exploring men's experiences in a feminist culture, concluding that most of what felt like disadvantage was merely the discomfort of having one's "sense of entitlement" removed. Get over it, men, was the clear message. See Rose Hackman, "'I didn't choose to be straight, white, and male': Are modern men the suffering sex?" *The Guardian* 5 September 2016. https://www.theguardian.com/world/2016/sep/05/straight-while-men-suffering-sex-feminism

[13] For an excellent overview of male confusion and withdrawal—and their negative impact on women—see Milo Yiannopoulos, "The Sexodus, Part 1: The Men Giving Up on Women and Checking Out of Society." *Breitbart* 4 December 2014. http://www.breitbart.com/london/2014/12/04/the-sexodus-part-1-the-men-giving-up-on-women-and-checking-out-of-society/; and Milo Yiannopoulos, "The Sexodus, Part 2: Dishonest Feminist Panics Leave Male Sexuality in Crisis." *Breitbart* 9 December 2014. http://www.breitbart.com/london/2014/12/09/the-sexodus-part-2-dishonest-feminist-panics-leave-male-sexuality-in-crisis/

[14] A 2013 study by two economists at MIT found that far fewer men are pursuing higher education than women: women born after 1975 are "roughly 17% more likely than their male counterparts to attend college and nearly 23% more likely to complete a four year degree." Because education is intimately related to lifetime income and social status, the prospects for men—and particularly for their sons, as the study explores, because boys in single-mother households are more negatively affected than girls—are bleak: "Recent cohorts of males are likely to face diminished employment and earnings opportunities and other attendant maladies, including poor health, higher probability of incarceration, and generally lower life satisfaction" (7). Such results are not unique to America, the authors indicate. See David Autor and Melanie Wasserman, "Wayward Sons: The Emerging Gender Gap in Labor Markets and Education." *Third Way*. 20 March 2013. http://economics.mit.edu/files/8754. Accessed 15 February 2017.

[15] The idea that masculinity is "toxic" or in some other sense harmful and pathological has now become widespread. Many colleges and universities in North America offer programs for young men to unlearn or re-think their deformed humanity. For an overview of such programs, see Lily Dane, "Look out, Men: Your Toxic Masculinity Is Now the Focus of Progressive Wrath." *The Daily Sheeple* 18 January 2017. http://www.thedailysheeple.com/look-out-men-your-toxic-masculinity-is-now-the-focus-of-progressive-wrath_012017. The University of Regina, which hosts a Man Up Against Violence program to encourage men to take responsibility for ending violence against women, offered a "Masculinity Confession Booth" in March of 2017. It encouraged both men and women to 'fess up to the manner in which they had reinforced what is called "hypermasculinity": *"We have all reinforced hypermasculinity one way or another regardless of our gender!! ...Come and share your sins so we can begin to discuss how to identify and change our ways !!!"* For the most explicit delineation of masculinity as a form of sickness, see the Institute for the Prevention and Treatment of Mascupathy. https://mascupathy.org/what-is-mascupathy/

[16] For an overview of the anger stirred by my anti-feminist talk at Queen's University in 2014, see "Institutions of Higher Indoctrination," *Studio Brule*, 21 October 2014. https://www.youtube.com/watch?v=-jEQYHAFfjg

[17] Two feminist activists (one a university professor) argued on Steve Paikin's TV Ontario show "The Agenda" that protestors had the right to shut down my talk at the University of Ottawa because it was anti-feminist. "The Agenda," 13 May 2014. http://tvo.org/video/programs/the-agenda-with-steve-paikin/free-speech-at-what-cost

[18] The website SAVE (Stop Abusive and Violent Environments) provides a voluminous compendium of fact-based articles documenting the lack of due process and the denial of the presumption of innocence for young men accused of sexual misconduct on university campuses across North America. For a good overview of the problem that now confronts those who care about equality before the law, see Sonja Sasser's "The War Our Sons (and Daughters) Now Face on College Campuses." *Politichicks* 3 February 2017. http://politichicks.com/2017/02/war-sons-daughters-now-face-college-campuses/. See also an editorial by KC Johnson and Stuart Taylor, "Students Accused of Campus Sexual Assault Are now Guilty until Proved Innocent." *Los Angeles Times* 3 March 2017. http://www.latimes.com/opinion/op-ed/la-oe-johnson-taylor-campus-sexual-assault-20170303-story.html

[19] Some men are even willing to insist that women have a *right* to hate men. See Anthony J. Williams' blog post, "Women have a right to hate men." https://medium.com/@anthoknees/women-have-a-right-to-hate-men-df41b4de3842#.txs66147k

[20] Michael Kimmel has made a career of belittling men who object to feminist theory and arguing for their need to reform according to feminist dictates. See Michael Kimmel, *Guyland: The Perilous World Where Boys Become Men*. New York: HarperCollins, 2009.

SECTION ONE – THE PERSONAL IS THE POLITICAL

Chapter 1 – A Son of Feminism

Pat Kambhampati

An immigrant to America from India compares his experiences with racism to his experiences with gender discrimination in order to show why the latter harmed him more severely.

I write this chapter for my father and for my sons. Why should their lives matter any less than the lives of women? This has become the unexamined question of our time. As a son of feminism myself, I offer my life as a case study in the hope that my sons' lives will be different.

I was born in India to a progressive leftist family. We moved from India to the USA when I was four, speaking no English. I started school at age five in Minnesota in 1975. It was the era of Gloria Steinem and Marlo Thomas style "Women's Libbers." My mom and teachers seemed enthusiastic about them, and so was I as a child. We were all big Mary Tyler Moore fans, and the women's movement seemed cool. In 1985 I attended an elite private school with a lot of wealthy families and some middle-class Asian immigrant families. The leftist-feminist atmosphere did not admit much intellectual variance, and by the time I got to college, the lack of intellectual diversity was even stronger, and the focus on gender feminism above all other ideologies even more apparent.

For my entire youth, from 1975-1992, I was surrounded by feminism and feminists and it was all fine with me. I agreed with the idea of women's rights and had empathy for my feminist friends. But little things bothered me even as a child. Already, back then, I was a rationalist egalitarian and so I wondered, why feminism? Why not egalitarianism? I had no idea how much this question would come to define my life and the lives of others.

From 1992 onward I spent my life as a reason-driven egalitarian. It is easy to discuss ideas and write words, but it is harder to live principles. When my wife and I had children, I wanted to share fully with her, in large part out of a commitment to fairness. As a grown man with a family, I now have my elderly mother living with us. I mention these points because experience has shown me that any man who questions feminism is personally attacked, usually through allegations that he hates women or is a loser who lives in his mother's basement. On the contrary, my mother lives in my basement because I am committed to caring for her and for all the women in my life.

What does it mean to me to be a son of feminism? The simplest answer is that it means that my life is fundamentally less important than it would be if I were female. It is right there in the name. I do not want to hear any clauses or conditions or assumptions. It is right there in the name. When I hear of women's liberation, I think it is offensive that my father is assumed to have enslaved my mother. When I hear of women's rights, I see that your daughter has more rights than my sons, and no one cares. When I think of campaigns to end violence against women, I think why not campaigns to end violence in general? And it is this last part that becomes particularly personal and will be the focus of my chapter.

It all came to a head in 2013. That was the year the Berlin Wall broke for me, the year I finally heard feminists say "Let them eat cake." In that year, I experienced a life-threatening event (albeit for the second time) that was for me the final straw. Suddenly I needed confirmation that my life mattered, not because I had made significant work achievements—which I have—but because it had value on its own.

In 2013, feminists were everywhere on the internet, making angry claims about rape culture, online harassment, safe spaces. Everything was "rapey."

Hearing such language from (mostly) straight white women of the first world finally gave me the impetus to ask, "What about me? Don't I matter as a colored male? Or do only white females matter?" Perhaps it was my Rosa Parks moment. I was tired of sitting at the back of the metaphorical bus.

As an Indian, I understand the caste system. That has helped me to understand other forms of caste as well. Even as a young person, I could see caste where others did not. I was born a Hindu Brahmin, at the top of one caste system. When I observed the culture around me in the 1970s and 1980s, it became clear that I was fairly low on the "value of life" caste system practiced in Minnesota. Since then, I have transitioned to a high point on a different caste system, that of academic success and professional accomplishment. So my life does matter in the classic male sense of the achiever, the provider. But what if I were less successful in my work life? I think of those men, the men immigrating and driving taxis, the men working in construction, working on fishing boats. Their work is low-paying, degrading, often dangerous and dirty. In what sense do their lives matter?

Here are my specific memories of childhood as a son of feminism. My main point of comparison is to experiences with race and racism. As an Indian immigrant, I encountered a world in which I had to play the role of the "nigger" and the "Injun" to neighborhood boys whilst being beaten and chased. Those experiences were bad. They were formative in my life to this day. But the key point is that others cared about such experiences; racism was not simply accepted and approved. Indeed one's family always cares—if they are aware. And by 1980 people generally cared about serious racism. By 2017 dealing with racism has devolved into mere virtue signaling. But that is not the point of this story: the point is to compare my fairly egregious experiences with race to my similarly egregious experiences with gender.

In school in the 1970s, all the teachers were women and they evidently preferred girls and at best tolerated boys. Teachers would say, "Never hit a girl," which raised the question of "Don't boys matter?" In any altercation between a boy and a girl, the girl was always believed. In grade school there was a gang of girls who would chase down boys in the playground and grab their genitals. It was always a pack against one. Later on I learned that this is how girls tend to act as predators. At no point did any teachers ever intervene in such attacks. Indeed I could see how these feminist-seeming teachers ignored and dehumanized boys. I could see this because I was smart and well behaved, and was always in the background watching. I noted how my more outgoing male friends were ignored. I never forgot that.

In grade six, I attended middle school at one of the best schools in the United States. At age 12, I was tricked into following a group of three older girls down a hallway, where they pinned me down and molested me. At this time of life, boys tend to mature more slowly than girls. To make matters worse, I was the youngest in my class, the smallest, and very immature emotionally. These traits are common for boys who are intellectually advanced, as I was. But at that time there was no sense of caring or compassion for boys at all, certainly not for those of us who found the world an intimidating place. Certainly not for those of us who were gentle little kids who merely wanted to learn about animals and aerodynamics and such. While that event itself is of some note, the more interesting point is that I kept no memory of it for many years and no idea that I even merited any empathy. Expecting empathy made about as much sense as a Hindu Untouchable thinking his life mattered as much as a Brahmin. I did not even remember what had happened to me until much later.

In ninth grade I attended one of the top private high schools in the state. It was filled with CEO kids, and kids who would go on to Ivy League colleges. As older kids, we were apparently suitable for indoctrination, and it being a progressive school, we learned about all the bad things men do to women. My female classmates were aspiring feminists. At an elite school attended by future Wellesley students, the young women discussed gender in feminist terms, and the boys simply had to listen. Mostly I ignored all that and kept doing what I did: BMX, computers, science, and punk rock.

In 1988, I left my private high school to attend another fancy private school, this time one of the best colleges in the US. Here, things got even more extreme. For Freshman Week in college I arrived with excitement to meet people, hopefully even to talk to girls. That week included one of the first "Take Back the Night" marches on a university campus. I recall hearing girls say "All men are potential rapists." When I questioned the logic and rhetoric, I was verbally attacked for it. It is generally considered that verbal abuse can be as harmful as physical abuse, but our culture tolerates women and girls verbally abusing men and boys all the time. I recall female students at the student center discussing cutting edge feminist ideas as expressed by radical activists like Andrea Dworkin and academics such as Catharine MacKinnon. Both emerged from Minnesota in the 1980s and were all the rage when I was a student. Both women said extreme things about men, and I never heard any girl speaking against them. Nobody ever said their hatred of men was a bad thing. I only heard girls saying how exciting it all was.

In this context of anger and blame, the feminist anti-porn movement emerged. Essentially the feminist movement in the 1980s took the opportunity to demonize all of male heterosexuality. The girls from school took the most outrageous examples of pornography and pasted them all over the halls to show how terrible male sexuality could be unless controlled by women. No man dared speak against the man-hating messages. Only girls' lives mattered. Only girls' feelings mattered. Only girls' sexuality was a good thing; boys' was a problem to manage. The net result was that I simply turned off my sexuality. I did this for much of my life.

Through this process, from age 4 to 22, I had no conscious awareness of what had been done to me personally and socially. The reason is simple: one only asks questions that are within the bounds of acceptability. Untouchables in India do not ask, "What about me?" and boys in feminist environments do not ask, "What about me?"

Following college, I went on with my life in science in the 1990s. My father died of a sudden heart attack when I was 22, so I never had a father figure to talk to as I entered adulthood. In the 1990s, I saw my peers transform their mothers' 1970s Women's Lib culture into modern feminism. I saw them discuss violence against women, the sexual assault of women, women's reproductive rights, the sexual objectification of women, all the ideas subsumed under the umbrella of patriarchy theory. I would ask about violence against men, men's reproductive rights, men's right to parent their children after divorce, the objectification of men. All of these questions were met with mockery and hostility, always on an emotional level and never on an intellectual level. As a science-oriented boy, I could dance the intellectual arguments like a ballet dancer. But I had no abilities at the emotional angle that seemed to be the only part that mattered. Nothing mattered more than the feelings of women, especially of rich straight white women.

That was the message from the 1970s to the 1990s. We boys learned it well then, and we never spoke of it afterwards.

The 1990s era of feminism in the universities was my era, my formative time. Then it seemed to go away. I went on and lived my life, tried to achieve, and was successful. I took a tenure-track position at an elite Canadian university. In 2008, the stress and intense work associated with achieving tenure caused me to become diabetic, which resulted in a number of near-fatal hypoglycemic events. The second was in 2013. When I recovered from this crisis, I could no longer go on ignoring my culture's hateful messages about men. I wanted to feel that my life mattered—not my career, not my life because of my career. My life on its own merit. I had never felt that. I know my dad never felt that. He had the male privilege of dying to provide for his family. He did not even get a proverbial gold watch upon retirement because he never made it that far.

2013 was a magical time in a nightmarish sense. Consider artistic images from James Ensor or Francis Bacon for impressions. 2013 was the year of "Yes All Women" and "rape culture." It was the era of internet third-wave feminism. Men had privilege. Men benefited from sexually terrorizing women. The harm to a person like me who was actually molested by girls was deep. Imagine Clockwork Orange as a point of reference. I had internalized all the dehumanization over the first 40 years of my life. But no more. Having nearly died twice, and having two sons of my own to protect, I could no longer accept it.

2013 – 2015 was the period in which I finally spoke out about feminism and men's humanity. I did it because of the reasons above. What I saw on Facebook and YouTube (first with Janice Fiamengo and Karen Straughan) was that others were questioning too. Others were having their Rosa Parks moments. It seemed to happen like a wave. When we spoke of our experiences we received hatred, scorn, death and rape threats from feminists. Even then, I thought that feminism could be reformed. I had no idea that the questions I and others raised on social media from 2013 to 2015 would be akin to pulling a thread on a sweater and watching the whole thing unravel before our eyes.

In hindsight, the internet discussions of feminism at that time seem a kind of Arab Spring. This was a time when people who had long been ignored by feminism finally stood up and stated their "lived experience," that notable phrase that was the centerpiece of feminism but which only included the lived experience of elite white women, the women and girls from my rich private high school and college, the modern version of the suffragettes, concerned only about themselves.

My own inclination is to focus on the ideas and practices of treating humans equally. I do not like to focus on feelings, even mine. I prefer to think about principles. But this book is about personal experience, so I will not belabor the intellectual arguments against feminism.

What was the role of feminism in my life? Feminism was a cultural force that had the effect of dehumanizing me in a manner far more severe than the experience of racism that people make TV movies about. The key difference between feminism and racism is that people cared about the effects of racism on us. But nobody cared about the effects of feminism on its sons.

Until now.

Chapter 2 – My Father

Krish

The author explains how, after his father's suicide attempt, he came to re-evaluate his family's understanding of male responsibility and female powerlessness.

I turned my back on my father, and I now feel ashamed for having done so. That was my own behavior and is my own responsibility, but I subscribed to the culture of my family, which I now reject wholeheartedly.

Our family is aggressively liberal and values emotional reality over analytical truth. Among our many biases, we go to great lengths to attribute blame to men and virtue to women. There seems to be a belief that masculinity is "toxic," a disease to be cured. "Kill the Indian, save the man," has become "Kill the man, save his inner woman." In this gynocentric worldview, men are defective females. Men's weakness is despised, their sexuality demonized and their merit denied. In a twist of irony, honest admission and accounting of gender differences is regarded as sexist, and we blindly enforce cultural norms that favor female interests. Perhaps a healthier attitude would be to admit the differences between the genders, the virtues and unique challenges both face, and account for these differences with empathy and understanding.

I personally value gender equality, but our current worldview is very much opposed to it. A simple way to observe the bias is to ask the question: why are more men in prison? The answer is obvious: because they commit more crimes. Why is virtually every new invention created by men? The answer is just as clear: because women are oppressed and men are dominating them. When something good happens, God is great, but when there is a problem, the Lord is working in mysterious ways. It is incredible to see the number of women who derive material benefit from male brilliance and sacrifice, then turn around and denigrate those who achieve results they themselves have never even endeavored to contribute towards. It is cultural blasphemy to admit this.

This culture finds it ludicrous and laughable that men can also face problems of their own, as the conventional wisdom considers women the sole victims of society. It is true that many situations favor men and that men hold more positions of leadership or overt authority. However, while the economy favors a male disposition, social norms favor the feminine. Why are the majority of suicides male? My father almost succeeded in taking his own life, while my sister and mother have never attempted to do so. I have stood beside my father while I watched his heart flatline in the emergency room. Why did my father feel that death was preferable to life? The politically-correct narrative forbids truth, stifling inspection by blaming his actions on personality and psychiatric disorder.

I too blamed my father. I blamed my father for traveling to India to get an arranged marriage, as I saw it as an act of cowardice. All the marital issues he faced were, therefore, his own fault. But women are far more discriminating in their love than men are. Perhaps I should also have considered how many American girls in the 1970s would have given a shorter Indian man the time of day. While plenty of women are frustrated by unwanted romantic attention, how many would prefer the feeling of becoming an adult without ever having been desired?

What's worse, where could a man like my father find sympathy for this misfortune, which was beyond his control? He grew up in a world starved of the most basic forms of affection. I believe this to be his greatest male "privilege": he internalized the understanding that he would only become worthy of romantic affection if and while he was in a position of prominence, which forced him to take far more risks, create, and work harder than those around him to earn similar social validation. Through my own romantic experiences, I've learned a similar lesson, albeit to a much lesser degree.

When my parents would fight, I was quick to label my dad as the oppressor. He would yell at my mom and tell her how to behave. There's something about watching your mother cry that makes you ready to do whatever needs to be done to fix the situation. I could feel her desperation and immediately sympathized with her pain. She was an abused housewife struggling to calm a crazed and angry man. While this is part of the truth, it is far from the full picture.

With my sister, too, the view was too simple. He was the angry father and she was the innocent victim-daughter. He was pressuring her to succeed in school and he controlled her activities. She was fighting for her independence. He threw a pan at my sister once and demanded she leave the house, which we all considered an unforgivable act of violence, cementing our perception of him as an abusive man.

Missing from our calculation was the fact that he was sitting in his own house, and she was acting in remarkably emotionally aggressive ways towards somebody who was recovering from depression and clearly under extreme duress. Women are entitled to emotional "safe spaces," but as a man he could have no expectation of peace in his own home.

There is a difference in how men and women naturally relate to others. Men express themselves physically: with my guy friends, wrestling and roughhousing are casual. Bruises are a part of life, and conflict is without animosity, just like banter. However, we talk less of our emotions, because it is selfish to burden others with one's own pain. Women tend to be the other way around: when women get in your face, scream and blame hysterically, that's psychological violence because it makes it impossible to be calm or happy. In this male worldview, my sister is a particularly abusive individual: I would literally rather take a physical beating than drive alone with her during one of her tantrums. As crazy as that may sound, aggression can only be measured comparatively, based on what the recipient would prefer. I believe throughout his life, a major reason for a man like my father to bury himself in his computers has been to disassociate from social tension and instead live in a world that is logical and sane.

It was my mother's passion to raise us, and she devoted herself to managing the household and looking after my sister and me. It was my father's steel but my mother's warmth that forged me into the man I am today. To a degree no outsider will ever appreciate, any accolades I earn are the result of the strength her love has given me. I can only imagine how hard it must have been for her to manage Dad's temperament. But on the other hand, if mom was so abused, why did she not leave? Because the image of an abused woman garners sympathy, we forgive her lack of agency and attribute her decisions to others. Why could she not provide for herself? That suggestion is absurd because we all knew that she was nowhere near as capable of self-reliance as my father, who was happy to care for her. We again blame her upbringing for this asymmetry in performance, entirely ignoring the fact that she was the beautiful and popular child of a wealthy landlord, with enormous luxury and privilege handed to her, which my dad had to earn for himself. In marriage, she was looking for a man who was strong, successful, and could provide for her and face the world on her behalf—all of which Dad could and did do. The reality, which our politically-correct culture prevents us from admitting, is that she valued security and material comforts, lacked personal direction, and has fared far better in life with my father than without.

There is a consistent sexism here: my father and mother each had distinct roles and were required to manage each other's neuroses, but her emotional outbursts were forgiven and her shortcomings were attributed to upbringing or other people rather than to her own character. We bestowed no such excuses on my father. We held him responsible, as the man of the house, for his own actions and those of others, instinctively expecting him to be in control and maintain composure.

My sister was as tempestuous as Dad, but was triggered differently. Dad typically was overzealous in his enforcement of rules that he believed to be in our best interest, while my sister was triggered more by an emotionally self-centered worldview. My sister's response to input was simple: if somebody approved of her, they were right, and if they made her feel bad, they were wrong. It was dangerous for any of us to challenge her self-image of perfection, no matter how reasonable the criticism. My father and sister's poor communication and terrible relationship is both of their faults. However, the expectations required of them were starkly different.

In the unwritten social contract, being a father means that you must provide for your daughter, ensure her safety and that she has every access to opportunity; she expected all of these and her expectations were met in spades. What are a daughter's obligations in return? Dad had spent 30 years of schooling to become a surgeon, and was commuting to his private medical practice for an hour each day, working to afford a private school education for a daughter who forged her own report cards to hide the fact that she wasn't attending classes. And if she was so deeply unhappy, what stopped her from leaving, living separately, providing and working for herself? A good friend of mine grew up in a trailer park where his drunken stepfather would often whip him with a belt. At the age of 14 he ran away, staying with friends and taking up work. I met him at SpaceX where he was happily designing rocket engines. His abuse was far starker and yet he remembered his father with far less resentment than my sister seems to harbor towards ours.

To this day, 18 year old boys enter into a draft in which they may be expected to fight, kill, and die for others. My sister was a young adult with every benefit of intelligence, affluence, education, and beauty. In the worst case, why did we not just assume there was a difference in personality, suggest that my sister sever ties, provide for herself, and amicably part ways with my father? In this sanctimonious culture of false egalitarianism, we give lip service to equality yet infantilize women as helpless victims rather than see them as individuals responsible for their own happiness.

Dad had glaring social faults which we all openly acknowledged and condemned. But he also was brilliant, hardworking, and used his rare talents to fulfill a burden of competence not required of others. He received plenty of abuse in his career, due to dishonest business partners and stresses from work, which he had to face alone.

Furthermore, when my mother or sister was upset, they could complain and receive sympathy in a way that my father could not. While he was never particularly good at expressing himself, this is also because others were less interested in listening, and because he was in a social role where he was less permitted to express it. Men must stifle their emotions out of necessity, because to a greater degree than for women, their social worth is measured by their ability to provide and the extent to which they are in control. If you're entitled to receive affection only when you're the one helping others, crying is seen as selfish and effusive and only diminishes your own character.

In effect, we value female emotional pain over male material contribution. Though extremely sexist, the reason for this attitude is pragmatically useful. Male sacrifice is foundational to any productive society and therefore encouraged, whereas female suffering is unnecessary oppression. If a soldier dies in combat, he's a hero; if a woman is forced into prostitution, she's a victim. A modern understanding of patriarchy laments a world in which women were confined to household labor, but conveniently forgets their husbands in the coal mines, dying from black lung.

Dad was in a marriage where he had to provide, yet was likely deprived of romantic intimacy. As an aside, I've noticed an interesting pattern in suicidality—I have yet to see a suicide attempt by a man with a good sex life. I believe sex is an instinctively and particularly important part of male mental well-being; if it significantly influences whether a man desires life (or will risk his own in its pursuit), then perhaps it should be treated as a legitimate biological need. Men are naturally hardwired to believe that sex is at the core of a good relationship, while women tend to crave emotional support and commitment. Both views are essential to romance and neither is intrinsically better. Yet while everyone knows that a woman can never be obliged to provide sex, our culture is asymmetric in nonetheless expecting men to be committed to provide financially and emotionally. Had my father strayed into an affair or paid for sex, he would be seen as a monster. We would blame him and side with my mother. In a divorce, we would expect him to split his wealth evenly, and furthermore celebrate his loss as a victory, ignoring the fact that he made far more personal and significant contributions to its creation.

The result was that he was locked into a stressful and demanding career, with asymmetric responsibilities to fulfill his side of a social contract from which we all derived benefit. He was simultaneously encumbered in two permanent relationships in which he must provide significant value towards others yet ultimately be denied very reasonable needs in return—for romantic intimacy or emotional affection. Rather than being able to rely on family support, he felt a need to shut it out, as his wife, daughter, and sister ignored his grievances and held extractive attitudes to his social role. By what means could he reach a reasonable resolution?

In reality, neither my sister nor my mother responded positively to logical engagement. Mom's sense of logic is rooted in her ephemeral emotional state, and as her emotions change, so do her beliefs. My sister is more capable of logic, but, (at least at the time) was so myopically obsessed with her own emotions as to be incapable of empathy towards others. The latter is a common female behavior which I have observed repeatedly in my own romantic life; the women I have loved both succeeded at the highest levels of education and were remarkable humans in their own right, but both had a far greater affinity for emotional reasoning over logic. This was taxing, because when they would react emotionally to situations, it placed the burden of calm rationality squarely on my shoulders and inhibited accurate communication. I think I speak for many men in wishing for great gender equality in women's willingness to hold themselves accountable to being reasonable. Admission of this grievance is considered sexist, and therefore again blames the male for female behavior. If Dad's rational conversation did not work, could he yell? Yelling at a woman was considered verbal abuse. What if he gave my sister a smacking for her poor behavior? Knowing my sister, news of her having been assaulted would have spread across our school within hours and those who never met my father, knowing nothing of the situation, would side against him. Any system of law, including social norms, must provide appropriate ways for conflict to be resolved constructively; otherwise individuals must look outside the rules to get it. I am fully confident that if we lived in a culture that had the capacity to acknowledge the issues Dad was facing, and gave him reasonable mechanisms of recourse, he would not have been driven to such an extreme form of desperation.

Dad was not crazy and he certainly was not a criminal. He was not an abusive drunk who would beat his wife when she burned the casserole. He wasn't a philanderer and clearly took his duties as a husband and a father very seriously. He loved his patients, and made his living as a doctor returning vision to those nearing blindness. Rather than squander his wealth on himself, he spent it so that we would have access to all the opportunities he had not had. If we had grown up in poverty, or had the faintest understanding of hardship, we would have considered Dad our hero. His failure was to be so thorough in solving the material problems of our life that his very presence became our greatest inconvenience.

Considering the situation in its entirety, I believe it is rational for a man to want to leave this situation of servitude even at the expense of his own life. Why were we all so unwilling to consider this?

When my aunt and uncle stepped in to help my sister and me, their intentions were genuine and we desperately needed it. But while my Aunt was loving toward me, in retrospect it is quite apparent that she fostered lifelong hatred toward my father that, at an emotional level, was in part motivated by a desire to inflict emotional pain upon him. In the time of our greatest vulnerability, we were assured that my father had always been crazy, his legitimate grievances ignored. It is no small aggression to try to forcibly confine a man to a psychiatric ward (which would have ruined his career), actively attempt to dissolve his marriage, appropriate his wealth, and foster a relationship with his children in his stead. Afterwards, we had the gall to consider his lack of compliance with our efforts as further proof of his guilt.

We were the bigots. We were so dogmatically attached to a worldview we craved to be true that we would literally rather watch our closest kin die in misery than actually listen to him. There are places in the world where women are stoned to death for premarital sex. Although our tactics differ, I can no longer say we are superior. Even skinheads and Neonazis lack the sadistic inconsistency to imagine themselves the saviors of the people they discriminate against most violently.

To my Aunt – I asked you directly if you could think of a single positive thing men do that women tend not to. You looked as though I had asked you to swallow battery acid, and gave no response. I repeated the question, and again, nothing. As I reflected, I realized that I have never heard a female member of my family concede a single positive generalization about men. I find this strange, because I can think of many things I love about women; I feel incomplete without their love in my life. Is it true that there is literally nothing good about men? And if you think so, was that relevant when you lamented my father's inability to "finish the job"? You care for boys, but I no longer believe you have the slightest love for men.

Perhaps I grant my father grace because I see myself filling his role. Although I have little wealth today, I am confident that I will be able to earn by the merits of my ideas and their diligent execution. I am naturally inclined to derive my sense of self-worth from my ability to be a source of stability and peacefulness for the people I love. But that seems foolish when those very people would denounce me and ignore all the good I do. I have come to realize that while those closest to me will care for me so long as I remain a boy, if I ever self-actualize as a man of prominence, I will become an unwitting patriarch in a family whose culture is defined by a hatred of such. Any success I experience will reaffirm their belief that the world has favored men, and I will descend to the bottom of a social hierarchy where value is determined by one's ability to claim victimhood. I will be expected to perform in the interests of others to a greater degree than they can or will do themselves. Alternately, if I pursue happiness on my own terms, I am sure to be the target of hatred as I violate a social contract I never consented to. I find the idea of controlling others abhorrent; but neither do I consent to live in a world which is so deeply biased against me. With great sadness, I have come to accept that if I am to live in a world that treats me fairly, I must sever ties to my family.

I genuinely wish I had more women in my life who see the humanity of men. My closest friends are brilliant, passionate and creative guys who are devoting their lives to building companies and solving research problems they are passionate about. Most are socially awkward and meek in politics. When we try to talk about the things we love with women we meet, the women generally get bored and move on to somebody more interesting. After years of hard work, most of us will fail. I wonder what will happen if we succeed. Will women blame us as they suddenly notice that we exist? In the meantime, I wish more would spend the time to understand what drives us and share in our love for our craft.

Chapter 3 – Finally Awake
After Fifty Years of Feminism

Allen

The author presents his Everyman story of how a divorce and its legal, cultural, and familial effects destroyed his illusions about gender equality.

What has my life been like under Feminism?

In order to answer that question I need to go back five decades, to the mid 1960s. This was when Second Wave feminism began to appear in the media and affect North American culture. Fortunately for me, I lived in a rural area about a three hour drive from Toronto, so until my late teens when I traveled to attend university, I remained blissfully unaware of the new feminist ideology spreading across the continent.

I was born in 1948, during the Baby Boom. I was the third boy of four children, with a younger sister, and we lived on a mixed farm in Western Ontario. Our family would have been described as traditional. My parents' roles were different but complementary. As soon as we three boys were old enough, we were expected to work on the farm before and after school. My younger sister helped in the house. In short, I had a simple, somewhat harsh, traditional childhood with parents who didn't divorce. Our farm had a wonderful bush and a little creek running through it. Our farm community was slow-paced and everyone knew each other. Neighborhood moms and dads were like additional parents.

Life was hard on the farm with many things still done by hand in the 1950s and 60s. Miraculously, we grew up relatively unharmed by all the demanding physical work. I went to a one-room country school for my first eight years of education (1954-62). I grew taller and stronger than most of the boys. During playtime at school, the boys bonded with the boys and the girls with the girls, but as we hit puberty (grades seven and eight), the girls wanted the boys to like them and the boys wanted girls to like them. Heterosexuality was assumed. We occasionally played "spin the bottle" when safely out of sight of the teacher.

In 1962 I traveled by bus into the nearby town to attend high school, a big change from my one-room schoolhouse. I joined the school band and the basketball team and stayed in town at my grandmother's house in order not to have to go out to the farm so often. As for boy-girl stuff, it was heaven. Gender roles were still firmly in place, and I had the good fortune of being tall and involved in both sports and the arts (basketball, school band and drama club). I think I lost my virginity by age 15. It was an age of innocence—and stupidity. Unprotected sex was common and, if pregnancy occurred, the girls were the ones shamed and blamed, usually having to drop out of school and be hidden away until the child was born, and often giving the child up for adoption at birth. I managed to escape small town life without being forced into a "shotgun wedding."

I starred on the basketball team, was president of the school band, was class president twice, and was in the Drama Club. My high school life was a 'Happy Days' dream. I was 'cool' and popular. By the end of high school I had had several dating and sexual partners.

In the fall of 1968 I was accepted into the Theatre (Acting and Directing) program of the new Fine Arts Department at York University. I minored in English and added a Minor in Film by the time I graduated in 1972. York attracted a lot of young staff, many from the U.S.A., and it was truly awesome to attend such an open, progressive liberal arts university. In my freshman year, American draft dodgers and activists crossed the border under the benevolent eye of our anti-war Prime Minister Pierre Trudeau. There were anti-war protests on the campus; Bobby Kennedy and Martin Luther King were assassinated that year. There was a full blown youth revolution under way. It was also the peak of the Sexual Revolution. The chant on campus was not "Down with The Patriarchy" but "Down with The Establishment." Women had the pill, so Free Love was proclaimed. It was a sexual bonanza for me.

From the day I arrived, the parties, drugs and drinking started. Marijuana and hashish as well as more powerful drugs—psilocybin, mescaline, LSD and several other mood-altering concoctions—swept the campus. Older conservative practices like curfews for girls and denied access to women's dorms were mocked as old fashioned, and we romped freely into each other's residence buildings to party and stay overnight. If a couple left a party together holding hands and were both inebriated and or/high, the fact that they were going off to sleep together implied "consent." Stories I'm hearing now about consent not being possible due to the woman being drunk or a girl regretting sex the next day and charging the boy with rape were never in our thoughts in 1970.

The topic of feminism definitely came up during my years at York. Girls would bring up the subject of women's inequality. Books like *The Feminine Mystique* were popular and there was a push to study more contemporary women writers in the English program. There were even some feminist activism on the campus. This was when I first heard the term "double standard." At that time guys could do pretty much whatever they liked in public, at work, at school, and in relationships, but girls were expected to defer to boys. I acknowledged they had a point, although I recall arguing that I hadn't personally arranged things that way: it was just the way things were. I was quite sympathetic to the unfair experience of girls and I wanted women to be more equal to men. I even referred to myself as a feminist.

When I think back on the late 60s and early 70s, I remember those years with fondness. But what started out as movement to bring about a better balance between the sexes became co-opted by second wave feminism and has long since ceased to be about equality or balance. Rather, it is about women dominating in every sphere and claiming the female gender as superior to the "defective" and "toxic" masculine gender. In recent years this has turned into an all-out war on men, seeking at the very least to marginalize us and, if possible, to destroy us completely.

All this freedom and independence, this glorious sexual smorgasbord as an undergraduate, was about to change.

***

In 1972, the year I graduated, I met my future wife. In 1973-74 I took my B.Ed. (Bachelor of Education) at FEUT (Faculty of Education, University of Toronto) to become an Intermediate - Senior high school teacher (Dramatic Arts and English). I got my first teaching job at a good collegiate in a Toronto suburb in September, 1974. In the spring of 1974 my future wife and I moved in together. In the summer of 1975 we were married. I was 26 and she was 22.

My (Non) Choice to Marry – Reverse Proposal

As an undergraduate, I had many girlfriends and sometimes was involved with more than one woman at a time. I suppose I was what they now call an alpha male. I transitioned into a beta provider when I married. The woman I married had almost no sexual or even dating experience. She was somewhat overweight, which might help to explain the absence of relationship experience.

She had also taken the Theatre Program at York, so we had something in common. I liked her fresh face, healthy lifestyle (didn't drink or take drugs), good health, curvy body with hourglass figure, and large breasts. In a nutshell, she had white, middle class good looks. She had never been a party girl. She had not slept around. She was therefore "marriage material." She was also very intelligent and had a love of the arts like me.

In 1974 I was enjoying co-habiting with her, but she had a different plan. She told me one day that she knew she wanted to have children, and she should get busy with that soon. Since I hadn't asked to marry her yet, she needed to let me know she would likely need to "move on," to find a man who was ready to have children ... unless I wanted to ask her to marry me, in which case she would say "Yes"! And then she and I would have kids. And that is indeed what happened. We married in July, 1975. I was innocent, trusting and naïve.

The one thing I downplayed at this moment in my life was the fact that her parents had had a very destructive divorce—carried out by her mother on her father—in the early 1960s. In order to understand a lot of what happened to me as a "Son of Feminism," you will need to hear about my mother-in-law.

My Mother-in-Law

My wife's mother was an only child and had been psychologically abused by her mother, who hated the fact that she was a girl and hated the fact that she had a child at all. Her father was away as a traveling salesman all the time. She attended a private girl's school in Toronto, and went on to earn a BA and then an MA in English Literature at Victoria College, University of Toronto.

After that she met my gentle, kind and caring future father-in-law, who had a PhD in Electrical Engineering. They met at a United Church youth group, married in the late 1940s and moved into a new house in the new suburb of Don Mills. They should have been the perfect post-war nuclear family. My wife was the middle child of three. In the early 1960s my wife's mother took it upon herself to abduct the three children and hide away at a friend's house for three weeks, leaving my father-in-law in a state of total desperation and anxiety. When she did surface, she insisted on a divorce. She simply did not want to, or could not, cope with a man in her life. The damage done to my wife and her siblings was horrendous. My wife's mother was quite literally crazy. She was diagnosed later in life with "borderline personality disorder and paranoia." She acted out her craziness at every opportunity; yet I married her daughter. I was going to be the "Knight in Shining Armor" who would rescue her from the clutches of her emotionally disturbed mother and we would live happily ever after.

My wife's mother was very interested in feminism. She hated men, repeatedly bringing books to my wife and raising the topic all the time when she visited. I didn't think much about it then, but now I see that my fate was very much tied up with the spread of Second Wave feminism, an ideology I invited into our own home with my misandric mother-in-law.

Despite having some very significant challenges and difficulties in early life, or perhaps because of these hardships, I was both an idealist and an optimist. I was trusting of others and ready to help, especially those less fortunate. It's little wonder I chose to be a teacher. I am thankful I still have these attributes. Even though it has meant I've been used, exploited and hurt, it's still better than being jaded, cynical, pessimistic and cruel. The innocence, trust and naiveté were both a blessing and a curse when it came to my marriage relationship. I simply assumed that my future wife was trustworthy. What I didn't realize—or if I did realize, I downplayed it—was that my soon-to-be wife was "selecting" me on the basis of my biological features for strong healthy offspring and my likelihood of being a good provider and protector. And that is all she was selecting me for. When she announced she was separating from me and divorcing me in the spring of 1990, it crashed down on me that she had no love for me and never had. I was merely a provider, biologically and financially, so she could acquire children for herself.

This same woman, whom I worked hard to provide for, callously and abruptly ended our marriage after 15 years (1990).

It is noteworthy that my wife pulled the plug on our marriage after almost exactly the same amount of time (15 years) as her mother had. I believe it was unconsciously programmed into her to "eject" me at the same time her mother had left her husband.

The only serious issue my wife and I had had was a conflict over disciplining the children. She essentially didn't believe in setting any limits or giving consequences. There was a lot of very wild acting out and manipulative behavior from the kids as a result. All that my wife had to offer as a reason for separating and divorcing me was to say at a Married Couples' counseling session: "I don't feel loved anymore." It was calculated on her part, planned in advance with her (feminist) woman friends. Our youngest son was then eight years old, so she calculated with confidence that everything would fall into place for her. I would be required to pay spousal and child support, and with the kids all now in school, she would not be overburdened as a single mom. I had a good permanent teaching job, and she knew from talking to her friends that she would get everything she wanted in divorce court, including full custody of the children. In a word, I was "used" for 15 years to produce three gorgeous, healthy children, and then discarded like an unnecessary utility once the kids were past early childhood.

I was ordered by Family Court to provide child support ($150,000 over the next 15 years) from 1990 until my youngest son graduated from university in 2005.

In the spring of 1990 I moved into a single room in a boarding house so the children could continue life essentially the same as before the separation. I rode a bike to work at the nearby high school and left the one car with my wife to take the family around. I felt totally helpless about the situation and developed a lot of anxiety-type depression. I learned that I was not alone. Many men in my city were going through the same thing. I sought out counseling and workshops for support and was fortunate to have two doctors start a men's group that met weekly to do activities like express our frustration and rage by hitting pillows with a tennis racket—the only thing to do in a culture that had absolutely no concern for the losses men go through when they are forced to leave their home and see their children for only a few hours a week.

All three of our children were deeply disturbed by our breakup and developed a lot of psychological issues over the ensuing years. Our oldest had a phobia about going to school and had to complete almost all her high school courses remotely from home. Our middle child (a girl) was sexually abused by an older adult in the family home and under her mother's watch. She developed anorexia, was severely depressed and suicidal and, now in her 30s, still struggles to lead a normal life. Our youngest son went right off the rails, acted out in elementary school, was diagnosed as ADHD, and was medicated and put in a behavioral program. He is still acting out and abuses drugs and alcohol now. My children relate to me only when necessary, after several requests for a response. My ex was very successful at teaching them to avoid and ignore me, to have as little to do with me as possible.

Through the 1990s I worked very hard to be a provider for my children. It was not easy. I received no support from social workers, health care professionals or friends and family. The general feeling I got from everyone was that I must have deserved to lose my marriage. The media was full of domestic violence stories, and men were always and only the perpetrators.

When I went to court (in those days we men referred to it as "The Injustice System") I found myself literally laughed at by judges. They simply pulled out the FRO (Family Responsibility Office) "Schedule of Payment" based on my gross income and ordered me to pay monthly amounts according to that 'Schedule.' I wanted Joint Custody, but at that time, for Joint Custody to be considered, both parents needed to agree to it. Because my wife didn't support Joint Custody (big surprise), the Court deemed it "not in the best interests of the children."

Demonized in the Community

All through the 1990s and until I retired from the teaching profession in 2005, I experienced an ongoing social stigmatization that was just under the surface, never overt. While I was married and a classroom teacher (1984-90) I was fully accepted everywhere in the community. But once I appeared at work, at church, and in the community as a "separated" and then a "divorced" man, I seemed to carry a dark cloud of suspicion over my head. I suspected they were thinking when they saw me: *The poor woman probably couldn't stand to live with him any longer. Thank goodness she had the strength and courage to end a bad marriage!* On the other hand, my wife was shown a lot of support when she started her teaching career and around town. She was now referred to as a "supermom" since she was carrying on parenting without a man to help with the kids. (My wife did not work until the mid-90s when she trained to be a high school teacher too.)

To make matters worse, this aura of criticism and stigmatization in the community was added to by my wife. When I would encounter a mutual friend on the street downtown, I'd notice the person would cross the street and avoid me. My wife had spread lies about me such as that I had a bad temper (I was loud and shouted during family arguments). She even opened a file with the Children's Aid Society to investigate me for possibly being violent with the children. This claim was ordered dropped by my lawyer when we found out about it. But of course the damage was done. The lie could now be spread around town, affecting my reputation at work and elsewhere in the community.

From the early 1990s until I retired in 2005, it gradually became clear to me why I was never able to move up in the school system. There was a nebulous cloud over my name. My ex-wife had a lot of support in her school teaching ventures, but my career stagnated. I also learned another reason I was not chosen for advancement in the education system. I kept hearing that the board was seeking female applicants for new positions of responsibility in order to address what they called "gender inequality." This happened multiple times through the late 90's and until I retired.

I always received top grades when my teaching was inspected by my principal, was highly creative, hardworking, rarely off sick, a big strong man with a wonderful speaking voice, passionate about the subjects I taught, loved the kids, and they loved me. I even had a good sense of humor, a tremendous asset in teaching. I should have been able to advance in the system, but I didn't.

As we approached the year 2000, I was at my prime as a teacher in terms of experience, knowledge and ability, yet I was never chosen when I applied for transfers to other schools into positions of greater responsibility. When I retired in June of 2005, I retired as a classroom teacher from the same school I had been working in for over 10 years. As a male high school teacher between 1974 and 2005, I was a "Son of Feminism".

Parental Alienation

Since 2005 when my son finished undergraduate university and my support payments ended, my relationship with my three adult children continued to shrivel and diminish to the stage where I now have no interactive relationship with any of them. It began with my oldest daughter. After a weekend visit with her and her boyfriend in 2010 I literally didn't have any response from her for four years. I saw her new baby in 2015 when she brought him to show to my mother and me. Facebook or email communication between us is perfunctory and brief. Yet she has a deep and robust relationship with her mother. My other daughter and my son have also dropped out of my life even though they both live in Toronto, only three hours away. They are also both actively involved in relationships with their mother. My ex-wife has been relentless at teaching them to avoid me and discount me as much as possible. My three beautiful grown children are totally estranged from me despite my many attempts to reach out to them—asking to visit them, or them to visit me, asking them how they are doing, offering them support, wishing them the best in life.

My ex-wife never truly supported my "Access Agreement" for visits with the three children. I saw the girls only on Wednesdays and every other weekend a handful of times in the early 90s. I saw my son longer and more regularly for a number of years, but I remember him announcing to me when he was about to turn 16 that *he didn't need to visit me after he turned 16 if he didn't want to.* His mother had clearly been informing him of his "rights." When the girls stopped coming early on, I brought forward the issue in court. The answer I received was that it was difficult to enforce visitation orders because of the many variables:

child may not feel well, there is a special event on that weekend, etc. Child Support payments, on the other hand, were totally enforceable. They were garnisheed directly from my monthly pay and placed in my ex-wife's bank account.

Not having a father figure in their life has definitely had an impact on all three of my children, in my opinion. They all lack any moral or spiritual energy or direction. They strike me as emotionally shut down with little passion or zest for life. They all lead uninspired lives with no interest in benefitting society as a whole. The heartache and pain I feel goes on every day of my life. I practice Buddhist meditation and find it is an excellent way not to be "attached" to my feelings of sadness and loss. The situation with my three adult children is getting worse as the years go on. It's a major reason I'm involved with local men's organizations. I not only want to help other men and boys, but I also need help and support due to the parental alienation I suffer.

Chapter 4 – The Broken Promise of Equality

Eisso Post

The author looks in frank detail at the damaging contradictions, false claims, and broken promises of feminist discourse about male-female sexual intimacy.

This story is about how second wave feminism affected my love life in a very negative way. It is relevant to our present time even though I wasn't living on an American campus but in the Netherlands in the last century, and even though the term rape culture didn't yet exist (though objectification more or less did).

I won't deny that I wasn't perfect in my contact with girls. On the contrary, I'll admit I had enough troubles with that to begin with, even before feminism became conventional wisdom. Lots of boys have trouble, some more than others. That's all the more reason not to be negative about male sexuality, not to suggest that men always get what they want anyway and there's no harm in making them a bit less confident about it. There is harm, a lot of harm, in that.

If you can call anybody a son of feminism, it's me. In my early teens, moderate 'emancipation groups' like Man Vrouw Maatschappij (Man Woman Society) and Dolle Mina (Crazy Mina) started in the Netherlands. While I was growing up, becoming an adult, and trying to get myself something like a love life, the movement radicalized.

At first, it all sounded good to me. I thought that I wouldn't mind working half a week for money and have a girlfriend earning the other half of our income (or live in a commune or whatever). Even better, I'd love women to be no longer getting 'chased' by men, but instead admitting they liked making love as much as men did, and taking as much initiative themselves. Always having to take the initiative seemed like a pain to me—as later it indeed proved to be.

Already at sixteen I was much too optimistic, and at the same time too strict, about the feminist ideal of gender equality. I once touched a girl, stroked her shoulder, and kept on doing it, but she didn't do anything back. She accepted everything I did, and perhaps grew a bit impatient for more, but she didn't respond. Girls and boys being equals, I could only conclude she wasn't interested. This should have been the first girl I made love with, but instead it took some years before that happened.

Something Rotten

I became a university student without really having had a love life, more than kissing a few girls a few minutes each, mostly when I was drunk. I had never held a girl in my arms for hours, let alone anything more intimate.

I welcomed feminism when it became part of the student movement. Before that, but after the hippie movement had died, left wing activism was all about economics and class struggle. Feminism gave us the chance to think about what society, social change and yes, the revolution, could mean for our own lives, our contact with other people, love, sex. And no, feminism was not against men, neither was it puritanical. It was only against violent or authoritarian or disrespectful men and their sexuality. For someone like me, who was very respectful and tender, it could mean nothing but good. It took me some time before I realized there was something rotten in the queendom of feminism.

It didn't take too long before it became clear that some feminists *were* outright misandrists, and they weren't marginalized groups or small cults either. The feminists I knew personally were not—or I wouldn't have known them personally (because those man-haters hardly even talked to men if they could help it). But my feminist friends weren't as indignant about misandry as I hoped they would be. I did know women with posters on the walls of their rooms saying: "Before we talk about misandry in feminism, we should talk about misogyny in society," "A woman needs a man like a fish needs a bicycle," and "When God created man she was only joking." Except for the first one, I didn't even think they were unacceptable. One must be willing to take a joke.

The anti-sexual tendency in second wave feminism was subtle and complicated. It wasn't at all inquisition-like. It was about a thousand remarks and views being rubbed in, day after day, year after year. No one, except the above mentioned misandrists, said explicitly that the sexuality of heterosexual men was bad and shouldn't be expressed. Feminism was supposedly against sexual violence, not against sex.

At the same time, complaints about women being considered "sex objects" became more common. The idea seemed to be that you must not want to make love with a woman because of her sexy appearance, but because of her personality. Men trying to pick up women in a bar or at a party were considered at best superficial assholes who didn't have a clue what real love or sex was about and at worst sexist harassers.

The prevailing wisdom was: "How can you want to have sex (or even just want to kiss) with a woman you don't really know, whom you hardly have had contact with, no deep conversations and all?" The prevailing wisdom also was: "Why do men think if they have close contact with women, deep conversations and all, it must always end with sex?"

(Even though it didn't end that way at least 90% of the time.)

I bought this line or argument for years, more or less, even though it was totally unclear how a legitimate feminist love or sex relationship could come into being at all. It must have been something like: two people being together for hours, looking each other in the eyes and all of a sudden, without anybody saying or asking anything, knowing they were made for each other, or at least had *that* special contact at that moment—something super-romantic like that. Maybe it even happened that way, sometimes. But not very often, and not to me.

And feminist songs, articles, speeches about male heterosexuality were, however denying the fact, more and more shaming of just that: male heterosexuality. It even seemed to me, in the way they described it, that they borrowed from the puritan Dutch Calvinist tradition we hoped to have overcome (while at the same time not applying that puritanism to lesbians). But, as I said, hardly anybody ever explicitly said male heterosexuality was something bad, even though they probably took their theories from hetero-haters like Andrea Dworkin and Adrienne Rich.

Feminist Slut Shaming

The narrative at that time was very much that one night stands and sex without love were a man's thing, that a man trying to push those things on a woman was degrading her to his level. Female sexuality was more profound, more feeling, more person- than body-oriented.

You'll understand I was a bit surprised when thirty years later women demanded the right to be sluts and declared "slut shaming" typical behavior of patriarchal men. In the eighties, I would have loved women to be sluts and wouldn't have dreamed in my worst nightmares of shaming them—and I don't believe I was the only man like that. As far as I remember, feminists were the ones shaming sluts for practicing sex that was too "masculine" for a true liberated woman.

And then, the "friendzoning" cliché (but no less true): it struck me that heterosexual feminists weren't very interested in how supportive, feeling, and emancipated their boyfriends were at all. If it wasn't exactly a disadvantage to be a feminist man, it certainly wasn't an advantage either. Talking with feminists about that, you got the predictable answer: "Are you only nice to us because of *that*?" which is a worthless answer for several reasons.

First, it doesn't really answer the question. If women want men to be a certain way, they have the power to make them that way. Just deny love and sex to the non-feminist men and the whole world will be feminist within a few years. Women must pay a price for it, but that price is perfectly in line with their own feminist narrative: women should not date a "sex object," but a man who is good for them. If they say that's their own business and nice boys shouldn't feel "entitled" —all right, but stop complaining about men altogether if you refuse to do the most crucial thing you can do to right them.

Then, it's legitimate that boys want love, want sex. Doing something for that proves they *don't* feel entitled. They realize something is wanted from them in return. Then what *should* they do for it but be nice, supportive, open, all those things women say they are looking for in men?

And it's not about expecting girls to spread their legs every time you shout: "Down with patriarchy!" It's about wanting to have good contact with girls, have fun together, support each other, know what's important for the other and be thoughtful about that—and hoping sex will be part of that. Not because you're entitled, but because you're young and full of hormones and sex should be an important part of your life and you wonder what you're doing wrong if it isn't.

Neither is it about getting rejected two or three times. It would indeed be very childish to complain about that. It's about feeling powerless about not, or hardly ever, having sex for a long time, while at the same time hearing women complain that "good men are so scarce." It's about feeling you must be repulsive if you do your best to be the way women want you to be, and apparently still are less attractive than the majority of men who, according to those women, are no good at all.

A subtle way of belittling sex was always the statement, "Sex is not so important, good contact with good friends is much more crucial, don't be so superficial." Always said by women who were never short of somebody in bed if they so desired. But, at least, in those days you could talk with girls about sex without that already being called harassment.

Oh yes, and I almost forgot to mention the dream I was talking about at the beginning of this story—the dream of equality, of women taking as much initiative as men. Well, they didn't. (One exception: a woman friend once put her tongue in my mouth without warning, while we were in a bar listening to "Purple Rain." She wasn't that attractive, but nice enough and I enjoyed the experience.)

I talked about it to a girl I knew and the whole issue of girls taking the initiative surprised her. No, she had never thought about that at all. Well, I had to realize it wasn't easy for girls to do that. It was very scary for them and it wasn't expected of them. So I should realize it wasn't their fault. I didn't have an answer to that and only later I thought: do girls realize how scary it can be for boys to take the initiative? And yes, it is more expected of boys, but that expectation often takes the shape of: here come the horny bastards again.

A Very Rational Person

I'm not saying that I was perfect and that my difficulty was the world's fault or feminism's fault. I was a rather shy and awkward boy. I must have been a pain in the ass sometimes, behaving indecisively and nervously. But I was not bad; I was willing to learn, willing to improve myself. And trying just that, and trying to accept and express my sexuality, was like climbing up a hill that got steeper and steeper as my feminist environment got more and more dogmatic and aggressive. In a way, I had even become shyer since I touched that girl at 16. I wasn't able to do things like that anymore without getting very drunk first.

My biggest handicap was that I'm a rational and cerebral person. I take what other people say seriously and believe they mean it, and I find it hard to say things I don't mean.

Of course, a lot of this discourse about how men should behave and how women wanted it to be was a ritual. A set of rules for people to feel good about themselves and have a group to belong to, more than really to follow; and people used it that way without realizing it. Stupid though such behavior is, it's quite normal, especially for young people. Like good Catholics, they "sinned" all the time and then confessed later they had a long way to go before they could really live up to their ideals. They didn't realize they never would, because they enjoyed the way they did things, and there was nothing wrong with it. It just didn't live up to totally unrealistic feminist theories.

But I couldn't say one thing, let alone think it, and do another. It sometimes was bizarre to hear people, men and women, talking about their problems, not knowing how to stop their "sinning" (of course without mentioning that word), while I was brooding all the time about how to start it.

Assertiveness: Second Best

By the time I was in my early twenties, I had had a two week relationship, had had oral sex once, and apart from that still not kissed more than a few girls, and again, mostly just for a few minutes or less. There was no progress. My loneliness, my despair, the amount of horrible moments in my life grew bigger and bigger.

The older girlfriend of a friend of mine proved a great support at that moment. She was a bit of a busybody and quite dominant, but interested in helping other people and good at it. I'm still very grateful to her.

What she mainly taught me was assertiveness. Assertiveness is not an ideal way to handle these things. It's not flirtatious, it's not spontaneous, and it's not impressive. It's essentially making clear what you want and giving the other person room to react to that, reject or accept it. It is very much second best, but for somebody as intimidated as I was then, it was not so bad.

Not that girls ever said *yes* when I said "I want to make love" or "I want to kiss you," except for one in the USA. Partly because of the above mentioned lack of spontaneity, partly because they seemed not to want to take responsibility, whether traditional or feminist women. But it opened perspectives. Some said no but later started the kissing themselves. Some started complicated, indecisive monologues, but then I was daring enough to say: "All right, I'll start the kissing now, tell me when to stop." It didn't bring me much, but it brought me quite a bit more than the years before, especially kissing girls without getting drunk first, which made it a lot more enjoyable.

And still I hadn't got the feminist narrative out of my system. I was particularly haunted by the idea of being with a girl and realizing she might like to be with me but not in a sexual way. Worse: that it might be disappointing for a girl if a man wanted to be with her for sex and not simply for talk or fun or whatever. That all men wanted that and that all girls were in despair because no man approached them as "human beings." This was a horrible blackmailing narrative, for who wants to disappoint a girl, especially a girl in despair, especially a girl you like so much that you want to make love with her?

Even when I was together with a girl whom I daringly had once complimented for her beauty and who had been very pleased with that, nothing happened. It might have been a very pleasant night or even a relationship, but at that moment I was too paralyzed.

Another time, a girl came to my place for dinner. She was beautiful, sexy, and full of naughty flirtatious humor. But she was also attending a school for social work or something, and just before she came to my house, at school she had seen the film "Not a Love Story," a feminist anti-porn movie full of violent masculine sexuality. Though she wasn't negative to me, she was so shocked by it that it was clearly not the moment to try something with her.

Still another girl said I confused her because I "didn't give her the chance to play the female/the (little) woman (*het vrouwtje*, hard to translate)." No doubt I didn't. I had learned all my life to treat girls and women as equals, to take them seriously. I had learned that flirting or "cheap" compliments were out of the question. Apparently, again, I was more sincere in this than other men; in her world I was an absolute exception, almost a freak.

Growing Older

All the same, I probably grew a bit more confident over the years. At 28 I had a relationship that lasted a few months. But it was all too little and even more: too late. For not long after that relationship broke up, something started to play a role I only realized a lot later: I grew older. People around me had relationships, lived together, even got married and had children. I was still behaving the same as I did the years before, so my love life changed suddenly from a rather dry steppe landscape to an outright desert. There was no time anymore to try things out; it was time to find somebody to stay with for at least a long time, maybe for life, even though I didn't feel experienced or settled enough for that.

Looking back I think: when your love life involuntarily hasn't really begun at 20, or maybe even at 18, you're in trouble. Something really should happen, and quick. You need all the support you can get, you need reaffirmation that your feelings, your longings, your sexuality are good (not just not bad, but *good*). You don't need any monitoring or criticism, let alone demonizing. The only restrictions you need to know are to respect others and not use violence. But essentially people already know those things.

At 35, I finally got into a relationship that lasted longer, about twelve years. Only a few months before that, I read a book about the differences in men's and women's brains. I had always thought they were the same and that difference was a sexist myth. It may have been coincidence that the relationship started soon after that, or perhaps not.

In the beginning the relationship was quite good; later it became mediocre. I didn't want to break up, knowing too well what it is like to be alone. Still, it broke up and I'm alone again. I look around and realize I'm living in an astonishing world. On one hand, women don't pretend anymore that they don't like sex or even casual sex. They claim to be proud of being just as horny as men, something totally unheard of in the seventies and eighties.

On the other hand, male sexuality is demonized more than ever. There was of course already talk about "harassment" in the eighties, but now every expression of male sexuality can fall under that category. Maybe as a result of that, there's hardly any talk about sex anymore in daily life.

When I was young, all the above-mentioned dogmas were rampant, but you could at least talk about them and about how sexuality felt for you, also to girls, also to feminists.

Not long ago, in a volunteer project I worked on, a woman asked me how my life was. I honestly told her about it, my loneliness, and yes, also the sexual part of it. She listened to it and encouraged me to talk. But her girlfriend, who coordinated the project, had a severe personal talk with me afterward. She told me not to talk to this woman or any other volunteer about these things, because it upset them. She said her girlfriend "could not make clear her boundaries" —we're talking about a 30 year old woman. She had the nerve to say, "It may be a bad thing that sex is a taboo, but you have to admit it is." I should have answered, "Good thing my generation wasn't as narrow-minded as you, or you wouldn't have an open lesbian relationship like you have now." But I didn't want any trouble. This woman is very charismatic, a great organizer, and she's done very good things on this project. But, as I found out on Facebook, she's also one of the worst SJWs around.

A few points. I realize very well that this is *my* story. Lots of men, whether calling themselves feminists or not, managed to have quite a good love life in that same period and enjoyed themselves very much. I'm not saying feminism made that impossible for everybody. It was also my personality, my character that didn't fit in with the era, one way or another.

Still, I've met men with comparable stories. And there's a lot of loneliness in our society, for which I partly blame the current lack of trust and respect between men and women. Well-meaning institutions organize dinners for lonely people instead of addressing these issues.

Not long ago, I read the book *De mannen van Nederland* (The men of the Netherlands) by the French woman Sophie Perrier. I had to laugh and cry about it. Women from 22 different countries, living in the Netherlands, complained about Dutch men. Those men never tell you when they think you're attractive, they say nothing to you in the streets, even in a bar when you are most sexily dressed; you can sit there all night without anyone approaching you. When they touch your elbow and you withdraw it, they won't try again, as if they don't want to invest any energy in you. A woman I talked to confirmed that her female foreign friends had the same feeling, for the same reasons: "Dutch boys are assholes."

What these women don't know, of course, is that the situation says a lot about Dutch women, how they disciplined and intimidated their men.

Then again, the question: is sex that important? Reading this story, it may seem as if all my social contacts during decades were one big attempt at getting laid. That would have been maniacal, and of course it wasn't that way. I've had fun with lots of men and women, talking, making music, going on holiday, joking, playing. There were moments to be grateful for. But there was also something missing.

So yes, to me, in the most desperate moments, it also seemed that everything I did was one big attempt at getting laid, because everything else seemed trivial. If there isn't any sex at all in your life, it becomes very important, more important than you wish it would be. I can imagine that some people have enough sex in their lives but no other form of closeness, no honest talks, no signs of sympathy, etc., and that they keep missing something. But believe me, the other way around is just as bad.

And then, sex is a good stepping stone to other forms of closeness, a necessary stepping stone to being "more than a friend," whether for a few weeks or forever. If the sex isn't there, the other thing won't be there either. Sex, even rough sex, can awaken deep, warm, happy feelings of love. I hardly ever felt so much love in my life as on some occasions, lying with my face in a woman's crotch, looking, smelling, tasting.

I would have accepted all CEOs, government leaders and prize-winning artists to be women; I would have accepted all affirmative action leading to that, if they'd only stopped demonizing male sexuality.

So—is it reasonable to say feminism fucked up my life? Yes.

Chapter 5 – Deadbeat Dad

Frank Farmer*

The author explores how his generation of New Men were destined to fail as husbands and fathers, and how the Deadbeat Dad is the ultimate creation of Cultural Marxist Feminism.

In 2004, I was standing on the Brooklyn Bridge in New York City on a windy night, drunk, waiting for a gap among the passers-by so that I could summon the strength to throw myself over. I had lost my job, my visa was about to expire, and I had just walked away from my wife and kids. The one idea obsessively circling in my mind was this: I have failed as a father, husband and provider and I will never see my children again. I will only cease to be a blight on other people's lives when I kill myself.

In retrospect, I see that I wouldn't have managed to go through with the task that night. The fact that I was crying on the bridge was a sign that I hadn't achieved the cold detachment of dissociation that is usually required to see suicide through. The thought of my children held me back. No matter how much I hated myself, I couldn't put them through the aftermath.

My close encounter was amateurish. The choice of bridge was inept; if I had jumped I would have fallen only twelve or so feet into the lanes of traffic that flow slowly below on either side of the pedestrian walkway. I might have landed on a yellow taxi stuck in the nightly New York log-jam and sprained an ankle, or, at worst, got myself into trouble with a driver I'd inconvenienced.

I'm making light of something both horrific and personal, which is a process we men often go through when it comes to all those emotions that cluster round admitting personal failure.

I'm also wary of assigning blame, of saying it was the fault of this person or that. Nonetheless, looking back on this near miss thirteen years later, I can honestly say that one major thing, something I chose willingly, led me to the edge of the bridge.

I would call it Marxist Feminism or Cultural Marxist Feminism. My generation of males—Generation X—were an experiment in fathering in the Cultural Marxist Feminism mold and we were pre-programmed to fail. We were part of the historic creation of the social pariah known as the Deadbeat Dad.

Mainstream websites, papers and gossip pages have for two decades used the Deadbeat Dad to sum up all that is wrong with modern man. The name, originally a feminist slur, has passed into common parlance. There are even academic studies on what is now seen as a natural phenomenon, as if a deadbeat was lurking within every man. Homo Deadbeatus is regularly described as a selfish man, frozen in juvenile stasis. According to the urban dictionary a deadbeat dad is: "A father who does not provide for a family that he was part of creating. Does not have morals or a responsible enough nature to realize how difficult he is making life for his family."

In 1998, the Clinton Administration turned the slur into a legal formulation with the "The Deadbeat Parents Punishment Act;" an act that over five years extracted an extra $5 billion predominantly out of divorced fathers.

If the Deadbeat Dad had not come into existence, Cultural Marxist Feminism would have had to create him as he fulfills all the goals of their project. He is the final collapse of the nuclear family and his existence requires the absolute and unquestionable intervention of the State amidst all parties within the family.

I was such a man in the years after my 2004-5 divorce. Like many other fathers of my age, I had become unemployed. Between sparse temp contracts, living in a student-level apartment in a poor part of town (with vermin and with a roof actually collapsed), I attempted to pay child support from my unemployment benefit. All the time, I struggled to hide my sense of uselessness from my kids whom I saw, once or twice a week, under conditions suitable to my ex wife, to whom I had granted full custody.

There is some solace, I have found, in depersonalizing the experience and in seeing oneself as piece of data. According to the General Household Survey in the UK, the percentage of lone parent households that are mother-headed is 91%. Family courts award mothers sole custody in 71% of cases, while joint custody is awarded in 21% of cases and fathers sole custody in 7% of all cases. In the U.S.A., men lose custody in 84% per cent of divorces.

It is very common for mothers during custody battles to receive state funded legal aid, while advice from lawyers to fathers is that they can't win and so should avoid costly custody challenges.

The failings of the Deadbeat Dad unable to pay his child support payments or to provide a safe home for his children (for example if he has a roommate unknown to the children's mother) guarantees that the State plays a huge part in raising and monitoring his children. His "failure" enables the existence of ever larger government departments of child care and child assessment, emboldening the State to intervene. The State oversees and polices the father's contact with his own kids; it threatens imprisonment if the conditions and schedules of the Deadbeat Dad's payments are not met. Through the

Deadbeat Dad's failure to earn enough to support the family, his children are forced into state controlled kindergarten and after-school care while the mother works; or if the mother cannot work, the State takes total control by providing her income and the maintenance, education, socialization, health, diet and surveillance of her children.

The Deadbeat Dad is not an historic error but the deliberate and successful realization of the Cultural Marxist Feminist project to replace fathers with an ever more powerful State.

What most of us don't realize, however, is that the Deadbeat Dad is also the direct result of a much more upbeat and apparently positive project that began in the 1990s to create feminist males and New Men. I know this because I chose to be both a feminist male and a New Man.

Standing on the bridge, what seemed so tragic and fated for me was the realization that it all began with me trying to be one of the good guys, a left liberal who believed in equality.

My history of involvement with Marxism and Feminism is long and goes back to my teenage years. As an arts student, I was a member of the Trotskyist organization the Socialist Workers Party. I graduated with a feminist dissertation on "The Male Gaze." I was part of the New Queer Cinema movement and was a gender bender who chose to take part in the great experiment to become a New Man.

The New Man rose to prominence in the 1980s and was jokingly referred to as an evolutionary step, a new kind of man who was "happy to do the washing up or change a nappy." According to the *Oxford English Dictionary,* it wasn't just about task-sharing but was part of a new way of being: The New Man was someone "who rejects sexist attitudes and the traditional male roles, esp. in the context of domestic responsibilities and childcare, and who is (or is held to be) caring, sensitive, and non-aggressive."

I prided myself on being an exemplary New Man and married a strong woman. The marriage, I told myself, wasn't like a normal nuclear family; it was postmodern and in part ironic. Even though I soon had two young kids and a mortgage, I had a tick-the-boxes list of things that set me apart from the old Patriarchal man, whom we'd been taught to see as uncaring, authoritarian, and violent.

I ticked the box on being there at the births of both my children. Doing night-time bottle feeds with expressed milk. I took the babies out for neighborhood walks in their strollers. People often stared—"Look, a man with a pram!"—and this filled me with feminist pride. Look at me, I thought, subverting Patriarchal gender norms.

I cooked nearly all the meals and apologized for not doing my fair share of the laundry. I also acknowledged that one day all men would do these things without seeking praise for them.

There were many guides on how to be a New Man in the media at the time and I absorbed it all subliminally and made attempts to be sympathetic to female emotions and ways of communicating. Our Socialist leaders in the UK appointed the first ever Minister for Women, and she was the Marxist Feminist Harriet Harman. I recall thinking that she was a heroine leading us to a better future. In a later essay entitled "If I ruled the World," Harman stated: "I'd forcibly narrow the gap between what women and men earn … I'd make child care part of the welfare state and oblige all governments to guarantee child care for all children …"

The dominant idea through the 1990s and the early 2000s was that as feminist males, it was our duty to accept that equality meant a lowering of our status, wages, and sometimes quality of employment. Rather than fight our way up the career ladder and work those extra hours as our fathers had done, we'd leave the office at 4:30pm because we had child care to catch up on.

Through all of this was some subconscious idea that penance was being enacted. Men like me knew we could never make up for all the oppression that women, as a subclass in the Marxian sense, had suffered over millennia, but we tried to say sorry by domesticating ourselves. We asked our wives and we asked feminism, "What can we do to make things right for you?" The world of work changed too, to accommodate women's needs; the culture of the lifelong sole breadwinner was replaced by the unisex flexi-time worker. Real wages dropped when women flooded the market in the 90s, but this seemed like a necessary sacrifice on the road to equality.

My then wife and I were constantly assessing whether the share of daily chores and professional achievements was equal, and if not what could be done to remedy it. We even made the mistake of trying to share sleep deprivation with a newborn. A lot of this was cute and upbeat, something never before attempted in human history.

This is not intended as a critique of my ex-wife. She was in many ways more generous and pragmatic than I and far less politically doctrinaire. My nervous breakdown was my own doing. My problem was the mindset I took into the marriage. The Cultural Marxist Feminist project I bought into undermined me every step of the way. How can you fully commit to a marriage if you have Kate Millett's radical chant in your head, as I did:

"And how do we make Cultural Revolution?

By destroying the family!

And how do we destroy the family?

By destroying the Patriarch."

In this world of flexible parenting and multi-task roles in which families came to require the earnings of two working parents to stay afloat, when one of you stops earning due to the new volatility in the un-gendered workplace, then the work/parenting balance collapses.

This is what happened to me. To us. After working in short term freelance contracts for a decade I grabbed at something that looked like a big steady job, but I failed and I fell. The Cultural Marxist Feminist in my head mocked me: "You tried to be a Patriarch, now you're fucked; it serves you right."

In 2003-04, the double standard towards men, wages, and parenting came into full force. The number of divorces hit an all time high in the UK. Freelancing men, New Men who fell out of work, were suddenly deemed no longer fit to be fathers.

The long term marriage commitment and the world of short term contracts proved to be incompatible. Marriage remodeled itself on the labor market; it became a short-term deal until one partner fell afoul of the low wages and no-commitment, zero hours contracts.

A divorced New Man, it turned out, from the 2000s onwards had to be a detached breadwinner with limited contact with children—"Stay away and provide the money." This, ironically, had been almost exactly the Patriarchal Alpha Male provider role, the 1950s father, that we had been determined to overturn in the 90s. If we had known that all that was ultimately required was a sperm donation and a performance as financial guarantor, we most likely would never have given up our full time jobs to be New Men to start with. We would never have embarked on "the deconstruction of gender stereotypes."

Surveys show that the majority of No Fault Divorces (80% among the college educated) are now initiated by women

(69% in the general population.) The primary stated reason for divorce is "dissatisfaction." This is a code word for something much harder for liberal society to admit, the failure of male partners to be providers.

So New Men were divorced for ceasing to be the Alpha Males that they had sought to replace. Out of the four couples I knew who married at the same time as me, three are now split. In two of these situations the men have been labeled as Deadbeat Dads and have faced legal challenges over child support payments and access.

The State plays nasty tricks on Deadbeat Dads. The first involves teams of lawyers and free legal aid for women, a whole system set up to make the no fault divorce as smooth for the woman as possible and to deprive the father of any rights, including visitation, until the paperwork is done.

The legal advice I received was to do what I was told, quickly, and not to contest anything. It didn't really matter what the terms were in the agreement. The message from the lawyer was that there was only room for flexibility on the mother's terms. Sign it.

Most fathers, as I was, are too overwhelmed by the insinuated threat within the legal jargon that you will be deprived of access to your children to look over the small print. Most fathers, in a state of shock at suddenly no longer being part of the family home, are keen to get the paperwork over with so that they can begin the negotiation on visitation rights. They are told not to rock the boat and that this is the way that things have operated since the 1980s.

According to the way it is set up, a father can't contest the primary care being automatically given to the mother and if he does, he will then be calling for psychological tests for himself and the mother: the suitability of the mother to be a parent will have to be called into question. This is perceived as an aggressive move, and most fathers do not want to have to cast suspicion upon their ex-wife's ability to be a good mother. So the vast majority of fathers do not challenge the legal status quo, and as a result they get to see their kids on terms that suit the lawyers and, in the second instance, the mother.

In many cases the No Fault Divorce has come about because of a changed financial situation. So you have a father with no money having to find a place to live, acquire a new job, and pay legal fees. His new place will be substandard, to save money so that he can make the Child Support Payments. The State or the mother can then rule that the abode of the secondary caregiver is unfit for children to visit. If you mess up on this front then you may be restricted to supervised visitations. If a father falls into arrears in payments, mothers feel they are within their rights to deny access until they have been paid, and this sours relationships between the child, father and mother. Mothers actually have no right to do this, legally, but it is common practice.

Living with the emptiness of your new daily routine as a solitary man who used to be a live-in father is a threat to health. You are haunted in the hours by the schedule of your children's lives. You are not there to make breakfast for them, to take them to school, to pick them up in the car, to help with homework, to put a sticking plaster on a knee, to play ball, to build Lego, to tuck them into bed, to read them their bedtime stories. You can't make any long term plans together, as you are only there as a guest on the mother's schedule. You are like an uncle—Uncle Dad.

Of course, for generations this has been the curse of the divorced father, but it is even harder for the man who tried to be a gender-equal New Man.

Trying to negotiate a better deal can also be dangerous.

The way things are set up, simple domestic arguments about the hand-over of kids or advance scheduling can spiral into a situation that could lead to a restraining order or the removal of visitation rights. Any confrontation with the mother can result in accusations of breach of visiting agreement or be construed as aggressive behavior. Even worse, it can be defined as domestic abuse under the emerging "primary aggressor" laws, designed to make sure that men and only men are arrested in domestic disputes.

In such cases, no evidence of violence need be presented for an arrest to take place and the male is considered guilty until proven innocent and is held until court appearance. Such a set of laws was enshrined in the Violence Against Women Act (funded to the tune of $1.6 Billion under the Clinton Administration in 1994). VAWA is built on the false assumption that only men are perpetrators of domestic violence. It is an act that the Concerned Women of America described as "creating a climate of suspicion where all men are feared or viewed as violent and all women are viewed as victims," and which the American Civil Liberties Union described as "repugnant" with respect to the unconstitutional extension of pre-trial detention.

Fathers arguing for equality of treatment have to tread very carefully so that their protests, often on the front door-step of the mother's (the family) house, cannot be interpreted as in any way aggressive. Since the 1996 Family Law Act (UK), even shouting can be construed as domestic violence.

Many fathers undergo mental collapse during the process of having their interactions with their children managed by the State. But they are advised not to seek mental health advice or care as this will go on their medical records. In the case of a father's renegotiation of visitation times with his children, or of a custody appeal, a health record with evidence of mental illness would be used against the father. So these men have to go through severe depression without medical help. They are afraid even to ask their GPs for advice after having been advised not to seek psychiatric help by their lawyers.

I had no choice in this matter. My mental collapse required immediate intervention. But had I appealed for joint custody, I would have lost on three counts: being unemployed, not having a suitable home, and being on record as receiving anti-depressant treatment and cognitive behavioral therapy.

The Deadbeat Dad very often has trouble with money and finds it hard to get back onto the career ladder he has fallen off. The sheer numbers involved in setting up a new home, buying duplicate commodities to those that were in the family home, paying child support, paying rent on the new place and your share of mortgage on the family home, and paying alimony if required—all these can clean a father out, leave him on a treadmill close to the poverty line. This lack of agency and sense of being trapped turns depression into more dangerous forms of mental ill health.

I say all this in the third person, I talk about fathers and deadbeats because I really don't want to make this about me, even though many of these processes are things that I, and men I know, have been through. The need to generalize here is in part therapeutic; I can talk of "we" and "they," not just of the solitary, struggling "I." Above that, it is important for we men to see the systemic processes that are in place, that rob us even of the autonomy of a fully functioning "I," that make the "I' into something that is either to blame or to pity.

For the Deadbeat Dad there is also the desperation caused by having somehow been criminalized and then having to police one's own actions, causing a deep rooted paranoia about oneself, a conviction that being male is in itself the crime. You must be on guard against these flashes of insight that tell you the system is rigged against you and you must not give in to anger, because as feminism has taught you, anger is uniquely male and all men are by nature violent. This sense of being caught in a no man's land between one's awareness of feminist programming and the reality as a disempowered man is typified by the following quotation from the book *Viros*:

"Ask yourself: why do you pay her? When she already has full custody of your children? Are you paying her as if she was a nanny and the children were a job that needed doing, a burden? Your children are not a burden. They give value to your life. They are a joy and a reward that you are deprived of. Being denied access to your children is a far greater burden. She makes you pay money in order to see them for one day a week. A fee for admittance. A fee as if they were a sideshow. What other people do you have to pay to see? A doctor. A lawyer. A prostitute. You slave to pay her to see your own kids for an hour. And with the money you give her she puts the kids in childcare, so they see neither parent."

If the primary goal was to destroy the nuclear family and to place the state in a position of control over each member of that family, then no plan could have been more cunning than the creation of Deadbeat Dads.

Recently divorced men between the ages of 30 and 50 are the demographic that suffers from the highest rates of suicide. A world-wide report aggregating information from over forty scientific studies, conducted in 2012 by Samaritans and entitled "Men, Suicide and Society; Why Disadvantaged Men in Mid-life Die by Suicide," found an approximately four times greater increase in suicide amongst men than women after divorce. They also discovered that the highest suicide rate is now among men aged 35 to 54, the age that, prior to the 1970s, was the safest period in male life. The spike in suicides appears generational and connected to the changes in male female relations from the 1970s onwards.

"Since the 1970s, several social changes have impacted on personal lives, including rising female employment, increased partnering and de-partnering, and solo-living. As a result, men in mid-life are increasingly likely to be living on their own, with little or no experience of coping emotionally or seeking help on their own, and few supportive relationships to fall back on."

Add to this irregular work patterns, insecure or temporary work, and debt burden from lack of full time labor, and the changing nature of parenting at a time in which the divorce rate doubled and you have a generation of men cast adrift.

Historians ask, "Where did the New Man go?" The answer is that he became the Deadbeat Dad. Then the Deadbeat was beaten and he died out. He became a silent increase in suicide data.

If, back in 2004, I had not had a mindset that embraced two decades worth of Cultural Marxist Feminist ideology, my marriage might have survived. But I smashed the marriage and walked out in disgust at myself. I was not pragmatic or level headed because the ideology I lived and breathed told me that marriage as an institution was historically doomed to fail anyway and that all men were intrinsically less moral, less good than women. I walked out of that marriage with a head full of deterministic apocalyptic Marxist Feminist fury. With a sense that historically, as a man, my time was over.

When you are involved with Cultural Marxist Feminism, as I was, you believe that you are an agent of social change in the outside world. But you are mistaken; you have it the wrong way around. The primary task of Cultural Marxist Feminism is to transform you, to make you a disenchanted, alienated person cut off from all social ties, utterly alone and living in a state of rage for which you are taught to blame the status quo. It makes you into a person who is unable to take care of yourself, unable to have or maintain a family. Cultural Marxist Feminism succeeds by creating human wreckage, creating people with a mindset that alienates and destroys social bonds.

The proof of this covert plan is that advocates of greater freedom for women, easier divorce, and more women in the workplace in the early 1970s were themselves Communists. For example Betty Friedan, who described the nuclear family as "a comfortable concentration camp," was outed in 1999 as a former member of the Communist party, an identity that she concealed for decades while pretending to be a typical suburban housewife. The first No Fault Divorce law was put into place by the Bolsheviks in 1917 with the expressed intent of destroying the "bourgeois institution of marriage." Kate Millett's communism was more overt, while the Maoist origins of the postmodernist feminists have only recently come to light. These radicals were not interested in the slightest in female liberty; it was a smokescreen to smash the family.

I don't blame specific individuals, my art tutors, my former fellow New Men, my ex-wife, or any of the other women in my life. I blame myself. I blame the self that surrendered its agency all too quickly to this belief system. If I was just a good feminist and a good New Man, I told myself, I would be contributing to a better society. But I was a useful idiot. I caused harm and spread it.

Cultural Marxist Feminism took me to the edge and, thankfully, I stepped away from it. I climbed off the bridge and I walked around the perimeter of my children's lives, entering in when I could.

From that position and over all that time, I learned to see very clearly.

Fifteen years on from my collapse, I see that new studies (published in TIME magazine, 2015) now admit that Deadbeat Dads weren't so bad after all and that contrary to public opinion, mothers were just as much in arrears in child support as fathers over the preceding decade. Even when we were penniless, we fathers contributed, through the giving of food, clothing, play, driving and time (known as contributions "in kind"). We contributed through teaching and giving what a child needs most of all; the sense that their first footsteps and attempts are valued. We gave, without even trying, the eyes of men who will protect and love unquestioningly, with no conditions attached. We gave the gift of humor, and shared sadness, and a bit of courage and ingenuity in having to make-do. We built things together and we shared the imaginary world that allows man and child to marvel together at the known and the unknown. We shared the gift of seeing ourselves in each other and of feeling ourselves grow and change over time. We learned how to say goodbye and hello with gratitude for every moment.

All of these simple human interactions, which come so naturally, lie beyond the plans for a socially engineered Marxist Feminist future. They are the things that stand in its way.

* Frank Farmer is a nom-de-plume.

Chapter 6 – One of the Lucky Ones

John Savage

The author presents his school experiences, from his earliest years to his graduate training, to show how even an unscathed life can be shadowed by experience of cultural bias.

I consider myself a fortunate man. When I see what many men go through, mine has been a fairly easy ride by contrast. Though it has not been without trials, setbacks, loss and grief, these have generally been of the sort common to men throughout the ages. I have, thank Heaven, not had to silently endure any of the soul-destroying horrors that so many others have under feminism. Yet even I have realized that "male privilege" is a myth and have witnessed the escalating war on males. And so I offer this sketch of my life, not as anything special, but rather as a representative account, what feminists might call the "lived experience" of one of the more "privileged" members of my sex.

My formative years were, I imagine, typical of many British males of my generation: I was born into a stable if not always harmonious middle-class home during the early 1970s, sent to a nursery school (of which my recollections are few and hazy), and thence to a state primary school. In that school, and later in the junior school adjoining it, my "socialization" as a boy began in earnest.

The primary school was staffed and run entirely by women. Most were older women with children of their own, and were of a pre-war vintage; they were typically rather motherly, benign figures who appeared to show no partiality to either sex. There were, however, exceptions. One in particular was a woman who would materialize when one of her more aged colleagues had broken down (these temps were called "supply teachers", though exactly what they supplied is to this day a mystery to me). Tall, stiff and starchy, with a long, disapproving face and permanently downturned mouth, she reminded me back then of the character Beaker in *The Muppet Show*, and left me with my sole enduring memory of the time I spent in that school.

I was seated in her class next to a girl who'd been in my ear about something or other which I can no longer remember, but which had exasperated me sufficiently that I saw no course other than to pinch her on the back of the hand. Not my finest hour, to be sure, and doubtless in the eyes of many merely evidence of the routine abuse females suffer at the hands of males, but I was only about five and had never before (and have never since) resorted to such measures, so I can only assume that I was sorely tested. To my surprise, the girl immediately burst into tears and presently I was looking up into the teacher's implacable countenance.

After a brief inquiry and the revelation of my crime, she instructed my victim to pinch me back. I offered my hand, and the girl pinched me. It was rather a feeble effort and so the girl was commanded to pinch me again, only harder. She tried a second time, but evidently this too didn't comply with the supply teachers' penal code, and so the teacher herself demonstrated how to pinch a small boy properly. I remember watching her long, painted nails digging into the skin on the back of my hand, and the look of grim satisfaction on her face as she surveyed the mark they left. Of course she suffered no adverse consequences for her actions; had anyone in the class thought them a mite harsh, nobody said so. I was too ashamed of my own transgression to mention the episode when I got home, but looking back, I think that had I told my dear old mother, she would have stridden smartly up to the school and taught the teacher a thing or two about pinching.

I don't relate this incident in the hope of garnering sympathy—it could be argued that my punishment was deserved—but rather to show that a female teacher was quite comfortable doing this to a young boy, and to ask how likely a male teacher would have been to dig his fingernails into the hand of a young girl who'd pinched a boy. The scenario is so improbable as to be absurd. Had it taken place, the school would have been a-chatter about his aberration and he would have lost his job (and possibly also a few of his teeth, depending upon the disposition of the girl's father).

On moving up to junior school, I found myself in the class of a young, clog-wearing feminist, perhaps my first encounter with the species. I remember her as a scrawny harridan with bad skin and a bad temper, whose arresting body odor would engulf me whenever she leaned over to mark my work. She can't have been long out of teachers' college, and student radicalism apparently coursed yet in her veins. When on duty at break time, she would swank around the playground, linked arm-in-arm with a long chain of girls, herself front and center, as though she were leading a Marxist solidarity parade (other female teachers did this too, curiously enough, though perhaps without quite the same revolutionary mien: I could never figure out why girls would want to walk slowly around with the teacher during break, when one could play a game instead, but then girls' games were tepid confections with chalk and elastic rather than the heroic struggles of Barbarians or British Bulldogs). I knew intuitively at the time that there was something odd about her behavior.

I hated being in her class. I kept my head down and was a good pupil, and so avoided drawing her attention and wrath. But others were not so fortunate. One, a slow boy from a poor background, but who was otherwise no real trouble, was subjected to an explosive and very humiliating outpouring of her simmering disdain for males. She erupted at him for some misdemeanor or other (maybe laziness, as he was simply sitting quietly at his desk). I can still see her look of naked contempt for the boy and recall snatches of the things she snarled at him: "You *disgust* me!" ..."You're like a *slug!*" ..."From now on, I'm going to call you *"slug"*!" Quite what effect this had on poor Michael, I don't know, but again, nothing happened to her as a result of her tantrum.

My time in this woman's class ended badly. She had a close colleague, also a young feminist; not quite as volatile. In order to dispense with the cumbersome designations "my teacher" and "my teacher's colleague", I shall refer to the former as Euryale and to the latter as Lamia; far be it from me to embarrass these estimable educators by disclosing their real names. Lamia was put in charge of taking our class to the local park. I'd been under the false impression that my mother would collect me from the park at the end of the day, and so I stayed behind, waiting for her to arrive (I sat on a bench chatting with the warden about the park's wildlife). Lamia had failed to notice this, since she hadn't bothered to take a proper head-count when leaving the park, and, since she did not realize that I was missing from the group, she was at a loss when my mother arrived at the school to pick me up and asked where I was. After searching the school, my increasingly frantic mother took her car and drove down to the park, immensely relieved to find me waiting for her. I explained that I'd thought she was coming to collect me and so the confusion was cleared up, and lessons learned.

But then the following school day, Lamia came into our class and sternly summoned me out of my seat to stand before her and Euryale. She then wiped the floor with me, verbally, until I, despite my best efforts, started crying. When her comrade was finished, Euryale coldly thrust a box of tissues under my nose. I dried my face and returned to my seat feeling about two inches tall. I couldn't understand what I'd done to deserve such a lambasting, when even my mother herself had understood I'd made an honest mistake and so had not been cross. And again, would two male teachers have dared so to treat a small girl? Even had I been wholly responsible for the incident, it might still have been dealt with calmly and sensitively, but for the feminist predilection for self-righteous histrionics.

I actually told my mother about this, as it was so humiliating: she was incensed that the teacher had sought to shift blame for her own failure onto me and was set to raise merry Hell with the school. But alas, my father (who was seldom a dependable ally) stopped her, saying that it would only make waves. My mother was not a firebrand—she was a kind, gentle woman—but when stirred by injustice she'd come out swinging. She was of the same generation as the older primary school teachers, born a few years before the war, and had married late. She loved my brother and me more than life itself and certainly had no time for misandric young females. Speaking of which, Lamia eventually married and produced a daughter, whom I later met; she was her mother's only child and was raised in her image. I remember how she, as a young teen, would follow her mother around wearing a pink shirt emblazoned with the slogan, "Not if you were the last boy on earth."

My final year in that place was spent under the stern eye of another female teacher, but though she was strict and rather fearsome when roused, she was also of the old school (and again, grew up during the war, before feminism really got going). Though initially wary of her temper, I came to like her and was happy in her class. Looking back, there was a very marked divide between the older women and the others: the older women were impartial, treated boys and girls with equal kindness or severity, and were altogether more likeable people than the younger women, whose female chauvinism, I now realize, was often evident and unabashed. Most of the older generation grew up in the chapels and were shaped by the Bible, whereas the younger women grew up in the Sixties and were shaped by whatever had been poured into their heads at college. I sometimes wonder what happened to the character of the school when that older generation retired. I'm glad I wasn't born a decade or two later.

The following year I began secondary school. Like most British children, my secondary education meant attending the local mixed comprehensive. Built in the 1960s, it was a blot on the landscape, its appearance as grievous to the eye as incarceration there was to the heart. The makeup of the teaching staff was very different from that to which I'd grown accustomed; there were a lot of men, many of whom were surely necessary in an enforcement role, owing to the increasing size and strength of the boys. Looking around at some of the older inmates filled me with foreboding: though but a year or two my senior, the females were all stockinged calves and thighs, swaying hips and swelling breasts, whereas the males were muscular, pustulated and desperate-looking, neither boy nor man, trapped in an agonizing and frustrating hormonal limbo. Both males and females alike talked endlessly about sex and its overtures— who had "got off" with whom—and the place reeked of thwarted pubescent desire. I, with my hairless little body, felt like a petunia in an onion patch.

There was an established social hierarchy in the school, more or less a cacocracy: the worst of the worst—the bullies, social climbers and assorted opportunistic backstabbers—set the tone and formed the in-crowd, and everybody else had to curry favor with them or suffer socially. Both sexes were part of this mafia, although in my own year the worst persecutors and the most miserable victims tended to be male. There was little sense of brotherhood; just cold-blooded, internecine competition.

Then puberty, the inescapable plague, began to grip my year. Teenage boys are often stereotyped as sexually incontinent, but although I was as red-blooded as the next male, the life of a rake never appealed to me (nor, so it seemed, to most of the boys with whom I chose to associate). Alas, there were a fair few lads around my age who did live to drink themselves speechless and to fornicate like spawning frogs. But then, so did many of the girls. The latter revelation came as a shock to me: having been used to male company, I'd been long aware of the ignoble depths to which all too many males sink, but was of the opinion that girls were on the whole more sensitive, more civilized, and generally better people than boys (an opinion formed less from experience—I had no sisters—than from accepting the prevailing cultural narrative). But I was to be horribly disillusioned by the things I saw and heard.

I remember one girl in my year talking graphically about a boy's strange-looking penis: another girl who'd had a sexual encounter with the boy had described it to her, and she was now sharing it with the class. I'd been under the impression that the fairer sex was not like this; indeed, only the worst of males would ever regale their friends with gossip about the appearance of a sexual partner's vulva, much less bruit it abroad (such things always struck me as a reprehensible betrayal of trust). In the quarter of a century or so since that time, I've heard many similar things (and far worse) from feminists. And sadly, women in general seem gradually to be following suit, boldly affirming their "liberation" by being lewd and shameless.

I ended up at university (more by accident—or lack of imagination—than by design). Though the architecture was better, it more or less picked up where school left off. We were no longer "pupils," but "students," and now lived away from home in accommodation of our own, yet the collective mindset was essentially that of the sixth form. Sex and drinking ranked at least as high as academic study.

School had left me with a strong aversion to English and essay writing; besides the mandatory Shakespeare (which I quite liked), we'd been given the most dismal modern fare to read; thin, depressing novels depicting the meager lives of working-class heroes. Consequently I chose the mathematical sciences in the hope of never having to write another paragraph. Thus was I spared much of the feminist brainwashing that passes for scholarship in the humanities these days (although I notice that even the sciences are now succumbing to the rot). I also remember thinking it not at all out of the ordinary that there were only a handful of young women in my classes, or that all the teaching staff were men; I knew that my subject held little appeal for the vast majority of females, since one had only to mention it and their smiles would freeze and their eyes glaze over. The only thing preventing females from entering my field was the fact that almost all were bored to the core of their being by the mere thought of it.

Despite the licentious milieu at university, I noticed that male sexuality was generally denigrated, whereas female sexuality was celebrated. Even before I got to university, I'd been culturally conditioned for years to believe all manner of dogma about the sexes and their sexuality; for example, that masturbation was almost solely a male vice, the bitter lot of losers who could not attract a woman, and that moreover male masturbation was both repellent and ridiculous. Females did not masturbate; they did not need to. And when it occurred—unlike common, beastly, male self-abuse—female masturbation was unicorn-like, rare and beautiful: a tender, quasi-sacred act of "self-love." If a female did decide to masturbate, it was not because she couldn't get sex from a male, but because she didn't *need* a male: it was—as is almost everything females do nowadays—"empowering."

On completing my degree, I—for want of something better to do—embarked on a PhD, also in the mathematical sciences. During this period, my path crossed that of a PhD student in the humanities. She asked whether I would proofread her work for her, and I agreed. On reading what she gave me, I was shocked at how poor and ideologically driven it was. Badly structured, unsound in argumentation and extremely light in actual content, it was rendered in a feminist *langue de bois*, presumably to mask its lack of substance. Though I am no writer—I chose figures over words, after all—I found her prose so choked with jargon and so turgid as to be practically unreadable (although her politically correct euphemism was at times unintentionally comical). I could scarce believe it would pass for scholarship at all, yet for this she received a PhD and is now a professor. I remember sitting outside with her and her fiancé one summer evening as she rehearsed the sins of my sex. I listened and said little, but later thought that had I so dilated upon the baseness of women, she would have promptly denounced me as a male chauvinist pig.

It was experiences like this that finally led me to question the *status quo* and to think more objectively about what I saw and heard. I began noticing that men and their feelings just didn't matter anymore. An example: BBC Radio 4 broadcast a woman's program in the mornings, and sometimes I'd listen to it. One guest they interviewed was a male prostitute who'd been featured in a documentary on BBC television a few days before. The aging feminist hosting the program asked him what was the most female clients he'd had in one "session" and was told that he'd "done" all seventeen women in a hen party, including the bride-to-be.

I imagined how crushed the groom would have been to learn that on the eve of his wedding, the woman he loved was with this creep. And how did the feminist presenter react? She tittered. Had a woman been on the show relating how she'd been devastated to discover that her husband had visited a prostitute on the eve of their wedding, would the presenter have tittered at that?

In time, I realized that male humiliation was for most people little more than a source of entertainment. Somewhere along the line it had become socially acceptable, fashionable even, to ridicule men and masculinity without mercy, although when directed at women such cruel "humor" would be condemned as misogyny.

I felt angry whenever a woman was mocked for having small breasts; whether by loutish men or by busty or catty women. Yet I noticed that in the media, women with small breasts were seldom ridiculed, but men with small penises were mocked constantly. The male member was a laughing stock, derided and despised. So much so that even men with totally normal genitalia were now racked with insecurity and depression on account of their "manhood." (I remember seeing a lousy documentary following three men who had crippling anxieties about their penile dimensions, only one of whom had a penis classed as below average in size. The documentary showed him trying to be "more" for the woman he loved, consulting a specialist who gave him a torturous-looking steel frame on which he tried in vain for weeks to stretch his hapless organ. Of the two other men, one had been scorned by a woman because his average-sized erection wasn't as big as her former partner's and the other had simply become convinced that he was inadequate, seemingly through the messages he'd absorbed from the wider society. Ironically, this was screened on a television channel that routinely broadcasts "comedy" comprising the sexual ridicule of men like these three tormented souls.)

I also noticed that men who dared complain of being sexually humiliated in this way were typically told "it's only a joke" or that "size doesn't matter" (whilst the behavior of many women told them the opposite), or were simply belittled further, informed that they were "fragile" or "insecure" (despite a mass-media onslaught which was effectively geared to produce precisely such insecurity).

Then there were those cases in which a woman took a knife and sliced off her partner's penis. The woman was always painted as a heroine, her partner's infidelity or abuse cited as grounds for keeping her out of jail. If a man had *ever* taken a pair of nail-scissors and performed a clitorectomy on his wife/girlfriend, it would not matter if she'd been the most unfaithful, abusive woman on the planet. He would go down in history as a monster and straight to jail, probably ending up in solitary confinement for his own safety. Yet women laugh openly at male victims of such crimes, even on national television. When I considered how so many women apparently hate the male member (I bet the Germans have a word for it — *Gliedhass* or something), I began to wonder whether that old fraud Freud might have had a point after all.

Why is there so little basic compassion for men? All my life I've seen males defending females, and this is their reward? And whilst female "self-esteem" is a national concern, receiving lavish, solicitous attention, with endless government-funded initiatives to support girls and women and cater to their multifarious wants, what about boys and men? Whenever men protest against their portrayal, highlight their own suffering, or request that more empathy be shown to males, they are seen as unmanly, un-masculine (and many women shame them for it). What to do?

I have no answer; but surely the work of cataloguing the wrongs done to boys and men is a step in the right direction. Being myself (as stated earlier) one of the more fortunate of my sex, I was, although conscious of pro-female bias in the culture, unaware just how bad things had become for so many males today—a truth which feminists seek to obscure or flatly deny—and I am thankful to have had my eyes opened. If attitudes are to change and boys and men are to receive more humane treatment, then the truth must come out.

One important point to note in closing is that it would be inaccurate to impute all injustice against males solely to feminism: a great deal of the misery inflicted upon men and boys arises from the wider, far older and much more deeply rooted phenomenon of *gynocentrism*, of which feminism is but a particularly malignant modern outgrowth. Many of the double standards I experienced growing up were due largely to "traditional" or "conservative" views on the raising of boys, which effectively prize females over males. (Peter Wright and Paul Elam have written some excellent articles examining gynocentrism, which provide context for our current malaise.)

Finally, I sincerely hope the efforts to help men and boys never emulate feminism; it has shown itself to be no more than officially endorsed sexism, a poisonous gospel of male original sin and female original virtue; infantile playground taunts dressed up finely in pseudo-academic language. Given the movement's track record, one wonders whether the very word "feminism" was ever anything but a portmanteau of "female chauvinism."

Chapter 7 – Warning: Don't Care, Don't Try

Anonymous

The author describes how his mother's mental disorder and abuse, and the unwillingness of those around her to see it, have permanently damaged him and his sister

My father, a Flemish immigrant, died when I was four.

That meant that my mom had to work and raise her kids alone. She went through a very tough time, and that helped no one at home. She slowly became a kind of monster craving for power over us and sympathy from the world, and nobody could see any of that. They saw only what she wanted them to see.

My sister and I were young and did not understand most of her behaviors, but we had no choice but to accept them as normal adult behavior.

Not so long ago, I watched a documentary about bipolarity and I finally knew what was wrong with my mother, and what had been wrong with her for the last thirty years. Still, a few details did not fit with bipolarity. For example, my mother was quite a rude person with my sister and me, making us think of ourselves as bad people. At home, she had heavy mood swings. But outside the house—in public—all of a sudden she was soft and kind with us.

We also noticed that she could not stop telling her story, over and over again.

I don't deny that what happened to her as a result of my father's death was terrible. But years passed, and still she could not have a conversation without mentioning it; my father's death, *her* loss. Every December 18th, she would always find a way to say it; I've been completely alone for exactly X years today.

She had no regard for my sister's and my feelings. In fact, she was so focused on gaining sympathy for herself that she told everyone she would meet what bad kids we were, how difficult we were to control. In time, she managed to have us treated with electrotherapy because of how bad we supposedly were. Everybody supported her. She had become addicted to that support from people, and to their sympathy; people would let her talk for hours without interrupting her.

The result for us was that we went to several doctors and were treated in various ways. We still don't know the reason why because, when we ask her about it now, my mother claims to have forgotten.

To this day, I am destroyed by the experience of her sickness. My sister survived better than I did, but it's fair to say that we are both misanthropic and nihilistic to the point where we can imagine guys like Nietzsche looking down on us from heaven. We developed addictions to drugs, alcohol and other things, damage control addictions. Even now, we cannot feel an interest in ending these since everybody around us thinks we are failures anyways.

My mother, who is half-Jewish, used her so-called war trauma as an excuse for behaving badly (for example, taking great pleasure in insisting beyond all limit on having people eat large amounts of food) even though she was born in 1950.

I would like to give cis-gendered straight white or non-white males some advice. I experienced it and managed to get away from it.

In case you are nice, and for one reason or another kept naive, kept under control in some emotional way, you want to fix all problems. You try hard not to cause problems. You do your best to be kind and cool and quiet and polite and so on. But women in your family seem not to understand your position, whatever you might say and however you put it. They misunderstand and act hurt. They accuse you.

It's hard to imagine, but you must consider the possibility that they do it on purpose. It's like a game for them, a way to control you. Don't try too hard because you'll end up exhausted and depressed, struggling with an addiction when you grow up, but still trying to fit in.

Women lie. Women play. They tear you in two; one part of you wants to tell them to go fuck themselves, and the other prevents you from doing that at any cost.

The cost is your mental health. I kept on being empathetic, repressing the demon in me. Step by step, I arrived at a door, which I opened for just one second in order to take a look at what was behind. What I saw was schizophrenia. Keep that door closed and get away from it.

It's time for you to go exclusively into self-preservation. Smoke less weed. Drink less alcohol. Do a little sport and learn breathing. Forget about finding love. Ideally, you should even forget about finding a job. You are confused to the highest level imaginable. Finding quietness must come before socializing again because you've been hopelessly wrecked. Save yourself.

Chapter 8 – 58 Years Trying to Be a Man

Angelica Perduta

A transgender woman explains why she rejects the feminist narrative of male privilege.

I was born a male child in Ottawa, Canada in 1956. My parents were religious and did not identify as feminists; nonetheless, feminist dogma would play a detrimental role in my life, and I cannot say for sure whether my transgender identity was innate or exacerbated by growing up in a culture of misandry and male deference to women.

At age three I realized that I wanted to grow up to be like my mom, not like my dad. I wanted a baby in my tummy just like mom had. I was devastated to be told that boys couldn't have one. I responded defiantly that in that case I would have a turtle in my tummy instead.

Throughout my childhood, I was intimidated by the rough and tumble of other boys and felt no desire to compete with them. Girls would not include me either, so I ended up always alone.

My primary school teacher was a middle aged feminist. Woe betide any of her pupils who accidentally called her Mrs. instead of Miss. She blamed a global patriarchal conspiracy for the suffering of all women and delighted in any opportunity to shame and demonize the boys in her class in retribution.

At age seven I copied two girls in my class by painting my nails different colors with felt tip pens. The teacher was livid and declared me a "pervert." I had no idea what that word meant, but the tone of her voice was quite enough to tell me it was not something one ought to be. She dragged me by my ear up in front of the class to publicly humiliate me for my lack of masculinity.

It was not surprising that I lost interest in school or even in trying to make a good impression. I would slouch all day, eyes cast down, aiming to be as inconspicuous as I possibly could. By the time puberty set in, I hated my male body and its emerging secondary sex characteristics. I never developed sexual attraction to male or female and I really did not understand sex at all.

My father died a gruesome death when I was 16. Not long after, I tried to talk to my mother about having a sex change but she was horrified. She told me that I should accept my male duties. She told me to focus on getting a career that would support a wife and children. I had always wanted to do art and I was jealous that my sister was encouraged in that while I was denied it.

When I reached age 21 I decided that as I was legally an adult, I was entitled to make my own decision, and I sought expert medical advice. Alas, the experts declared I would be a mentally ill sex pervert, and prescribed aversion therapy against homosexuality, even though I had neither wanted nor had sex with anyone. This destroyed the last vestiges of self esteem that I clung to. I dropped out of university, turned to drugs and rapidly declined, but by age 24 summoned the willpower to get a job. I worked hard as a distraction from my low self esteem, but I still drank to excess and remained an asexual virgin with no real friends. Quite a few women did try to seduce me. I found them repugnant; all that most of them seemed to want was financial security by becoming a single mom in a welfare state.

One woman who had been an acquaintance for several years came to live in the house I had bought. She didn't have a job or any money, but she did have better qualifications than I. So I let her stay for free, hoping I would be helping her to get started on her career. What actually happened was that she decided to be the stay-at-home matriarch of my house. She took a part time job for some extra spending money for herself. She took it for granted I would carry on paying the mortgage and all the bills and more, even though we had no children.

She made me get rid of my paying lodger. She would not let my biker friends come round. She threw out many of my clothes that she considered too effeminate for a man. Why did I put up with it? Well, it was how the psychotherapists had taught me that a "man" should behave and how my father had behaved before me.

She too started demanding sex, and I tried to awaken the "natural, healthy sexuality" that the psychiatrists had told me would be there. One time I even bought a porn magazine, but it did nothing for me. She found it and gave me a stinging lecture about sexual perversion which devastated my self-esteem once again.

One day she became tearful and started giving me the silent treatment for weeks on end. Eventually I ventured, "Are you pregnant or something?" She snapped, "What do you think?" Actually, I had thought she was on the pill, but apparently she had decided to stop taking it without telling me. She shrieked at me that contraception was not only the woman's responsibility. I would have liked to have had a baby, but she wanted to make a point that it was her choice, and so I paid for the abortion.

She lived in my home for 12 years and then we got married in a church, because that's what she wanted. She got pregnant again and I told her this time that I didn't care either way what she did. I was convinced she would deliberately do the opposite of anything I suggested, just to assert her authority. She seemed to think that men needed training and to be put in their place at every opportunity.

During her pregnancy I did try to suggest she cut down on smoking and drinking and I myself quit to support her in that, but she dismissed me, saying her parents had smoked and it never harmed her. My son was born with mild fetal alcohol syndrome and has suffered from asthma all his life.

I loved him. I would feed my son, change his nappy, take him places, sing him to sleep and play with him, but his mother said he didn't need my input. She said he did not need two mothers. I secretly thought, just one mother would be a start, as all that she did with him was to plonk him in front of the television while she was off with her friends all day. When I came home from work she made me feel like an unwelcome guest in my own home. She ignored me every night while she talked on the phone to her family for hours. She dictated my gender role and started associating with a divorcee clique, planning effective divorce strategies while I was earning a living for us.

When my wife and I finally split, she took half of all I owned and never disclosed her own assets. She made many false accusations. She would only allow me to see our son for an hour every fortnight under supervision at an expensive contact center. I had no work at that time, and so I emigrated and left her and her new man to sort it out themselves.

I flew to see my son on a few occasions, but his mother would disappear with him the moment she knew I was around. The head teacher of my son's school would support her in that, and to this day I have no idea what she was told.

Eventually I did manage to take her to court. The judge allowed me to take my son skiing in France for a week, where we had a great time. Then a year later his mother phoned to say she didn't want our son anymore because her "real man" did not like children. Later I learned that he had tried to strangle my son.

My lad came to live with me in New Zealand, but a lot of damage had been done as he now believed I would be a child molester and a sex pervert. He believed he could catch AIDS from me (I am not HIV positive and I don't have sex with anyone).

At one point my ex came to visit him in New Zealand, suggesting that we should get back together. I told her I was not going to treat her like she had treated me, but that I was seeing someone else. She then made a point of meeting this person to tell her all the same lies she had been telling people in England. It resulted in this new woman becoming suspicious and, more seriously, in many intrusive investigations by authorities before they decided the anonymous tip-offs were false and the result of malice. My son lived with me until after the 2011 earthquakes and then I had to send him back to England, as we had no sewer, no electricity, and no water. His school was shut, the roads broken, liquefaction everywhere, my home damaged and the insurance refusing to pay. I decided that he would be better off back in England even though his mom was reluctant.

I had several other serious problems. I had failed in every aspect of my life. I went into deep depression that culminated in a serious attempt at suicide in 2013. When I awoke, all alone in pool of blood, I realized I was not cut out to be a man and I resolved to have the sex change I should have had back in 1977. I transitioned in 2014 and I've been happy every single day since then despite many other problems. I just cannot understand why anyone would want to be a man or have a relationship with a woman in the current gynocentric social and political climate.

***

I have in the above account tried to keep my interpretations out as you may see things quite differently. Yet now I will talk about why my story is related to feminism.

1. The Myth of Patriarchal Oppression

The imposition of gender roles that I experienced as a child did not come from a "patriarchy." The gender system was the woman's choice and men were subservient to women's needs. As a boy, I was marginalized in education due to sexual discrimination and denied the career choices I aspired to.

2. The Myth of the Male as Sexual Predator

I was not at all sexually motivated and tried only to please women. Women took it for granted that I should desire them sexually, and shamed or even blackmailed me when I didn't. They would cast aspersions on my manhood if I failed to please them on demand. Not once would they take "No" to mean "No," but as a personal insult. Twice I resorted to taking Viagra just in the hope of living up to a woman's expectations, but they always demanded more.

3. The Myth of Men's Greater Career Opportunities

In my experience, men are often work slaves. My wife did not use her training, she chose not to pursue a career, she chose to take it easy and swan about with her friends all day, yet she took it for granted that she was entitled to my full financial support even after we separated. At work it was seen as acceptable to make gender the overriding consideration in recruiting female management. These are NOT equal opportunities. These are blatant sexual discrimination.

Having lived as a man, I know what it is like to be a man. I hated every day of it.

Chapter 9 – Fear of Feminism

Argentarii

A father outlines his fears that feminism will sabotage his son and alienate his daughter.

I am not sure whether it's worth it for me to write a lengthy account of my problems with feminism, because having a family and children (one is a boy) and a bit of common sense, I have kept to myself all my views against feminism, cowardly as it sounds.

I am confident that I would lose my job and jeopardize my family's well-being if I spoke out, which fact alone is a good reason to denounce feminism; people are terrified of the backlash if you openly disagree. I work in an educational institution in the UK where feminism (alongside Communism) is taught academically, with plenty of propaganda, and where the students are given talks about how women are raped by men but not the other way around, and the usual garbage you know better than me. I've had a student telling me that all men, including me—a married man with a daughter—should take courses on how not to rape, and I have as a supervisor a feminist who teaches feminism and who could potentially get me fired if I said something incorrect, so I lower my head and think of my children's future as I take all the humiliation I feel.

Don't get me wrong; it is nowhere near as bad in the UK as in Canada yet, but it is slowly spreading everywhere, with most people not realizing what is happening.

My daughter is going to school while my son is still in a nursery, but I have had enough chances to see what is going on; girls are the "gold standard" in education. After a certain age, boys seem repressed; they look shy, they are not allowed to play hard games or anything competitive, and they are expected to be all smiles, sensible team players, with everyone getting a medal. Every single event I've been to at my school was about "Everyone wins!" no matter how crap they did, even in a race. Whenever there is an activity where children have to sing and act funny, I can see all the girls waving their hands (including my daughter), and almost all the boys blushing, looking at the floor as if they wanted to die there. Call me paranoid, but I don't like the way it looks, and my boy is next in line.

How else does feminism affect me? Well ... everywhere, all the time. I get bombarded with messages from the media, the TV and every other source reminding us men that we are aggressive, emotionless, insensitive, "privileged" ... and one of the most annoying, "perverts," the infamous man-stare rubbish. Seriously, we are biologically programmed to be hopelessly attracted to beautiful women, by any sign of fertility being displayed, and we now live in a (western) world where women dress as provocatively as possible, but we are supposed not to look? I'm totally against the "she dressed like a slut so she asked for it" line of thinking, but I do think that if women have the right to dress in a way that makes our blood boil, we at least have the right to look.

Anyway, back to the main topic. I will spare you the details of my personal circumstances, but I had several minor suicidal episodes, two of them involving the police. The worst one was going to an online suicide center when I was desperate and opened up about the problems I was having with women. The ultimate solution I was given at that time, by a woman, was to "read feminist literature!" I noticed she did it on purpose to finish me off, but the anger was stronger than my depression.

There is no need to interview hundreds of thousands of people to reach the conclusion; almost every single man on YouTube who speaks against feminism does so anonymously because he is terrified of what feminism can do to him; ruin his life and his family's (count me in here). This is really scary. You can't challenge or even discuss this cult without the fear of losing your job. Why are there thousands of teenage feminists posting videos about their cult without fearing anything? Is the Patriarchy attacking only men? This is a nearly Orwellian situation where this cult has almost everyone terrorized and afraid of admitting it—while all the while claiming that feminists are the victims.

I'm scared of seeing my daughter brainwashed into this cult, seeing me as an evil oppressor instead of the loving father who has done (and will do) anything for her, and I'm terrified of the potential damage feminism can inflict on my son if he gets indoctrinated when I'm not around to protect him. If I have to describe feminism in one word, I would say "FEAR"! Fear of losing my job, fear of having a daughter who hates me for being a white man, fear of having my son psychologically crippled by these irrational man-haters. I would gladly give my life to end modern feminism, just for the sake of my children.

I know this is just a rant, and not enough to be a proper account for a book, but I rarely get a chance to vent out my frustrations with feminism and, unfortunately for you, you are one of the few people who can understand how I feel (my wife doesn't!).

Despite being only a rant, everything I have said is true and I don't mind having it published ... as long as I keep my identity anonymous... in order to protect my family from feminists.

SECTION TWO – MEN RELATING TO WOMEN

Chapter 1 – Healing From Shame

David Shackleton

The author analyzes how he came to recognize women's unconscious power to shame men.

It feels like a regular evening as I walk into the Glebe Community Centre for the monthly meeting of the Ottawa/Hull Men's Forum. I have no inkling of the life-changing event that is about to happen.

It is February, 1990, two and a half years since my first wife left me, to my huge surprise. No, it wasn't that I thought we had a great marriage, only that I was completely unconscious of her truth or mine. But I am awake now and feeling strong. I have started a men's group and done a lot of work on myself in the last year. With the wonder of a small child, I have begun to see that the world is very different than I had thought, and that most men are still lost in the labyrinth of the male role. I am starting to see myself as a potential leader of the fledgling men's movement. And I have begun attending regular meetings of the Ottawa/Hull Men's Forum, described as a male-positive, safe space for men growing out of stereotypes of masculinity.

The organizing group of the OHMF has arranged for this meeting to be about male violence against women. Three women from the Ottawa Rape Crisis Centre have been invited to lead the group in an exploration of this issue. I arrive early; only a few men and the three women are present, sitting on chairs arranged in a circle. It is unusual to have women at the men's forum and so I ask them, "Are you leading the discussion tonight?" In a sign of things to come, the women sigh and exchange despairing glances, and one of them turns to me and says scornfully, "Hierarchy already! No, we're not going to *lead*, we're going to *facilitate*!"

Rebuked, I sit quietly. More men arrive; we introduce ourselves and the women are invited to begin their facilitation. They say that violence against women is a part of male behavior that men must help to eliminate. I certainly agree with that. They propose a debate and offer the contention; "Although not all men commit violence against women, all men benefit from it." At first, we are divided arbitrarily into two groups, for and against the contention. After a while, we are permitted to "cross the floor" if we wish, in order to take the position on the issue that feels right to us. The debate is orderly and also passionate. I do not need to cross the floor, as I am already in the group that I feel has the right of the matter.

I think about how men's violence against women has affected my life. I remember that when my wife left me she did so secretly, because, she said, "I was afraid you would be violent." Clearly, the fear of male violence was a major issue for her, even though I personally had never been violent. I imagine a world in which men are never violent against women. It seems to me that, comparing that world to this, there is not a man in it that would not be better off. More trusted, more loved, more respected, more honored, more happy, more seen and understood. Less feared, less ashamed, less defensive, less insecure. I know which world I would want to live in. There is no question that I feel diminished rather than advantaged by the violence of men against women.

The debate proceeds and some men have begun crossing the floor. To my surprise, they are crossing in both directions. Some are actually choosing the group that is arguing that they benefit from men's violence against women. I begin listening more carefully, more seriously to what they are saying. I had thought that this issue was obvious.

They are saying that they benefit from having their partner afraid of them. They are saying that someone in fear is like a slave, willing to obey them and reluctant to take a stand against them. They get to have their way much more often than is fair, because she is afraid to offend. I wonder what these men want from their relationships with women. Are they actually attracted to a relationship of fear? What about intimacy? What about happiness? Have they said these things to their wives? I cannot imagine that men in recovery, in the men's movement, would feel that they would benefit from fear on the part of their intimate partner. Yet it is so. For the first time, I sense a profound divide within the Ottawa men's movement.

The debate is over. It has been a valuable experience for me. I have much to think about.

But wait. The women have more to say. They stand up together and move to the center of the room. To my group, to the men who do not believe that they benefit from men's violence against women, they say this: "You men are worse than the men who beat their wives, the guys in the strip clubs and using prostitutes. You are pretending to be deconstructing masculinity, you are pretending to be growing into new and more whole, more conscious and responsible men, yet you are denying the very benefits you get from the violent, patriarchal system that you are a part of. You should be ashamed."

My God! I am reeling from this. I didn't see it coming. My heart is pounding and I can't think. What can I say? What can I do?

A man talks about his pain, about the way that he is also injured by the patriarchal system. The women interrupt him. "Don't tell us about your pain. Your pain is insignificant. You are the oppressor!"

Another man speaks of his experience with his ex-wife. "She accused me of sexually abusing my three-year-old daughter. How could I prove my innocence?" he asks with tears in his eyes. "I haven't been allowed to see my children for three years." "A woman would never lie about such an issue," he is told.

We seem helpless in the face of the angry accusations of these women. I have recently read Warren Farrell's *Why Men Are the Way They Are*,[1] and I try to describe some of his ideas about the equality of men and women, how men are victims of violence more often than women are. Even as I speak, however, I feel guilty and ashamed of the anger that I am feeling and that is probably in my voice, and I am ignored by the women.

Another man speaks more eloquently. "Your pain is real and needs to be heard," he says to the women, "but so is our pain. We do not deny your pain as women; please do not deny ours as men." He too is shamed in response.

The situation is incredibly charged. The women are clearly feeling unheard and angry, their worst fears about the men's movement confirmed before their eyes. The men are feeling shamed and devalued, accused by women who will not listen. We close the meeting in great awkwardness, with stiff thanks for the facilitation. The women leave in silence, obviously hugely offended. Some men huddle and talk in low tones, others leave quickly. I feel abandoned, alone again in the playground, the naughty boy standing in the corner, sent to bed without supper, punished and feeling

---

[1] Warren Farrell, *Why Men Are The Way They Are: The Male-*

guilty for not being how I "should" be. I compliment those men that I think spoke well, and leave.

I know that something pivotal has happened for me. I see that I am far from healed, far from secure and strong in my manhood. I don't know the nature of the wound I am carrying, but I know that it disqualifies me from leadership. I am not ready. I must withdraw from a public role in men's issues while I heal myself.

The Forum was never able to heal the divide that was exposed that evening. The drama played itself out over the next weeks and years. The women sent a letter to the Forum, protesting the way that they were "abused." The organizers responded with a formal apology, promising that they would make sure that it never happened again. They renamed the Forum "The Ottawa/Hull Men's Forum Against Sexism" and declared it actively pro-feminist. Men not of that persuasion were subtly (or not so subtly) unwelcome. The Forum continued for another three years, never again attracting the numbers it once had, before ceasing to operate from lack of attendance and lack of energy among the organizers. An offer from a new group to restart it on an unaligned, non-ideological basis was rejected by the holders of the name and the mailing list, who felt that they could not allow it to continue as other than specifically pro-feminist. It died, and has never revived.

I am either blessed or cursed with a passion to get to the bottom of things. Most days I think it is a blessing. For years I struggled to understand what happened that day. It seemed pivotal to the gender debate, as if the vast forces that move us had risen for a moment to the surface, like a great sea monster from the depths.

Gradually, some things became clear to me. First was that the three women were anything but powerless. In that encounter, they were both the formal leaders of the evening and also the emotional and moral center of the experience. They controlled all of the structure of the event. They felt to me like unshakeable rocks against which I and the other men battered ourselves in vain. Yet, as I replayed it over and over in my mind, I realized that they were sincere in their belief that they were victims, being abused even as they were defining the terms of the debate and overpowering the protests of the men. They did not experience their power over us as a feeling of power. I knew that this was important. They were incredibly powerful to us, yet they felt powerless and abused even as they exercised that power. How could this be, I wondered?

Slowly, I realized that I was the same. As I listened to women talk about men's power, about the oppression of women and the patriarchal advantages I had as a man, I saw that I didn't experience them as power. Indeed, my position that evening had been the denial that men's violence against women gave them any advantages at all. Yet clearly, the fear of violence seemed to dominate a lot of women's lives, and they saw violent men as very powerful. I began to get an inkling that power, between the genders at least, is very much in the eye of the beholder. And that this is very contrary to the way it *feels*. But I still didn't have an explanation for these facts. Nor did I have any sense of why this issue carried so much energy for me, why I experienced the accusation of those women as so powerful in my life. How could their shaming of me remain so devastating when I didn't agree with it, didn't think that they were *right* about me? What was the nature of their power?

In 1991, at a ten-day experiential, personal growth workshop, I found a piece of the answer. It was my first experience with people dedicated to discovering the truth about themselves, undistracted, over several days. For the first few days I risked little but watched very carefully. I learned that when people dropped their guard and confessed their fears and failings, they were not shamed but rather supported throughout the experience. What's more, they seemed to emerge stronger and with more self-respect, not less.

On about the sixth day, we did an exercise involving shadow fighting with opponents from within the group. We chose partners and mimed fighting, with or without imaginary weapons, and then changed partners and did it again. After several changes, I noticed a pattern. When my opponent was a man, I would fight energetically, striving to win. When I was in conflict with a woman, however, I would be more anxious and more restrained, and try strenuously to ensure a draw. I remember a moment of astonishment when I discovered myself fighting with a sword in my left hand. I am right handed, but I had taken an imaginary sword in my left hand because my female opponent had done so. Why was I allowing her to choose the weapons and the rules? I had never before had any awareness that my conflict behavior was different with women than with men. Was this a legacy of my childhood experience? I was intrigued.

On about the eighth day, the workshop leaders hauled three mattresses into the middle of the room and said, "OK, each of us is going to have a tantrum." "Right," I thought, "you've got to be kidding." I couldn't imagine myself doing such a thing at thirty eight years old. I made sure that I was toward the end of the line that formed around the wall. As I watched, I saw that people were really getting into it. One by one, they opened a door into their rage and kicked and screamed and wept. I decided that when it came to my turn I would give it a try and see what happened. I had no notion of any anger in me that needed to come out, but I had moved myself into a willingness to discover what might be there instead of a fear-based denial of there being anything in me that I didn't already know about.

As I ran out to the mattresses, I felt sure that I would end up feeling foolish. But almost immediately I found myself kicking and pounding the mattresses, and words began to pour out of me. Over and over I cried, "It's not fair, it's not fair." There was huge emotion in the words and a great sense of release. "It's not fair." I knew that what I was shouting was my outrage from my childhood, when I would argue with my mother and not once over many years (and still to this day) did she acknowledge to me being responsibly wrong about anything. Instead, if the argument began to go against her, she would end it with an unanswerable phrase like "You'll see when you grow up." Or, "You can't understand because you're not a woman." Or worse, "You're always completely unreasonable, there's no sense arguing with you." At one level, I was dreadfully afraid that she was right, that what seemed right to me was totally wrong, that I was self-centered and arrogant and unworthy, as she claimed. At another level, I knew that this was her defence because she knew that she was on shaky ground. Her unwillingness to ever admit it drove me crazy. I was incensed at her dishonesty. For twenty years I had carried that anger inside me, not suspecting its existence, but unable to really trust a woman because I expected her to turn against me and to deny all responsibility for her words or her actions.

The next day brought a new exercise. A rolled up blanket, tied with cord, was brought into the room. One by one, we were invited to have the blanket be whomever we wished, and to say and do what we needed to. Each person's session was contained within a formal ritual designed by the leaders, to identify the action as sacred space, as symbolic and not something that could or should occur in the real world, with the real person. This was deep psychological work.

My heart was pounding with fear as I contemplated what I wanted to do. I knew, now, that I had a great deal of rage at my mother. I knew also that I had never really expressed it to her, because of the power that she had over me, the fear that she would abandon me and throw me out of our home.

(When I was four, because I refused to run with her for a bus, she got onto the bus alone and left me crying in fear at the bus stop. Unknown to me, she got off at the next stop and watched me crying. She waited until she thought I had learned my lesson before coming back to reclaim me. I always ran after that.) And so I had never allowed myself to win a fight with her, but contained my anger and held back my rage, as I had shown myself so eloquently in the shadow fighting exercise. Could I give myself permission to say and do what was in my heart? Was I ready to go past my fear of abandonment, still real in me twenty years after leaving the family home?

I still didn't know as I walked out to begin my work. For a while I just walked around the blanket, looking at it lying on the floor, trying to find the courage to speak my truth and unshame my anger. I started talking to it, asking questions like "What did you think you were doing to me? Why did you never hug me or kiss me? Why couldn't you tell me you loved me?" Gradually, I began to feel my anger. I began to shout. "Don't you know how much that hurt me? Couldn't you see how afraid I was?" I began kicking the blanket and screaming, "I hate you. I hate you." I kicked it across the room, picked it up and slammed it down on the floor. I kicked it so high it lifted one of the ceiling tiles. With tears rolling down my cheeks, I stomped my mother's head into the floor. For the first time in my life, I experienced my anger without shame. At thirty eight years old, after spending my life till then unconsciously circling around her, I killed my mother and began the process of setting myself free and growing myself up.

A consequence of setting myself free in this way was that I became able to see and understand the operation of female power in society. The power that the three women had exercised in that debate about male violence was *moral* power, the power to shame good men into silence. Of even more significance was that they didn't know they had it.

They felt like victims even as they wielded huge moral power, power that I and the other men experienced as overwhelming. They accused us of abusing them, *and they got away with it*, the Forum renamed and re-missioned itself as a feminist institution in response to their shaming.

Is this the power of feminism? Is this how it has operated for the last fifty years? I think so. Women, from their role as the primary parent in almost all families, carry huge weight in the psyches of both men and women. The power that this gives them is the power to say what is right and what is true, and most of all what should be done about it. What is political correctness if not the social shaming of "incorrect" thinking? The success of feminism itself is the proof of this. After all, if feminists were right that men have operated a patriarchal conspiracy to benefit themselves and to oppress women throughout history and still today, then feminism could never have gained traction. If men really were patriarchally self-interested and oppressive, they would simply have said to the early feminists, "Shut up and get back in the kitchen." The fact that feminists succeeded in bringing women's issues to the forefront of social concern and, even more powerfully, suppressing concern about legitimate men's issues, argues for their power, not their powerlessness. That power is moral in nature, the power to shame. Indeed, that is what they have done; masculinity itself has been deeply shamed, named as oppressive, abusive, toxic. To take back this moral power, or even to see its reality, men need to look deeply into their own psyches and reclaim their moral authority.

The process of discovering the source of one's shame and recovering from it is not trivial. It involves looking deep into one's soul and learning to love what one finds there. It is fearful because what one expects to find is guilt, unworthiness, inferiority, everything shameful. It can only be accelerated through intensity, through the passion with which we pursue it. Sometimes, if we are willing, life brings us to moments when we are able to go deep and return richly blessed.

Chapter 2 – The Brave vs. the Privileged

Seth McDonough

The author explains why, as the victim of a brutal physical attack, he chafes every time he hears calls to end "male violence against women" even while he recognizes his own conditioning to care more about harms to women.

One of the great philosophical dilemmas that confronted the childhood version of me was determining which was an easier life; being a male person or being a female person. On the X chromosome, I noted, there was the biological expectation that one eventually give birth. But, on the Y chromosome, there was the apparent social requirement that one get into physical fights, both consensual and non-consensual. While girls could be cruel to each other, the threat seemed to be more often psychological. As a boy, the risk of violence was, as far as I could tell, omnipresent.

Despite my jealousy of what I perceived to be a violence-free life, I never questioned the convention that girls, in particular, deserved special protections. "Never hit a girl," seemed as unimpeachable a notion as gravity.

Today, the adult version of me is a critic of feminism, not because I have revised my concern for the safety of women, but because it occurs to me that male people deserve protection from violence too. As it is, our instinctive double standard in favor of protecting women has been multiplied by feminism's thesis, rarely challenged in academia, advocacy, and media, that women are forever under siege while men are privileged.

Stop Violence Against Women vs. its Corollary

A notable symptom of feminism's penchant for claiming that women's pain doesn't get enough consideration—while simultaneously ignoring men's pain—can be found in the phrase, "Stop violence against women," or, as I learned as a child, "Never hit a girl." Whenever I hear this impassioned call, my mind conjures a corollary: "Violence against men is fine." Clearly, my inference isn't a logical necessity. (Someone who says, "Let's end cancer" isn't necessarily implying, "But diabetes isn't worth worrying about.") Nevertheless, if one spends a few moments considering how our media and culture generally represent violence against the two sexes, it is difficult to escape the notion that we are significantly more comfortable with non-consensual and even deadly violence against men than we are with any violence against women, particularly if the latter is performed by men. (Indeed, some feminists will openly double down on the anti-violence double standard by calling for us to "Stop *male* violence against women.")

For anyone skeptical of the notion that we have an anti-violence double standard, I request that they consider Canadian citizens' call for a Public Inquiry into Missing and Murdered Indigenous Women and, in contrast, how little attention has been brought forward to contemplate missing and murdered Indigenous men. Researcher and political science professor Dr. Adam Jones notes that, according to RCMP police reports, two thirds of Canadian aboriginal murder victims are male. Moreover, he says that while the RCMP has not released data on missing Indigenous males, utilizing a global correlation between homelessness and missing populations, he estimates that First Nations males will also likely make up the majority of the missing Indigenous people. Nevertheless, the government and media that supposedly represent all of us rarely talk about the murdered and missing Indigenous men and boys.

Equal Gender Consideration vs. Me

I find our society's lack of concern for male victims of violence to be the most daunting of double standards: while it angers me every time I notice it, I simultaneously cannot resist participating in it.

The childhood version of me played lacrosse for many years. In one of my later seasons as a teenager (i.e. past the age when boys' and girls' average physical strength is roughly equal), my teammates and I peered through the mesh faceguard of one of our opponents and spotted the eyes of a girl. Lacrosse is a game of consensual violence, but when we encountered this anomaly (she was the first and only girl I am aware of opposing in my eight-year career) we were conflicted by two maxims:

(1) Lacrosse Strategy: When your opponent has the ball, and you're near them, you are obliged to try to separate their union via the physical imposition of your stick and/or your shoulder.

(2) Social Expectation: Never hit a girl.

As far as I could tell, without saying a word, we all decided that Maxim (2) overruled Maxim (1). (I estimate so because I did not see the girl hit with a stick or shoulder at all.)

My teammates' and my collective decision was in one sense unfair to that girl. It's hard to become a great agent in any sport if your opponents go easy on you. (Probably for this reason, she was—as far as I could tell—trying to hide her female status from us so that we wouldn't discriminate in favor of her.) But I don't know if it's fair to criticize us for following our cultural conditioning in this case.

We'd been taught since inception that violence against boys was okay, while violence against girls was a symptom of evil. And, while we had also learned from our coaches and sports-TV-viewing that winning at all costs was a crucial virtue, the instruction never to hit a girl seemed more unbreakable.

I don't regret my share of the gender bias that day. As much as I think we need to stop non-consensual violence against men, the thought of participating in consensual violence against women still scares me more.

Equal Gender Consideration vs. Our Stomachs for It

Our culture's greater concern for the suffering of women is, I think, an understandable consequence of our binary evolutionary upbringing. As meta-analyst and critic of feminism Karen Straughan points out, our ancestral societies had to have a thick skin for males going into battle against rival species or tribes. If you think you are immune to this increased comfort with violence against men, find a movie in which a woman is punched or kicked and compare your stomach's reaction to that with watching a man receive ten times that much abuse.

If I'm right that most of us are significantly more squeamish about violence against women than against men, one might argue that such divergent gender concern is artificially influenced by the fact that we are more used to seeing men assaulted in the media. I do not doubt that increased exposure has desensitized us to the pain of male victims, but I suspect our biology is playing a significant role in our reactions, too. And, even if it is not, the point remains the same: we are more comfortable watching a man getting beat up than we are with a woman receiving any aggression at all.

While I understand and participate in this preferential concern for female victims, I believe it's time to resist our biological and cultural training a little, and expand our compassion catchment area to include men.

Feminism vs. Nuance

Feminists will, of course, deny that we care more about women's victimization than men's, but they are left then to justify why there are so many publically-funded resources to "Stop Violence Against Women," and so few looking out for the rest of the population.

Consider the two most talked about categories of violence against women, domestic violence and sexual assault. While both may involve greater numbers of women, even the most female-centered feminist acknowledges that men are sometimes victims in both areas. So shouldn't excluding men from the lead slogan against these domains of pain be as untenable as excluding female war veterans from post-traumatic stress therapy?

For those advocates who are egalitarian at heart, instead of dividing candidates for their concern into gender-worthy and gender not-so-worthy, why not simply help anyone seriously suffering in any particular category they're concerned about, and let the gender percentages fall where they may?

Perhaps the distinction that justifies this gendered anti-violence advocacy is that, while men are victims of such violence, too, they are in less danger when they are, because they are better equipped—via their generally superior upper body strength—to defend themselves. If that is the justification, it seems we are ignoring (A) cases where particular perpetrators and victims of violence do not fit into that average, (B) male on male situations where one is much stronger than the other, (C) weapons and their penchant for equalizing physical power imbalances, and (D) male victims' possible aversion to defending themselves against their female aggressors because (1) they've been socialized not to, and (2) they think that the justice system will be biased against them if they do. (And before one dismisses such a self-imposed unwillingness to defend oneself as one's own fault, one should note that it is parallel with the feminist argument that women are sometimes psychologically unable to leave abusive relationships.)

Feminism vs. Equality

Moreover, while domestic and sexual violence may more often injure women, is it not the case that men are the more common victims of most other forms of non-consensual violence (including stranger attacks, gay-bashing, and murder)? I do not argue for gendering these issues either since women will be victims of them, too, but if we're going to have an *end violence against women* reduction strategy for the areas in which women are more often hurt, what reason is there not to have an *end violence against men* category for the areas in which men more often need support?

Feminism vs. the Force

Instead, while feminism maximizes our instinct to get women and children to the life boats first, our media and governments lock the discrepancy in place with their unwavering commitment to feminism. Recently, for instance, when my city of Vancouver, in association with the YWCA, promised to open a new shelter "for single moms and their children," nary a pundit wondered aloud if there would be room for dads who might be in the same difficult predicament as the solo mothers. (Alas, in the pundits' defence, it probably wasn't that they didn't care about single dads; instead, it didn't occur to them that male people would need to be included in such an initiative.)

These sorts of women-centered projects surround us like the Force: "Because I'm a girl," "We need more women in STEM fields." And we need to celebrate "girl power," and "strong female characters," and "Ban Bossy" and stop "mansplaining." Meanwhile, "Because it's 2015," we need to help "women and children." "He for She!"

Feminism dominates everything and everyone around us, yet the mainstream conversation rarely notices its influence. I have never heard anyone in the Canadian media, for instance, question the fact that Canada has a "Status of Women" department, but doesn't possess a matching hub of inquiry for men. This not only denies that men currently have many high rates of suffering in Canada—homelessness, workplace death, suicide, and so on—but it discounts the possibility that men in general could struggle in future. By its lack of a matching Status of Men department, it seems that men's problems are not only institutionally invisible in Canada, they are also impossible.

Feminism vs. Gall

Again, this discrepancy of concern is played out in the successful call for a Missing & Murdered Indigenous Women Inquiry. To their credit, the usual feminist microphone, CBC Radio, did a story on the higher numbers of murdered Indigenous men. The news department interviewed a couple of feminist experts, who explained, that, while yes, murdered and missing Indigenous men are of concern, too, we shouldn't take our eyes off the group that had brought us to this success of attention; indeed, adding men to the discussion would detract from the needs of the women. So we were best to focus on missing and murdered women for now, and then sometime in future we could think about missing and murdered men. And that was good enough for CBC Radio News.

This line of obfuscation broke my gall-o-meter. Imagine, let's say, we lived in world wherein white children's organizations proliferated across the landscape. And imagine that these white children's organizations persuaded the public that white children were suffering unusually high rates of cancer compared to other children, and so they convinced the public to tell the government to start a hospital exclusively for sick white children. But then one day, let's say, it was noted that black children suffered even higher rates of cancer than the white children. And so the white children's organizations explained, "Oh, well, that sounds bad, too, but right now we really need to focus on the white children, and then maybe later we can help the black children."

Media vs. Equal Consideration

I wish this were an exaggeration, but our media has been so bamboozled by the notion that women are an oppressed sex who always need more help than men that they cannot see the obvious double standards that would scream into their ear pieces on any non-gendered (or race-focused) topic. If a study claims that 1 in 5 girls are suffering in a particular area, our media will already be shouting that we need to do better for our girls before they have had a chance to read page two, which reveals that 4 in 5 boys are suffering the same.

Violence vs. Me

Like many men, I have been the victim of violence. Along with my brother and one of my sisters, the university student version of me was one day walking home at night from a play. We passed through a school yard next to our house. There, we were surrounded, threatened, and assaulted by a large group of teenagers. They punched my brother and me several times in the head, while our sister, a karate instructor, tried to pull them off of us. At first I attempted to fight them off, but I soon felt dizzy from the assault and I figured I was making matters worse trying to resist, and so my siblings and I kept walking through the mini-mob as they threw fists at my brother and me. For a brief time, the teenagers left us, and we nearly got home, but then the attackers returned with large sticks.

The leader swung his weapon at my brother, who blocked the blow just in time with his arm. So the attacker moved onto me, but I didn't see him coming. However, I did feel the stick land at full force on my face, breaking my nose, and my orbital bone, and ripping a trench into my mouth.

I fell to the ground, and another of the attackers kicked me in the ribs. But I didn't feel that. I just remember thinking that I might be blind because I couldn't see through the blood that was pouring into my hands like rain.

Another of my sisters heard the violence from our house, and she rushed out to tend to me while our attackers threatened to kill us. Soon after, two of our neighbors came out as well, and they dragged me into their home, while the assailants threw rocks at us.

Men vs. Freedom from Fear

Since that violent day, I have often listened to talk radio programs, and whenever they discuss violence against women, a popular consensus among callers and pundits is that men have no idea what it's like to feel the fear that women do of being assaulted while walking alone at night.

I try not to play my registered victim card, but I must admit that every time I hear this presumptuous and compassion-deprived claim, I have difficulty not hollering at my radio.

Men vs. Privilege

Men are told by feminists that we are universally privileged, and not to feel too bad if we don't yet see our privilege because, after all, the privileged are naturally unaware of their own advantages. One wonders if such delightful accusers will ever ponder the obvious counter that they may also be privileged without noticing it.

I don't doubt there are distinct types of danger and/or fear that are more common to women, but men have genres of violence of which they are more often the victims, too, so

I'm not sure why these grand assumers have trouble imagining that men could experience fear of violence.

For the record, dear privilege accusers, men do not all wander the streets free of worries. After my siblings and I were attacked, I took my lacrosse stick with me wherever I went. My brother carried soup cans to throw at any would-be attackers. And I don't want to speak for all men, but I doubt I'm the only one who is not only aware of dangers to himself, but also feels a duty to try to protect those he cares about wherever he goes. And *that* is an additional fear. I'm not just scared for me; I'm scared that I won't have the physical strength to protect those I love. Moreover, I feel obligated by both society and my own moral code to stick up for strangers when they're in danger. That's a scary expectation to live with, and yet I feel shame when I don't do enough.

It is a self-loathing that our culture would not necessarily have spared me. After all, I am male, so susceptibility to fear is not a respectable option. In fact, perhaps the greatest insult you can give to a man is that he is a coward. (Indeed, if a crime is particularly vicious, police will call it "cowardly" as though that somehow makes it an even worse wrongdoing.) In contrast, for women, there is no such thing as cowardice: there is only danger, fear, and courage.

Shaming vs. Male Bystanders

In support of the cowardice-shaming binary, there is currently a popular project called the White Ribbon Campaign (supported by my own favourite professional football team, the BC Lions), which describes itself as "the world's largest movement of men and boys working to end violence against women and girls, promote gender equity, healthy relationships and a new vision of masculinity," and which calls for male bystanders to step in when women seem to be in danger.

"Don't walk on by if you witness harassment or an assault on the street or anywhere: assess the risk, then intervene and confront or defuse the situation. If you need to, ask for help. Call 911."

This isn't an inspiring-future-heroes project, but instead a shame-based, stop-being-part-of-the-problem campaign. Before providing the above instruction, White Ribbon headquarters tells male people to "Think about the kind of man you want to be," "Be a good role model and share with those around you the importance of respecting women and girls," and "Accept your role as a guy in helping end violence against women."

As a former victim who was helped by my siblings and my neighbors when I was lying injured on the ground, unable to see, I am touched by the notion of encouraging people to look out for each other. And yet I am also irritated by the coarse manner in which such campaigns call upon men to put themselves in danger's crosshairs.

First, it is another double standard that it is only men (regardless of their physical and crisis skills) who are asked to help, and only women who are considered worthy of concern.

Second, campaigns such as this seem to imply that the intervening bystander is an invincible species who cannot be harmed in the execution of his duties. On the contrary, those who try to help are putting themselves at risk, as they may find themselves in a physical battle with someone who is stronger than they are, or in possession of a weapon and/or allies.

Thankfully, the campaign does include a suggestion to call 911, but that safety option is not the main point. (If the campaign organizers were merely asking people to keep their senses tuned for dangerous situations and to alert the police whenever needed, why would they ask this only of men? Phoning 911 does not require the advantage of increased upper body strength.) No, the lifeblood of The White Ribbon message is that men should directly intervene as much as possible to have a better chance at redeeming their problematic and ever-sinning male selves.

Courage vs. Courage

Compare, then, how we treat male bystanders with how feminists have convinced us to talk about female victims of violence. As in the bystander circumstance, there is an opportunity for female victims to help protect future victims by immediately going to the police. But asking such victims to step forward is currently called "victim blaming" by feminists and those who yield to them in the media and government. (Note that there is no matching "bystander blaming" phrase aimed to keep would-be male interveners safe.) So, whereas male bystanders are expected to put themselves in physical danger to protect potential female victims, feminists have convinced our media that female complainants who take the emotional risk of speaking up in court are, by definition, "courageous."

Applying such heroic terminology to every female case tells women that standing up for future victims is going beyond our expectations. Indeed, while we disregard men's courage, we condescend to women by not asking any of them. Sometimes, I'm sure, courage is required to take an accusation to the police and to the courts, but why does our media insist on using the term "courageous" without having any evidence of whether it applies in particular cases?

In my case, I eventually stopped carrying my lacrosse stick, and I started to trust strangers again. But, if I'd been told by my friends and the media that I was a permanent victim, and that going to court was courageous, that would have been quicksand to my resilience.

Vulnerability vs. Virtue

Note, moreover, that while we have relatively little compassion for male victims of violence, we are expanding the definition of violence against women so that we can include more female people in our consideration. For instance, we often hear victims' advocates telling the media that the court process is *worse* for women than the assaults themselves. And the media always nods its head gently as if this weren't a shocking statement.

When I went to court to watch the sentencing of our lead attacker, a young man sat near me. I quickly recognized him as one of the gang. It turned out that he was the teenager who'd kicked me after I'd fallen during the attack, and now he was just a meter away with no one between us (until my dad arrived and took the intervening space). That was unsettling to me. But "as bad as" the assault itself? The suggestion is so ridiculous, I will not dignify it with a response.

Compassion is a beautiful virtue that can help victims, but so too is respect. Our universities are currently drenched with "trigger warnings" for alleged "micro-aggressions" and "language-based violence," and the students are given "safe spaces" where they—especially if they are female—can be spared ideas that they find scary. Such students are being taught to celebrate their vulnerabilities as virtues, instead of learning about the best ways to overcome them.

Equal Gender Consideration vs. Chivalry

In my story, before that stick collided with my face, one of the attackers bumped into my sister, and another attacker said, "Hey, we don't hit girls." The two aggressors quickly agreed on this point of ethics, and it was clear that they were looking for a way out of a situation that had escalated further than the camaraderie they were looking for when they had joined the assault squad. And so my sister courageously stood between the attackers and her brothers hoping to give those two strangely chivalrous violent offenders a reason to back down.

As these baffling characters—along with the White Ribbon campaign—demonstrate, our society still believes in chivalry. While "women and children first to the lifeboats" is officially an antiquated term, the phrase "women and children," is not, and it is still often substituted by the media and American presidential candidates for the gender-free term *civilians*.

Notice how many politicians and advocacy groups will do their best to emphasize how women are hurting in order to sway us to support them on particular projects. Women in pain tug at our compassion more than men in pain.

My anger bubbled against this empathy gap recently when a Vancouver anti-homelessness advocate noted that having shelter space is not always morally sufficient; for instance, she explained, "no woman" should have to go back to a shelter at which she's been assaulted by another resident. I don't disagree, but the corollary again seems to suggest that it's okay for men to sleep next to people who have assaulted them.

Stigma vs. Stigma

I have no doubt there are common negative female experiences that I am shielded from, and I have the empathetic flexibility to care about circumstances that are different from my own. I certainly don't want to remove the stigma against violence against women. If terrible people weren't motivated by chivalry-shaming, then the Western world could come closer to the misogynistic dystopia we are told we already have. However, I wonder if we could clear out some of the infantilizing emotional protections for women, such as trigger warnings for topics that feminists don't like, so that we could make a little room in the stigma to include some non-consensual violence against men.

Courage vs. Fear

Perhaps I acquired my unorthodox concern for male people from my mother, a now-retired superstar math teacher and principal, who always looked out equally for both the boys and the girls.

A few weeks after we were assaulted, most of my family was to attend an event, but since our attackers had threatened to return to our house in future, my mom decided it would be best if she house-sat for her children while we were away.

A couple of hours into her solo evening, my mother heard someone knocking loudly at the front door. She looked out the window to see a rough-looking teenage boy calling for help. He claimed that he and his friend had been climbing on the neighboring school, and that his friend had fallen off. My mom wondered if this was a ruse from one of our attackers, but she was not in the habit of ignoring youth pleas for help so she followed that young man into the dark. She soon found that his companion was indeed critically injured, and so she did as she always did and she helped save that wounded boy.

I have trouble thinking of my mother's courage that evening without tears touching my cheeks. And I forever hope to live up to my mother's example when I encounter women or men in danger.

Chapter 3 – Chain Male

Richard Odenwald

The author highlights a number of experiences, both trivial and profound, that have left him feeling at odds with his culture.

Submitting this essay has not only made me think about how feminism has affected my life, but also stirred up how I feel; why am I actually irritated? It boils down to this: men are still expected to be gentlemen, but women can be ladies only when they choose.

Many of my heroes are women. In Canada, these include Alexandra Morton and Elizabeth May. I have always judged people by what they contribute; it never occurred to me to choose whom to admire in any other way. I have found it inexplicable and offensive to have been under scrutiny for presumed chauvinism most of my life. Aung San Suu Kyi is a hero, but so is Paul Watson. Today's strident feminists allow no such openness of heart. Paul Watson is excluded because of facial hair.

It is not all women I am mad at—not my wife and certainly not my mother, both of whom I worship, or innumerable other hard working and fantastic female friends—but women who play a strategy, conscious or not, of wanting special measures extended only to their sex (women-only spaces, emotional indulgences, preferred access to jobs) while still claiming superiority in everything from parenting to geo-politics. For the purposes of this essay, I will use the tired, grating term *womyn* to refer to those women who won't or can't be honest about themselves and the current absurd state of vindictive hyper-feminism.

It seems that everything feminine has become admirable and good while everything masculine has become suspect, seen as prejudiced, narrow minded, exclusionary or violent. By age 18 I learned that, according to womyn, discrimination was something that came naturally to me as a white male. I later learned that no matter how hard I worked and how competitive the job market, I was overpaid and any success came from my being "privileged." As feminism got a firm hold on the public psyche as well as on public policy, the list of female virtues grew ten-fold while male virtues became taboo. Even male physical strength was under erasure as Hollywood starlets, who on the previous day were perhaps resting up in a Support Center, were beating up burly men in action sequences.

The original feminist movement had laudable and just aspirations, and it has unleashed great minds. Unfortunately, in its present incarnation it has given safe harbor to small and vindictive ones. Latter day feminism has served some womyn so well they won't err from course for the sake of truthfulness or even for their own son's fair fortunes. Perhaps worst of all, it has strained the natural ties of affection between the sexes and eroded the innate caring and adoration that men have for women.

Feminism gone wrong has created a culture something like living in a one-party state, where not only is behavior and declared belief under scrutiny, but even thought is carefully screened through a feminist filter. One gender keeps claiming the moral high ground, regardless of credibility. As a man I feel a perverse pressure. I must prove myself "open minded" and "supportive" and constantly agree that womyn's lives are harder; that they face discrimination, that a conspiracy exists at the top to keep womyn from high office, that more womyn should be hired in every field from engineering and medicine to ski instruction and radio hosting. There is injustice everywhere, victims in every ladies' room.

Furthermore, even in normal workplaces, there seems to be an unwritten rule that special consideration must be given to womyn: they are more sensitive, better informed, and mustn't be offended. We are even to believe in the Divine Feminine, although generally I have seen little of it. We are expected to believe that womyn are better candidates for everything—except, of course, carrying heavy suitcases or changing a tire in a snowstorm.

Ironically, all this politically correct feminist training seems to be having little effect on men even after 50 years. In my office, which is about 70% female, there are rare occasions when there is nobody but men in the room. We all take note and, frankly, breathe a sigh of relief. "Just men?" we say in effect, "Phew." This is not to say we don't like, respect, and laugh with our female colleagues, but when they are gone we do feel at liberty to talk more plainly. We can be politically incorrect, and it is a great relief. Sometimes we talk about the absurdities we live with and we dare to speak honestly. If a Professor of Womyn's Studies were in the room, she would either have a heart attack or call the police, claiming an unsafe space. For all the decades of "training" in correct feminist-based twaddle, we still talk the same way when unencumbered and, what's more, believe what we feel is true.

My male colleagues struggle to stay afloat just as much as my female colleagues. The workplace is demanding and competitive. If anything, my male colleagues are extended less "understanding." Womyn can bring emotions into the workplace, as well as cleavage, even when professional lines are muddied. Contrary to all feminist doctrine to keep sexism out of the workplace, a well-dressed figure, distinctly calculated to draw attention or admiration, is still used by many womyn to help gain a promotion, often to the chagrin not just of men but also of their (perhaps less conventionally attractive) female colleagues.

On a personal level, I can offer some examples of how feminism has affected my life. Such episodes could not, I believe, have come from any other time than our own.

At a dinner amongst friends, I mention hearing of special government funded programs to get more womyn into the trades, and I offer the observation that very few women *want* to carry lumber, rebar or concrete across noisy, filthy and dangerous construction sites. Do they want to join the legions of male workers with bad backs, carpal tunnel and painful early retirement?

Although most people seem to think it is a reasonable thing to say, they know that agreeing with it can quickly get someone into trouble. Instead, we agree on the fatuous idea of making everything more "inclusive." The lack of womyn on construction sites has nothing to do with native interest, with strong arms or injuries; it is a lack of inclusiveness or its evil twin, the catcall.

I think we will come to a time when the push to put women into physically demanding jobs to prove something will lose favor. Besides, the fact is that social engineering is not trumping nature; it's simply the case that white-collar jobs are safer and usually pay better in the long run. In fact, with girls doing better than boys from kindergarten through Grade 12 and higher, I fear a time when all the "dirty" work will be left to the men while the "smart" work will be dominated by womyn. Mothers of sons may want to look hard at this trend if they have big dreams for their little boys.

Looking back over some decades, I can share several episodes in my past work and private life that left me with a sense of injustice.

I was 23 and had applied for a job for which I was clearly qualified. To my surprise, the job was given to a female colleague who had been in the same program as me. It was a surprise because I knew her work had been, to put it kindly, not very good. It was only later I found out that the government job to which we had both applied had a policy that in cases of "equal qualification," preference would be given to certain "targeted groups," including women. I had understood affirmative action to be helpful in bringing minority groups forward, but women are not a minority group. In this case, nor was there equal qualification. It is a near certainty she got the job only because of her sex.

At that moment I felt that the injustices of the past were now being unfairly heaped on the heads of a single generation of men. Ironically, I found out some time later that she quit the job to start a family two years after landing it.

A decade later, working in the private sector, I was asked by the boss to come into his office for a meeting. I wondered briefly if I was going to get a promotion. Instead he said, rather awkwardly, that a member of our team had come to him to complain of sexual harassment. He found it as difficult to say as I did to hear. It was absurd. "Who said that?" I asked. He told me and we were both a bit stunned. "I have to ask you, is there anything to it?" I replied, "Absolutely not."

It was pure fiction. He thanked me and said he would talk to her again. A few very uncomfortable days later, he said that the whole thing had gone away. She retracted her accusation. "Seems she has done it before," he said. "Other female members of her department heard about it, came to me, and told her either she retracts the accusation or they would all speak out publicly in support of you."

I have wondered since: how did she get away with such a serious, indeed criminal accusation, with nothing more than being confronted for lying and being embarrassed? Were it not for a presumption of guilt in all men, such an accusation would not have got very far. She knew the gravity and effectiveness of her action and I presume had seen it work before. The times were in her favor. Sexual harassment accusations hang like a dark cloud over a generation of men. Some feminists, sensing the tide running in their favor, feel empowered to act irresponsibly. The motivation for her action remains unknown to me.

Perhaps more than anything else, feminism resulted in my choosing not to have children. Now, in my sixth decade of life, I wonder what I have missed.

When I was in my late 20's, I entered the work world and over the next 15 years a few relationships, and a marriage, the topic of having children came up again and again. And each time it was shot down by two things: can we afford it and what happens if we break up? The latter weighed the heaviest. All around me, marriages were failing, and in each case I heard the same thing; "You're screwed." This was a reference to how a man would be treated by the justice system. The justice system had not kept up with the times.

At one time, when men had default access to higher paying jobs, and a one-income family with a stay at home mother was the norm, alimony and child support settlements made sense. But when two income households became the norm, a father left to support a family after a divorce made no sense. His stress level was ridiculous, far greater, I believe, than was acknowledged. The courts rightly had the welfare of the children in mind but seemed to be missing the fact that as the cost of living spiraled upwards, driven in no small degree by two income families becoming the norm, heaping everything on the head of a divorced man was not doing the children any good at all. All the men I knew going through this nightmare wanted nothing more than the best of care for their children, but the economy had so radically shifted that the "bread winning" dad model was a quaint idea from another generation. It was generally financially impossible. To make matters worse, fathers, who were usually blamed and demonized for the break-up, were expected suddenly to co-parent in a way never before seen.

My colleagues were living in basement suites, working full time, while their ex-wives were living in the hard-won family home and enjoying their lives a good deal more than the men. Something was wrong with the picture. Hollywood had even coined a term for a luxurious house in LA occupied by a woman: "That's a three-marriage house," meaning it had taken three marriage break ups and divorce settlements for her to be living in such nice place. "Why get married?" began another joke. "Find a woman you hate and buy her a house."

I cannot lay all the blame for my aborted fatherhood on feminism. There were other, existential barriers, including being too self-centered to give up certain freedoms. But I can say that were it not for the very real threat posed by an unfair family court system and the image of my distraught male colleagues arriving at work with disbelief and betrayal etched on their faces, I would have stepped up to the plate and would probably have been a fine dad.

On a lighter note, the effects of feminism have even filtered into sports. Apparently, in the eyes of some womyn, participation in sport is an act of chauvinism. We are not talking about rugby in 1880 at Oxford, but solo sports like rock climbing or surfing.

In this critique of the male, participating in sports is somehow an "exclusive act." Going out on the water or skydiving has become sexual discrimination! When I pointed out that anybody could go surfing or skydiving (barring a financial barrier), I was told "but you feel entitled." I still can't make sense of that. I'd say I felt driven, motivated, excited, determined but not "entitled" over somebody else. In fact, I used to bemoan the lack of women in sport and spent a great deal of time introducing anybody who showed interest. I can understand that some people don't feel confident in picking up challenges, but that is not to say that those who participate are exclusionary or entitled. There is no credibility in this thinking, but perhaps a good term from the Bard: the green-eyed monster.

Exceptionalism of any kind has never withstood the test of time. The dampening effect of this feminist culture on the male psyche and ego is not subtle. I suppose that is the point; to crush men down. I can only hope that as the current excesses of female empowerment are examined honestly, progress will be made to creating an equally bright future for everyone, regardless of gender.

Chapter 4 – The Definition of Insanity

Joe Mossman

The author explains how his innocent attempts to become friends with a popular high school girl caused an uproar—while a genuine predator went unnoticed.

There is nothing remotely interesting about unrequited teenage love. It is the corniest of all cornball clichés, and only the worst of hacks would bother to write about it. I'm talking about the squirmy, male-to-female kind, that old chestnut about socially awkward boys pining for uninterested girls. In fact, I'll bet that if you built a time machine and started trawling the centuries for tales of blundering nerds pitching woo at aloof beauties, you'd start to wonder if the whole human race was a canceled TV show stuck in a permanent rerun cycle. From Ancient Sumeria to the Napoleonic Empire, the story would always be the same.

Until you hit the twentieth century, in particular the post-feminist *late* twentieth century.

Up until then, that poor bashful boy was harmless, a starry-eyed romantic dreaming of love above his station. Sure, he might have to contend with a jealous boyfriend or overprotective dad, but it wouldn't be because he posed any real threat. His sexual ineptitude would have made him the subject of pity at best, ridicule at worst.

Flash forward to the 1990s, though, and that timeless story mutated into something considerably different.

The '90s was the decade that framed and defined my own adolescence, so I'm legally obligated, in a sense, to love it; we had the best music (grunge), the best fashion (grunge), and the best movies (also grunge) ... but we also had a media-driven fear culture obsessed with uncovering new kinds of *stranger danger*, which dovetailed neatly with a pandemic of sexual paranoia. It was not a good time to be a besotted adolescent boy.

Her name was Alina.

Actually, it wasn't. I've changed the names in this story, and while it bothers me to have to do that, at least it gives me some creative leeway to provide some more appropriate monikers. I picked Alina for her because it's Greek for *light,* and that is certainly what she was: a beacon in the darkness. She was beautiful, a dainty little porcelain doll of a girl with freckles and copper hair and big dark eyes, but what really piqued my interest was how Alina seemed to exist outside the high school political sweatbox. She was nobody's target and nobody's bully, a mature, approachable girl who got along with everybody.

Nevertheless, I didn't dare approach her.

The problem wasn't that I was shy. The problem was that I was *socially incapacitated*. I'd been bullied throughout most of elementary school, and the one thing people still cannot seem to grasp about bullying is that it's not the abuse *itself* that causes the lasting damage, it's the authority figures who tell you that the name-calling and the beatings are a perfectly normal part of life, that *you're* the problem for making a big deal of it, that in effect you *deserve* it. I did everything in my power to defend myself, but I'm fairly certain the boy who had my number had something clinically wrong with him. I won't call him a sociopath, but he was relentless in a way that defied all the usual explanations for why bullies bully. In eight years he never got bored, never got tired, never took a day off from his life's mission, which was to make sure I was completely ostracized.

It worked. I soon learned that I was actually safer lingering unnoticed in the margins. The Three Commandments are: Do Not Speak, Do Not Move, Do Not Contribute. I reached a point where I stopped caring, then went a step beyond that and stopped caring about *not* caring, and by high school I had completely withdrawn into myself.

Of course, I was still a heterosexual adolescent boy with all the accompanying urges, but I knew there was no chance I'd ever have a girlfriend. A lot of the bullying had revolved around my appearance and perceived weakness; as a kid I was small for my age, skinny, clumsy, not the slightest bit athletic, the classic nerd. I shot up a couple of inches when I turned thirteen, but my metabolism changed and I filled out horizontally as well, growing an inexplicable potbelly that I could never entirely tame or conceal. And the picture didn't get much prettier north of the neck: I had an overbite, a receding chin poking out from between a pair of pudgy gopher cheeks, and droopy eyes. I felt ugly and twisted and freakish, and I came to loathe my reflection.

So talking to Alina was out. Sure, she was kind-hearted, a sweet girl who didn't seem at all full of herself, but I didn't think that would matter much. I figured that even if she *wanted* to reciprocate, she wouldn't dare, lest she be dragged into the mud with me, and I pined for her for nearly two years, through all of Grade Nine and all of Grade Ten.

By Grade Eleven, I couldn't endure it anymore. When we went back in the fall of 1993, Alina had changed; she'd walked out of Grade Ten a girl, but puberty had put the finishing touches on her over the summer and she walked into grade eleven a young woman. She was growing, she was moving forward. I wasn't, and that was my wake-up call. I had to act.

The trouble was, I still had no idea how to talk to girls. I had no idea how to talk to *people* ... but I did know how to write. So I had a friend pass her a note confessing my admiration, and expressing my desire to get to know her better.

She politely declined.

This is the point at which I was supposed to walk away and forget all about her. But I couldn't. By that point, it had become more than a crush. I had come to truly admire her; I admired the rareness of her spirit, her exceptional integrity and maturity. I didn't want to pressure her into being my girlfriend—I knew that would be wrong, and besides, my confidence levels were *way* too low to play Casanova—but I didn't see any reason we couldn't at least be friends. It's just that I was still too scared to talk to her. She'd gone back to ignoring me, and while I didn't think there was anything malicious in that, I decided that my best option was to send her another message.

When the Christmas holidays rolled around, I did probably the most daring thing I'd ever done in my introverted little life and sent Alina a basket of flowers, although I made sure it was a generic "Christmas Basket" and not a dozen red roses, intending it to be less a sexual advance than a tap on the shoulder, a little reminder that I still existed.

It didn't work. When the holidays were over, I went back to school with my heart boogieing its way up the back of my throat, expecting *some* kind of response, even a negative response, like Alina telling me to shove it, but she never breathed a word about it, not even a token word of thanks.

Of course, for all I knew the flower shop might have screwed up and sent the basket to the wrong address, and as usual the smart thing to do would have been to just walk up to her and ask her what was up. But I didn't do smart. I *couldn't*. Again, *shy* does not describe what I was. I was like a man sending up smoke signals on a remote mountaintop, waiting for the winds to blow in just the right direction.

Every Valentine's Day our school did a carnation drive. There were two colors to pick from: red for love and pink for friendship. I very deliberately chose pink and sent one to Alina. I thought it would be different this time; she and I would probably be in the same room when the delivery cart made the rounds, so she wouldn't be able to just pretend it never happened the way she (apparently) had with the Christmas Basket. That had hurt more than I can tell you, more than if she'd thrown the flowers in my face. I'd spent most of my childhood making myself invisible, and I'd gotten a bit too good at it. Nothing I said or did ever seemed to make any impact, and I was tired of that.

The night before Valentine's Day, I ate some bad fast food and, without getting into the goopy details, I ended up in no shape to make it into school the next morning. I spent the day stewing in my sickbed, convinced I'd missed my golden opportunity to break the ice with Alina, miserably certain the gesture would end up ignored and forgotten.

That evening, though, a friend—let's call him Brad—phoned me up in a tizzy. All hell had broken loose. The flower had touched off a firestorm of hysteria, and the powers-that-be were out for blood.

Our school had two guidance counselors, Adam Sawyer and Donna Moran. Sawyer was the talking counselor, the resident therapist who'd help you work through all those pesky teenage troubles *Degrassi High* claimed we were supposed to be preoccupied with. Moran was ostensibly the career counselor, though she often pulled double-duty in a therapist tag-team with Sawyer. Apparently, the pair had caught wind of my friendship flower, and wanted a word. *But*, since I was at home popping Gravol and yarking into a bucket, they dragged Brad in and squeezed him for info about me.

Questions included:

Does Peter have any other friends besides you?

Is Peter angry at Alina?

Has he said anything hostile about her?

Has he ever made any direct threats towards her?

Does he collect and arrange photographs of her?

Does he talk about her a lot?

And perhaps most alarming of all: Does he have access to weapons?

Naturally, my first thought was that this was coming from Alina, that she was starting to feel harassed and had run to the counselors for help. Not so. According to Brad, who was part of her circle (Alina and I had a mutual friend, that's the really crazy part, although Brad never lifted a finger to help build bridges with her, but more on that later), Alina wasn't upset. In fact, he didn't think she was even aware of what was going on. He'd been told that the alarm had been raised by a "concerned staff member." Don't ask me who or why or how that could have been, though considering what happened later, Sawyer tops my list of suspects.

I thought Brad was having fun with me. He *was* the kind of guy who didn't always know when a joke was crossing a line ... but when I went back to school I soon found myself in front of Sawyer and Moran, facing all those ominous questions. Was I angry, did I want to hurt Alina, did I have access to weapons.

They seemed satisfied with my answers (*no*'s all around) and let me go, but I was left feeling like I'd done something dirty, not just for making "romantic overtures" (their stodgy little term) but by simply falling for Alina in the first place. If a girl doesn't reciprocate your feelings, you are supposed to shut yours off *pronto* or else you're some kind of sexual deviant. They also kept building her up, reminding me what a smart and savvy honors student she was, insinuating that a guy like me (a mediocre student who did the bare minimum and had precisely zero extracurriculars) should really just ... well, *know his place*. They made me feel as if I actually *was* hurting Alina in some way, that I was trying to drag her down. And since I couldn't stand the idea that Alina might feel the same way, the first thing I did when I left that office was send her another note.

Two notes, actually, over the span of about two months. Crazy, I know. But I was mortified, horrified, terrified, *everything*-ified. I had zero self-esteem to begin with, I'd felt like a freak my whole life, and now people thought I was hoarding weapons and building creepy photographic shrines. The notes expressed my dismay at this absolutely *insane* misunderstanding, reassured her that I meant no harm ... and could she please, *please* just let me know that she understood that?

She couldn't. No response, not a peep. That was how she was; she never showed any indication that she was happy, sad, angry, scared, or even marginally aware of my existence.

At any rate, that *seemed* to be the end of it. I gave up on Alina, and didn't bank on hearing from the counselors again. Moran, at least, left me alone. But I was on Sawyer's radar now, and was about to become his special little project.

Less than a month after Grade Twelve started, I went into school to find that my locker had been broken into and completely cleaned out. Everything was gone, even the lock itself. Naturally I assumed it was a student, that somebody had discovered my combination and robbed me blind, until I found myself back in the hot seat in the counselors' office, being grilled not only by Sawyer but by the school board psychologist, who had been brought in to assess me.

Apparently, I had threatened to blow up the school on graduation night. I had no memory of this—probably because it never happened—but the accusation, coupled with the carnation kerfuffle, had fueled Sawyer's concerns that I was a troubled boy with serious anger issues. He even busted into my locker with bolt-cutters (completely unnecessary, as all combinations were kept in a ledger in the main office) to make sure I wasn't hiding any explosives. All he found was an unsold box of chocolate bars from a school fundraiser. But that didn't matter. If there was smoke, there had to be fire *somewhere*, and Sawyer (with the help of his psychologist pal) was going to find it.

So ... *was* there fire? I mean, why would anyone make such a serious accusation frivolously? Sawyer wouldn't tell me who'd leveled the charge—the whole thing was very Kafka-esque—but I had a pretty solid idea. We'll get to that in a bit, though.

The interrogation took most of the morning, and it wasn't long before Alina's name came up. My persistent "overtures" (God, I hate that word) were a further sign of my instability; again there was the sense that trying to persuade her to speak to me (let alone persuade her to date me) constituted an act of violence, despite Alina's apparent indifference. Again I was reminded that she was an intelligent girl who knew how to take care of herself, and that she had to take the *warning signs* that I was giving off to heart. Both Sawyer and the board psychologist seemed almost to *want* me to be a disturbed delinquent; there was an accusatory, leading quality to their questions (You don't have enough friends, do you? You spend too much time on solitary hobbies, don't you? You can't take rejection, can you?), and the festivities ended with an ultimatum: I could either submit to a psychiatric evaluation at the local hospital, or the police would be called.

Needless to say, I went with door number one.

(Sidebar: I realize I haven't said much about my parents thus far, and you might be wondering where they were during all this. I only had my mom—my dad died when I was eleven—and while she was always very supportive, she was also of a different era. I was born when she was forty-three, which not only meant she was nearing sixty when I started high school, it also put her a generation behind most of my peers' rebellious Boomer parents. She hailed from an era when people respected authority and did what they were told; if some officious twerp came along waving fancy credentials and claiming they had the power to, say, stuff your kid in the booby hatch, you believed it. She didn't like what was happening to me, but she felt she had to roll with it.)

The good news is that everything changed once I got to the hospital. The social worker and psychiatrist I met were an entirely different breed of mental health professional, nothing like the bullheaded authoritarians in the school system, who *say* they're there to help, their idea of help being to confront you in a whirlwind of judgmental bureaucracy. These guys seemed to understand from the get-go that this was a waste of everybody's time, and after a few formalities I was cut loose with a clean bill of health.

That did not, however, dissuade Adam Sawyer.

A month after *that* fiasco, Alina was in a car accident. It wasn't serious—no fatalities, mostly minor injuries, and Alina herself walked away without a scratch—but Sawyer was quick to take me aside and warn me not to speak to her or express my relief that she was okay. She was badly shaken, he said, and hearing from me would only make her fragile emotional state worse.

He needn't have bothered. I was done trying to talk to her, if for no other reason than I was tired of hearing nonsense like that. By that point I definitely knew my place, and when Alina and Sawyer both left the school at around the same time—Alina transferring to a new school, Sawyer landing a job with a youth counseling service—it was almost a relief.

When high school ended, I tried to let it all go. After all, that's what you're supposed to do, right? There's this attitude in our culture that childhood and adolescence don't count, that unless you've been molested by a priest or beaten by an alcoholic father, nothing that happens to you should stick. I tried to buy into that, but in the end I couldn't. The sense of *otherness* that I'd had drilled into me as a kid, that open wound had been salted by the experience with Alina ... and Counselor Adam Sawyer. As much as I despised him, part of me was terrified that he might have been right, that my feelings were sick, that *I* was sick, even though a deeper part of me knew that wasn't so. A deeper part of me believed that *he* was the crazy one, that *he* was the one with the problem, and sixteen years later those suspicions were borne out when Adam Sawyer was charged with second-degree murder.

They caught him red-handed. He strangled his girlfriend in a fit of rage and stuffed the body under her own children's beds with a bunch of odor-eaters. He tried to report her missing, but when the police came to take his statement they immediately realized something was wrong (I'm guessing the odor-eaters didn't cut it), discovered the corpse, and arrested him. And that wasn't even all. Once in custody, his entire past came to light: it turns out he'd been a con artist and a fraud most of his life, with a history of mental health issues, broken relationships, and numerous shady financial dealings. He pleaded guilty, and was sentenced to life in prison.

So, yeah, clearly someone in the Ontario Catholic School Board wasn't doing their due diligence when they hired him. But the question is not how this man ended up lording it over a bunch of vulnerable teenagers. The *real* question is why his behavior never raised any red flags. And if you'd care to skim back a few pages to the beginning of this little ramble, you'll notice I've already answered it.

It was the 90s.

The media fear machine wasn't a new thing, but by the 1990s it was running hot. Workplace shooters, school shooters, serial killers, and pedophiles dominated every six o'clock news-bite, cop drama, and paperback thriller, which all had the general public convinced that mass murder and sexual deviancy were the world's new normal. It also sparked an epidemic of armchair psychology as every schlub with a TV clicker fancied himself as an FBI profiler. A lot of the most notorious baddies inevitably turned out to be socially isolated misfits (you know, Quiet Guys Who Kept To Themselves, Mostly) so pretty soon any kind of social clumsiness or introversion became a red flag. Nerds weren't just nerds anymore. They were ticking time-bombs.

Even before all the drama with Alina, people were calling me *psycho*. I heard it every day, stuff like "Watch out, it's always the quiet ones who SNAP!" and "There goes the future serial killer!" and I'm pretty sure that was what led to the accusation that I was going to nuke the prom. There were a couple of guys who really pushed that label with me, and I always suspected they were the ones who (perhaps unintentionally) egged Sawyer on. People knew who I was and what I was: a pariah, mocked and bullied as a kid, reserved and quiet as a result. In any other era, that likely wouldn't have been a big deal, I'd have been the dork with the glasses and nothing more, but now ... now I fit a *profile*. I was the new definition of insanity.

But it was my unrequited crush on Alina that really sealed the deal.

Of all the criminal bogeymen the media scaremongers liked to harp on, the biggest and baddest was undoubtedly the stalker. Arthur Richard Jackson, Robert John Bardo, Richard

Farley ... there were dozens of them in the 80s and 90s. The term *sexual harassment* had also entered the public lexicon thanks to a few high-profile cases, and there was definitely some overlap there; suddenly, romance was pathology. Any man trying to win a woman's heart with gifts or flowers was now a "harasser" at best, a "stalker" at worst. This hysteria was both eagerly embraced by and aggravated by third-wave feminism, which coincidentally traces its roots to (drum roll please) the early 1990s, and is *very* much an extension of fear culture: all women are potential victims, all men are potential victimizers.

All I ever wanted from Alina was for her to acknowledge me. She saw everyone as an equal and spoke to them accordingly, even my own buddies. All I asked of her was to extend that same courtesy to me, although honestly I also wouldn't have minded if she'd told me to fuck off and die, because at least it would have shown that she saw me as *something*. She didn't have to be my girlfriend, or even necessarily my friend. I just wanted her to treat me like a human being.

But people acted as if that was itself obscene. And by people I mean *everybody*. Alina's friends closed around her like a fist, and I never got an iota of support from any of mine. Even Brad refused to put in a good word or act as an intermediary, and another friend—we'll call him Ross—claimed that Alina risked "ruining her life" if she spoke to me. I'm not sure exactly how that would've worked, but it sums up the general consensus: that Alina needed to be *defended*, that she was exceedingly fragile, and that I was exceedingly toxic, so toxic that even my sympathy after her car accident would have been poisonous to her. According to Alina herself (whom I've spoken to a few times in the years since), Sawyer actually warned her away from me, claiming that I was dangerous and that she should call the police if I ever approached her off school grounds.

I had never threatened her, never acted aggressively towards her, never said an unkind word about her to anyone. And yet no one thought these knee-jerk responses (call the cops on him, check him for weapons, send him to a mental hospital) were overreactions. Even my friends seemed to think Sawyer was just doing the job he was paid to do because hey, sure, *we* know you're not a psycho, Pete, but that's the world we live in. That was the culture; that was the zeitgeist of the age: so cynical, so utterly paranoid that Sawyer's own mental illness was rendered invisible. Boys were the bad guys, presumed guilty. Girls were the victims, completely above reproach.

I never thought Alina was a bad person. I always wondered if she might just have been really, *really* shy, in the same way that I was really, *really* shy, and I always tried to give her the benefit of the doubt. The irony is that the people defending her were the ones who made her sound awful; if I *did* question her motives, if I dared to suggest that maybe she was being a bit ... well ... *mean*, it was met with a chorus of protest. No, no, no, Alina's wonderful, Alina's smart, Alina's *perfect,* and that is precisely why she won't go anywhere near *you*. Sawyer, Counselor Moran, the board psychologist, Ross, Brad and the rest of Alina's friends ... they all seemed very sure of this. Which was quite a phenomenal feat of group telepathy, considering the one person they never bothered to consult was Alina herself.

She claims she never took Sawyer seriously, that she thought him silly, maybe even a bit creepy. She never saw me as a threat, and had no intention of siccing the cops on me. And I believe her. It was the others who made her into a victim, even though she didn't consider herself one. They were the ones who made her sound weak—of mind, of body, of character—in spite of her obvious strength. By putting words into her mouth they robbed Alina of her own agency far more than I ever did.

And that, right there, is the insidious paradox of third-wave feminism: empowerment through infantilization, telling women that they're oppressed whether they believe it or not, that they're being exploited whether they believe it or not, that they're in danger whether they believe it or not, and it's always somebody else's job to save them, usually a man. Feminists have basically come full-circle, having returned to a time when women were the "weaker sex," in need of constant protection. It truly is extinction-level irony, and the effects of that worldview are still being felt today, both on a cultural level and an individual one.

My whole adult life I've had problems getting close to women. I'm almost forty now and my relationship history includes one girlfriend in college; beyond that, nothing. No dates, no one-night stands. And it's not by choice, I'm by no means a MGTOW. I want—I have *always* wanted—to find a woman to share my life with. But that sense of worthlessness that was drilled into me as a child was set in stone during my adolescence, the sense that there is something wrong with me and that women, *all* women, will find my interest in them revolting. I can't open up. I can't flirt. I've let countless opportunities pass me by. It's Pavlovian, it's like Alex in *A Clockwork Orange* once the Ludovico Technique works its magic on him. I don't dare open my mouth, I don't dare assert my masculinity with a woman because I always feel like I'm doing something wrong. I don't feel as if women are my enemy; I feel as if I'm theirs.

I sometimes hear people talk about how women need to "go with their gut" in their interactions with men, how if they feel that a guy is giving off "weirdo" vibes they should cut and run with no remorse. Whenever I hear that, I think of me, *teenage* me, the shy, socially awkward geek who could only talk through notes and flowers. *I* was a weirdo. I was the kind of squirrelly eccentric all the cop shows cast as their villain-of-the-week, the creepy little troll feminists warn women to watch out for. I was the definition of insanity.

Then I think of Adam Sawyer, the tall, handsome, charismatic youth counselor. Married with kids. Coached hockey. Excellent rapport with his students. The epitome of *well-adjusted*.

And I think: remind me again which one of us is doing time for murdering a woman.

Adam Sawyer was crazy. That I can accept. But the question lingers: what was everyone else's excuse?

Chapter 5 – Twice Bitten

Paul, New Zealand

The son of an abusive mother and abused father narrates his search for self-acceptance

I grew up in the 1970s and 80s in England, in a family where female violence was normalized. My Nana used to throw plates at Grandad. He was a peaceful man. My aunties told stories of Nana's violence as jokes. Deep down I always felt the injustice for my grandfather but I was never allowed to voice it. Somehow, he was seen to deserve it though no one could say why.

Later, my mother's mental health issues made life hell for my father. She reduced every night of our lives to a screaming match. She would throw tantrums, sabotage family events with attention-seeking outbursts and tears, and continually mock my father while demanding everything from him.

Dad gave and gave. Several times I saw him breaking down in tears though he never knew I saw. He would retreat to the bath every night for hours, no doubt to mingle his tears with the bathwater. If you asked him about this now he would probably shrug and minimize it. My mother physically attacked him, and he defended himself with restraint and courage.

He never gave up on me and my sister, and he never gave up on Mum.

At around ten years old I began to argue with Mum. I saw how she treated Dad, and saw that she was toxic, and I defended myself by arguing back. This was a result of her starting on me. She began to tell me that I was evil, and she did so several times every day for years. I was not perfect; I started lots of arguments, I never knew why. I think I needed the stress, like so many damaged people need conflict and crisis. I felt normal when my mother and I were screaming at each other; it even made me smile though I simultaneously hated myself for it and for what it did to Dad, who just wanted a night of peace.

In adolescence through my late teens, she told me all the time that 'No woman would ever want you,' and that I was useless. As with Dad, everything I did was wrong. Harder efforts were met with harsher criticism. My mother was threatened by my education and often said that she would burn my books. She was an expert in everything, was critical of everyone, and could not admit to the slightest mistake in herself. Nightly screaming matches continued.

I have a vivid memory of one cold night, running down the street with Dad and my sister carrying blankets. We were trying to catch the last bus (a 1 1/2 hour journey) to Gran and Grandad's house. My dad had considered Mum too much of a risk for us to be around. I often wonder what he told his own parents about his wife's behavior.

Years later he told me of her phoning him at work when I was a baby (my sister around five years old), telling him to come and get her, as she had boarded a bus or train and was two hours away somewhere with no money to get back home. She had the kids and no money for food. She did not know why she had gone there. My dad did not drive, so it meant hours to rescue us.

He has more courage in his little finger than I have in my whole body. My mother spent a decade in and out of hospital. I was never told why, but learned when I was a little older that she was diagnosed with depression. My dad was also told she was schizophrenic. I think these were both wrong. I think my mother is bipolar with a personality disorder. She also had pathological hypochondria and demanded tests for almost every known medical condition. She was incapable of admitting she was wrong, and endlessly projected her own issues onto me and Dad. Dad had many whispered conversations with specialists and doctors. The conversations could not be had with my mother; it would only cause arguments and tantrums for months. Dad's giving kept Mum safe, so no mental health action was ever taken. He just took her home and coped alone.

Mum's standard line to me for years was "I was all right until I had *you*." I was always blamed for her woes: her depression, anxiety, agoraphobia; also her litany of imagined illnesses like leukemia and cancer. When Dad was actually diagnosed with cancer and lay in hospital with a 16 inch scar up his abdomen from emergency surgery, my mother sat at home crying to her friends about how ill she was, and I was vilified and shamed for suggesting that Dad was the one who was sick. I was 17 years old then, and I wanted out. My whole life I have always feared the death of my father over the death of my mother. He would cope if she died, but who would she turn her venom on if left alone? I felt bad about this, but I felt it for decades, and maybe that was what led me to move abroad, absolving myself of the responsibility.

I avoided relationships with girls for years, partly because I had internalized how useless and evil I was, and partly because I feared developing my mother's traits and ruining another person's life as she had done to Dad. This pushed me into depression and low mood for a long time. I did drugs and boozed and avoided women like the plague apart from one night stands and weird affairs with no future.

The sole reason I studied Psychology at university was to understand my mother. My whole life has been about understanding her. If there was a reason for her behavior, then I might not be the person she claimed I was, might not be evil after all. At 40 years old I am still convincing myself of this. My skin is paper thin. I live in my thoughts and logic because my feelings are too fragile. Like many men in my situation, I avoid conflict. My aim is to go through life as a ghost. Un-noticed. No footsteps. No trace. No arguments. I am an amateur musician and on stage with a guitar, the man I could have been comes through. I am funny, confident, gregarious, and I am told that my eyes light up. Offstage I seek isolation and invisibility; I take years to accept a compliment, and it still feels forced.

In the first month of my Psychology degree in 1993, I heard about *patriarchy*, about how terrible men are and how we control everything and are the source of all of women's troubles. I knew it was nonsense, but I was so damaged that I could muster no defense against it. So I went further into self-hate and isolation. Psychology failed to give me answers about Mum and simply condemned me further because I was male. I looked everywhere for the privilege that my course told me I had, but found only pain.

So I joined the club. I hated on white, straight men. I took social constructionism so far to heart that I could not say *hello* without analyzing it for two hours. The only thing not socially constructed was my guilt.

I read everything, and tore away every layer of constructed reality that I saw, peeling back the perceived sin: white, male, straight. I tried to make myself gay, and when that didn't work I tried to make myself impotent. I tore away at myself for so long that ultimately I came to see myself as invisible. I had no form. No worth. No words. It took me five years to build myself back up to the point where I could speak to people. Working with maternal, non-feminist women helped a lot.

I met my wife and married. I have three beautiful daughters.

When I went back to university at 28 to study Social Work, I was in good health. I had worked as a carer and a support worker for years and knew I was a compassionate man who cared about protecting other people from distress.

Then, on Day One of my Master's course, it started again: the identity politics blame game. White straight males are the curse of the world. In my program there were five men and many women. The men huddled together in the early weeks, and we all contemplated quitting, talking about it openly. We were blamed, attacked, and judged the culprits for everything wrong. All in our late 20s and early 30s, we had no idea what we had done that was so bad. We wanted to use social work to help people, and we were being vilified. Along with the radfems and tutors waving photocopies of Andrea Dworkin chapters, there were angry divorcees who projected all their husbands' failures onto us. Our small group of men planned getting t-shirts printed: WHITE STRAIGHT MALE – NOT GUILTY and WHITE STRAIGHT MALE – YOUR INSECURITIES ARE NOT OUR FAULT. We did not follow through because we knew that our careers would be over. I was clever and knew my stuff. Some of it I believed, some of it I didn't, but I played the game.

I went home to my wife every night of the course, trying to be positive about moving towards being a professional. But secretly I wanted to drop the whole thing. I could not help but think that a career in Social Work would subject me to another forty years of attacks. It all seemed to mirror my dad's marriage to my mother.

Feminism had destroyed my memories and denied my pain, had not allowed me a voice in its narratives of abuse. I went to my tutor and said that I had no right to be there because I hadn't suffered enough. The tutor said I had value because I had an alternative life story that was more positive than the clients I would be working with in my career. A lovely man, he didn't know about my mother and I did not feel I had the right to share what I had gone through. I didn't feel positive.

I had top marks on the privilege scale, apparently. This meant I could walk through the train station at night. Well, I had to; all the others had cars and I didn't. It was a horrible and dangerous train journey through unpleasant parts of town. I walked with my keys between my fingers and rehearsed talking myself out of muggings and planning escape routes, just as I had my entire life growing up as a skinny kid and a scrawny man. This is not male privilege; it is the knowledge that no one will protect you but yourself. I thought of my dad doing this every day for years while my mother was in hospital.

But I got through it. I went to work in disability work. There were many hardcore (often lesbian) feminists in the work; I respected them and they respected me. Disability work rarely raised gender issues; we worked hard and we were good. I was deeply stressed by the workload, and experienced burnout after trying to appease a lady with personality disorder for over a year. She had whole offices tearing their hair out—just like Mum. I never gave up on her until my doctor told me to take some time off. I had one-year-old twins at the time.

I continued to bandy around words like patriarchy, accepting ideas such as 'women can't be sexist' without question. I am a man damaged by a woman and put together by women. I am a man raised in a woman's image. Weak, servile, eager to please, afraid of confrontation, guilty of my sexuality and afraid of it, convinced I am unlovable despite ten years of marriage. Ashamed. Afraid of other men. Oh yes, deeply, deeply afraid of other men.

However, I had folk music and the blues. Years of folk clubs, singing old songs that talked of dangerous women, husband-killers, boyfriend-poisoners. I think my attraction to folk music at 17—the most uncool thing I could ever have done, and something I still love—was that the songs told stories that reflected my childhood. Unlike psychology or social work, folk songs told real tales of reciprocal unpleasantness between the sexes: Lord Randall getting poisoned by his girlfriend; ladies leaving their husbands for whistling gypsies; scoundrel lady-thieves in Black Velvet Bands tricking young men into stealing for them and getting sent to Australia. You know ... the truth.

And then, in the last year, it has all begun to unravel. In my family work, I have been seeing a host of solo dads who have all experienced violent and abusive female partners. These are the good guys, the ones who do not hit back and so do not figure in any statistics. I began to realize how often in my first couple of years in my current job I had taken the woman's side without hearing the man's; about how I had so internalized the *men bad/women good* narrative that I had rejected men's experiences. And then it hit me: this is exactly what happened my whole life with my experience of my mother. Psychology and Social work (and my aunties) had not even allowed my experience to be acknowledged.

So, I began to dig. I read legions of books by all the writers so well known to people who follow men's rights issues.

I read about the history of suffrage, and how in the U.K. in 1832 only 4% of men were eligible to vote. Even in the First World War, around 40% of the British men who fought were not entitled to vote, even though they were entitled to die. It was women who shamed men as cowards with white feathers, not other men. Universal suffrage for men in the UK occurred in 1918, only 10 years before the same came for women. I was lied to. It was all there in the historical records. It was never *All Men Oppress All Women.*

Rape was never legal in British law. Wife-beating was also never legal, and vigilante groups of men in both the UK and USA would lynch men known to beat their wives. Similarly, men known to be beaten by their wives were publicly shamed in the Skimmington Procession for not standing up for themselves.

This was unknown history fully documented, instances of and societal responses to violence from both men and women.

My great, great grandmother (in records I discovered) was a widowed single mother who fled Russia during the anti-Jewish pogroms of the 1880s. She landed in Manchester and worked as a cabinet-maker. She was clearly a woman of substance and did not require an ideology to be so. Similarly, there are histories of female business-owners going back to Medieval times. This idea that women could not own property or businesses is a fabrication.

There are also diaries written by 15th century Venetian women that report their promenading around town in finery while their husbands ran their butcher shop and plied other trades. Whilst singular, these stories show that there has never been a time when *all* men have oppressed *all* women. In fact, the relationship between the sexes has been pretty consistent: some people have it bad, some people have it good. All families are not alike. Some are patriarchal, some are matriarchal. Some are neither. Just like today: some men are violent, some women are violent. All things rest in all people.

The laws usually hurt the poor, not just women, such as the Corn Laws about which the Peterloo Riots and subsequent massacre by the yeomanry occurred in Manchester in 1819. Votes were increasingly given to men in exchange for military service, and only increased to 100% when a good proportion of men had been slaughtered in the Great War.

Women in New Zealand (where I now live) got the vote in 1893, 25 years before all men in the UK If this is an oppressive global patriarchy, it is giving its power away pretty easily.

Then I got to thinking about wider oppression. Were black male slaves a part of the patriarchy? Were my Jewish male ancestors who fled Russia with their mother part of the patriarchy? Was Dad part of the patriarchy, with his unbending duty, courage and commitment to his children in the face of a violent wife and a family that normalized violence towards husbands?

G.K. Chesterton, a great man, said over a hundred years ago: Feminism is the muddled idea that a woman is free when she serves her employer but enslaved when she helps her husband.

What I learned through all of this hidden history is that I had been sold a lie. There was no original sin of being male. Women were never forced to go to war or pressed into navy service. History also records more lenient criminal sentencing; in fact, it was not uncommon for a man to be sent to prison for his wife's crimes, as he was responsible for her. This can be dressed up as female oppression, but on a day-to-day basis, who is worse off, the "oppressed" woman at home or the man in prison?

The idea of *patriarchy* stems from cherry picking history and a whitewashing of both female privilege and male oppression.

And then came modern times. I began to study domestic violence, police policies, cultural assumptions, and media misrepresentation.

Hidden from the figures that fit the *men bad/women good* narrative are the men who do not hit back. Only male perpetrators and male self-defenders (who may make up a much higher proportion than we realize) are reported in official statistics. Dad isn't in those statistics. Grandad isn't in them. I am not in them, because I did not act out as a result of my abuse. I internalized it.

How many other men are not in those statistics?

In a nearby town recently I witnessed a woman attack her husband in a park full of kids. She chased him and hit him with her sandals. He was terrified as it carried on for ½ an hour. He just took it. His face was confusion and fear.

How many men who abuse alcohol, take drugs, gamble addictively, watch porn or do any of the other things that are used to shame men are actually victims of violent or abusive female partners? How many, like my dad, are in their baths?

I never understood at what point I went from an emotionally abused boy into a paid-up patriarchal oppressor. I always thought I had missed a meeting. Or perhaps I was not given the particular sixteenth birthday cake that cures emotional pain. Now I know the *patriarchy* is a conspiracy theory designed to shut men up.

I have three daughters. I want them to have a fair go at the life they choose. I want everyone to have a fair go at the life they choose. There are many ways in which people are oppressed and discriminated against. I want justice for all of them. But the one group that is not talked about is men. The great assumption of patriarchal theory is that every law or policy automatically benefits men as part of its structure; that men somehow occupy a place in society where there are no hardships, no struggle, no discomfort, no pain, no injustice. My story, and the story of the men I continue to work with in social work, is proof that this theory is a fairytale.

I was winded and beaten to the ground by my mother. Successive waves of feminist psychology lecturers and radfem social work tutors dragged me kicking and screaming to a cell and put me in chains. The whole misandrist and gynocentric culture in which we now find ourselves has whipped me and force-fed me my own pain three times a day ever since.

But I've spotted a key on the window ledge.

Chapter 6 – Men Who Worship Women

E.D.

The author muses on how, contrary to the feminist narrative, men don't hate women, though many hate how much they need women's approval.

I think feminism was originally attractive to men because we were told that it was about equality, and men liked the idea of equality. Women have always had social priority in terms of their safety and health, and men sacrifice themselves for women all the time. I realized myself that my life isn't worth as much as a woman's life in the general perception of our society. So the idea of equality was attractive.

Let me tell you what I learned. We men want to improve our physiques and our talents in the hope that women will desire us in the same way we desire them. But we find that if we get in shape and try to be as attractive as women are, there is still a weird game going on, and women don't desire us as we do them. They won't sacrifice for us.

When I was younger, I always felt that women were superior and that I was nothing unless I could be perfect. I wanted a perfect body, money, and to be incredibly talented so that I could equal the desirability of a woman. Subconsciously, I think, a lot of men believe women to be the superior sex, as I did, and we hand over to women the judgment of who we are as men. Putting all of one's efforts into trying to impress and make someone else acknowledge you is a form of worship. I can admit now, after doing a lot of psychological and emotional work on myself, that I worshiped women as if they were divine.

It is embarrassing for men to admit this because the cultural idea is that we are to be strong and self-directed. But the truth is that a lot of us believe we have to earn a woman's love. Women, because of their power to create life, don't have to earn love in the same way.

A lot of men get angry and miserable when they get in shape or get skilled and find out that even then, they cannot attract women in the same way men flock to a desirable woman. Nature is simply not equal in that regard. What we discover is that in a lot of cases (not all, I have met a few very real and intelligent women), women are programmed by our media culture to battle us when we approach them. We are locked in a competition in which each wants to have something that the other desires and to use that to get from the other what he or she wants. It's not true in all cases, but in many cases it is.

Many songs are written in worship of women, in longing for their love and attention. A miserable man is a man who tries hard to give his love and attention to a woman, and gets nothing in return.

Most men won't admit that because we are not supposed to care what women think. But let's not kid ourselves; it consumes us.

Because a lot of men can't get rid of that—the fact that their desire for women consumes them—they get miserable or angry with women because the societal rules to please them seem to be at an all-time high level of complexity. The irony is that if I as a man become disgruntled with women's behavior and demands, women will say 'You hate women.' But nothing could be further from the truth.

The so-called hatred of women that comes from disgruntled men in the face of feminism is really a frustration born of wanting to please them and have their blessing but finding instead that our culture has incited women to battle us in the most sensitive area, our need for their love.

There never has been a "war between the sexes." We men want women's love and intimate touch in our lives so badly that we will play by whatever rules are necessary. Our anger comes from the perceived lack of appreciation—any appreciation—for all our efforts.

With my ex, I worked so hard that I got heart palpitations and panic problems because I wanted the money needed to keep her satisfied. I was willing to damage my health to keep her.

When men try everything they can to get love and it doesn't come, they lose hope, becoming self-destructive, miserable, or apathetic. That seems to be proof that the pursuit of a woman's love is what drives most men to succeed, dream, and be their best. Many of us live and die for it. It is one of the most raw areas of our sensitivity, and some of us go to great lengths to hide it out of shame at the depth of our need.

For men it is deeply embarrassing, due to our cultural programming, to admit that women have that much power over us. Women are beings physically weaker than we are, pretty and frail, and it's ironic that big, strong men are so afraid of them because they desire them.

Some men are on a quest to establish their identity in a way that it is impervious to women's power. They realized at some point that everything they did was for women, and they are trying to bio-hack their motivational centers so that "I do it for me now, not them." Is it possible to undo biology? Look at MGTOW. The majority are angry men constantly saying out loud, "I don't need women, I don't need women." But what I hear is, "I hate the fact that I need women, it bothers me very much." MGTOW is interesting. It is a quest for male identity where the end game is not to impress a woman. It's a lovely idea, but unless the guy is a monk of some sort, it will likely be defeated by biological reality.

Most men don't put any of this into words because it is anti-everything we have been taught to be. Other men would call me weak for saying it. This is because they don't want others to see how dependent they are on the companionship of a woman. Women shame men for saying the truth, which is another reason why men don't speak out. It cuts deep.

Chapter 7 – Truth Hurts

Anonymous

The author describes the devastating personal consequences of being falsely accused of sexual harassment on a university campus

I'm thirty years old. Let's start there. I'm a thirty-year-old man who's never been on a date. Never asked, never been asked, never seriously considered the idea. I don't know what a kiss or even a hug would feel like, and I don't want to. I'm quite heterosexual, mind you, but the thought of any kind of romantic relationship with a member of the opposite sex seems less realistic to me than being elected President of the United States.

Part of the issue is likely down to simple biology. I'm the high-IQ, eccentric type, and while women are not a lesser race, they tend to cluster around the average in most respects, leaving those of us men who are at the extremes rather lonely.

Some of my isolation could be a result of the seemingly universal, vitriolic rhetoric directed towards young men, which seems to have affected me in a way that I hoped culture and social norms never would. "Internalized misandry," you might call it. It may seem to be esoteric legal scholars who have defined all sexual acts as rape of men on women, and all interactions between men and women as harassment, but even as a teenager I had adopted basically the same mentality.

So much negativity surrounds the subject that I could hardly imagine what a "good" interaction would look like. Indeed, I still can't. And being possessed of the universal love and goodwill that most men have towards women, I would rather leave them alone than cause them harm. With that in mind, I entered college, having heard so much about violence against women in the media (despite having no first- or second-hand experience with it whatsoever) that I became a psychology major, and was quite determined to unearth what madness could pervert the most powerful force in the world: men's protective instinct towards women.

Then again, maybe the reason I've stayed out of the dating market is that when I made my first entreaty towards a girl, the barest attempt at platonic friendship with (in my mind) the possibility to progress to something more months or years down the road, the result was that I ended up falsely accused of some nebulous misconduct, tortured for months with a string of lies that came to a decisive conclusion when I was attacked by campus police and both literally and figuratively kicked out of school.

Whenever I've thought I might be ready to move on, whenever I sit across from some admittedly attractive young woman and start thinking maybe it's time to take a risk, I flash back to the experience of gasping for air like a fish out of water, ignominiously and silently. When my chest muscles spasmed it felt like drowning, and despite all rational knowledge to the contrary, it felt like I was going to die. I've yet to meet a face pretty enough to make me forget it.

And for such a consequential set of events, I know remarkably little about it. I had gone to school alongside my accuser for two years, and as it was a small college and we were in parallel majors, we saw quite a bit of each other. I knew we were from the same area before college, and when we ran into each other over the summer, I had finally convinced myself that she was worth knowing and was pleased to realize she was even closer than I had thought. I followed up in admittedly awkward fashion by ringing her doorbell in the middle of a thunderstorm. It was a step I'd considered many times, but only the crack of thunder seemed enough to shake me out of the anxiety I carried even then.

And at the time, her response was surprised, but to my naive eyes unambiguously positive, as we chatted for an hour or two and I left with a sampler of her musical tastes in the form of a case of several dozen CDs and plans to meet again over the summer. I had been in a car accident some years earlier, and was still quietly and privately suffering the long-term consequences, but when I shared this fact with her, she empathized and hinted at her own pain, talking about discontent between her parents and a sense of alienation unbefitting an attractive, intelligent young woman. As a gentleman, I felt it inappropriate to ask follow-up questions.

I went to my first of many summer concerts back at college, but the night was drowned out by another storm and I saw the girl I came to see only in passing. If weather has any symbolic, predictive value, I did not catch on to it. This was early in the social media era, and my disinterest in online interactions left me waiting another month until the start of the semester. Upon returning to college, we encountered each other regularly. I returned her CD collection, having listened to every minute, and we talked a few times but I struggled to engage on any deeper level. In fact, my anxiety over the idea of interacting with a member of the opposite sex had not subsided during the intervening months, and I was drowning under the heaviest academic schedule I ever took, complicated by worsening chronic pain that I had only just started to get treated. That being said, I was hanging on.

The first time she went off on me was thus a surprise I was ill-equipped to deal with. We ran into each other on a path crossing the campus, and after exchanging greetings, she trailed off and seemed oddly withdrawn. When I asked her what was going on, she snapped at me that it was none of my business and she wasn't comfortable talking to me. She told me to leave her alone.

This struck me as unprecedented and mean-spirited. Then again, I'd been warned time and time again about the emotional volatility and irrational behavior of college-age women, and I was inclined to write this off as such. I suspected that she was angry at someone or something else, and that I was a convenient outlet for that anger, and I accepted it without question. I felt it my duty to be supportive, and to not make it worse. So when she asked me to leave her alone, I said yes, unquestioningly, and left it at that. I kept my distance and didn't speak to her for a couple of weeks. It was a bit upsetting, but I had plenty of other things on my mind, and I decided to prioritize understanding physical chemistry and cognitive science over figuring out her moods.

The next time we ran into each other, on the other major cross-campus path, I was inclined to walk away, though there wasn't really anywhere to go without turning around and going back to my dorm. But when her eyes met mine, open, and full of emotion, I cautiously kept walking. When she finally said hello, I asked cautiously, how she was doing, and she went off once again. It was not an outburst of anger this time, but of contrition. She apologized for shouting at me (an emotive exaggeration) and for shutting me out before explaining that she had "a lot going on" and that "talking to [me] was hard," which wasn't really much of an explanation. Nonetheless, I held steadfast in my stance on nonjudgmental acceptance, and said that I was happy to proceed as she saw fit, even if I couldn't understand why the two of us having a simple conversation was ever at issue. She accepted this proposition and said she would need "a little more time" before we sat down and talked.

We both relaxed a bit. We started to make eye contact again. Smiles were exchanged. Every romantically successful man had told me that you just had to hold fast through women's emotional ups and downs, and I was beginning to feel like a man.

And then, she looked straight down once again and mumbled, "You know, I kind of talked to Public Safety about you," sheepishly, as if she was admitting to having cheated off me on a test. "They told me not to talk to you." Alarm bells went off in every corner of my brain, and it took a massive exertion of will to suppress them. I calmly excised from my demeanor any trace of a smile and asked her directly what she had told them. Still looking straight down, she told me not to worry. I moved on slightly to ask what I could expect from them, and again she mumbled a non-answer about how the school counselor told her to do it. Why was she seeing a counselor? With my heart pounding and my faculties barely intact, I asked her if we were okay. For some reason, that was easier to answer. "Yes, of course," she said, and started to walk to class. Confounded, but tapped out, I let her go.

That day was the date noted on my expulsion.

A few days later, the landline phone in my dorm went off, and I was asked to pay a visit to the Public Safety Office. It seemed like the sort of request one doesn't refuse, so I walked down immediately. Two imposing men, slightly overweight and with an air of rural social conservatism about their appearance and behavior, were there to meet me. They seemed simpletons to my college-educated eyes, and I focused on trying to suppress any sense of condescension I might have towards them as I disarmed the situation.

The one in charge asked me, without context, why I was there. I volunteered the name of my estranged acquaintance, and they made clear that was the right answer. Still having gotten little out of them, I went on to explain that the girl in question and I were friends who had experienced a simple social misunderstanding. There was no ill will from either party, I assured them. We were not sexually involved, neither of us had done anything inappropriate, and we had talked the whole thing out. "Oh, really?" the subordinate officer asked. I gave the date of our last encounter, and asked them if they had spoken to her since then. I asked them to follow up with her, diplomatically reminding them that I understood that all issues with men and women needed to be investigated seriously, but concluding that if they simply talked to the girl in question, they would hear from her that there was nothing wrong. This felt like a leap of faith, given her erratic behavior and that we hadn't talked since then, but I felt it the right thing to do. I asked them if they had any more questions (any questions at all, really), and they dithered around for a bit before agreeing that the answer was no and we were done. I politely left, my attempted goodbye met by stone faces.

Days passed, and when no further calls came, I assumed they had followed my instructions and that I was clear. Nonetheless, I began to notice that the sense of breathlessness and fear that I had thus far in life experienced only when talking to a particular sort of girl had now become a daily norm. Every time I saw a girl who looked even faintly like the one I'd tried to get to know, I was ready to panic. Every time I saw anyone in a Public Safety uniform, or one of their cars, I wondered if they were coming for me. Campus police had a reputation for being lax and inept, but I didn't want to take any chances. I was already suffering from a great deal of pain in my back, neck, and arms, and between the fiendish workload and the crippling anxiety, my muscles felt like rocks.

After another week or so of scratching and clawing through life, I received an envelope from my R.A. It contained a summons to a disciplinary hearing, and when I looked for a charge, I saw something to the effect of "Conduct emotionally harmful to another, including but not limited to harassment, threats, intimidation, or coercion." I dropped everything I was doing and spent the rest of the day trying to figure out what exactly was going on. Clearly, it had something to do with the girl I was now avoiding, and the date given for the "offense" was indeed that of our most recent conversation. But I had stayed far away from her since then, and nothing in our distant glances was informative enough to act on. I had no idea whether the process was initiated before or after my talk with Public Safety, and nothing indicated whether she was specifically involved or not. Her name was not on the complaint, and given that the counselor she had referred to, the campus police, and now this disciplinary process all seemed to be independent actors, I was confused.

I read everything available about the school's disciplinary process. It was vague and unhelpful. I had taken Psychology and the Law, and through that and other venues had some notion of how judicial proceedings worked (or didn't). There was no indication of how a charge would move or not move to a hearing; indeed, the wording seemed to indicate that every disciplinary report could be investigated regardless of whether it had merit or whether the reporting student reconsidered. I found this reassuring because it left open the possibility that the girl in question had told me the truth, and that the inquiry was proceeding either against her wishes or simply as a formality to cover the school. I read and reread every relevant piece of the student handbook, prepared lugubriously eloquent statements on every facet of my relationship with the girl, and showed up at the hearing the following week ready to go.

The hearing was held in a general purpose student center, and I ran into my accuser outside. Again, I opened gently by asking her how she was doing, and she smiled weakly and said things were alright. I started to ask if I had done something to cause her harm, but she interrupted me and said, "Of course not," adding voluntarily, "I don't even want to be here." This seemed to confirm my suspicion that the proceeding was the school's thoroughness rather than a genuine inquisition, though I was hardly ready to relax. A Public Safety Officer walked up and separated us, and she gave me an apologetic parting glance.

Nonetheless, I walked into the hearing on edge. It was held in the office of a miscellaneous administrator whose primary responsibility seemed to be managing extracurricular student groups, with one of the Public Safety officers I'd met before staring silently. She read the charge out loud, making it no more specific. My "accuser," as it were, made a short statement, not mentioning our original encounters over the summer and saying only that she had encountered me a few times at school, had felt uncomfortable once, and that a counselor had suggested she contact Public Safety. Her main point seemed to be "I never felt physically threatened," which she repeated three times. She concluded by apologizing for raising the issue.

Reassured, I delivered my own statement, taking far more time and endeavoring to make it clear that I had never touched her, no romantic relationship existed, and that we were both in accord now. I said nothing of my own pain, her admitted instability, or any other inflammatory topics. I looked to the hearing officer. She had paid little attention and had taken no notes. Indeed, as she looked up I noted that on her desk in front of her was a blank club registration form. She asked one oddly irrelevant question about how I found out the date of the summer concert (which I had already stated that the girl had invited me to). Then she asked whether I held myself responsible for the charge. "I certainly didn't harass, threaten, intimidate, or coerce anyone," I stated for clarity, "but if she was ever uncomfortable in my presence I apologize." The hearing officer repeated the question, asking for a yes or no. Looking at the original text, "conduct emotionally harmful to another," I said, "Yes."

My act of contrition, it seemed, was complete. I was asked to sign a waiver, and did so hesitantly. The girl and I were dismissed from the room. I was called back in and, without looking at me, the hearing officer read a scripted statement that I had been found responsible for misconduct. Then, she read off a list of sanctions seemingly designed for a serial stalker. I was to have no contact with the girl, avoid parts of the campus, and to see a counselor for "evaluation." I asked her directly what this meant, and she refused to answer my questions, stating only that I would receive a written copy of the findings. And when I did, it answered no questions.

I was referred to a school counselor for "assessment," a process which included her frequently mentioning how the administration was going through transitions and I should be patient, deflecting my concerns about what had happened into talk of my declining health, and adopting a perpetual look of concern for my wellbeing. This being a small school, the counselor was the same one whom my erstwhile acquaintance had come to, and was ostensibly the source of whatever bad advice she had received. I played along, attending sessions well beyond the required ones in part to create the appearance of goodwill, and in part because I had no one else to talk to. But I certainly didn't feel safe.

I felt even less safe when Public Safety officers began to show up at my residence and classes with regularity, most creepily when I emerged from a night-time band rehearsal to find a car on the pathway with its lights trained on the exit, its driver silently watching my passage. I submitted an appeal, and met with an acting dean of something or other. He seemed reasonable, and just as importantly, male. He listened to my story, which ended with another plea to contact the girl and verify it. He promised to look into it. But when the verdict returned a week later, it included only minor changes to the logistics of my punishment, and no explanation.

In the meantime, I saw her almost every day. We shared a similar schedule, and she sat in the orchestra directly in front of me. Little change was evident in her behavior. She alternated between ignoring my presence and smiling emptily as if nothing had happened. My one approach to her (a violation of my discipline in and of itself) was a brief happenstance meeting at the school's one cafeteria, in which she claimed again that she knew nothing about anything the school had done and still needed more time.

But the clock was ticking. In earlier conversations she had indicated plans to study abroad after the semester, which would end any chance of righting the situation. I quit going outside except for classes, and spent hours in my single room in such a state of tension it felt as if I was crushing myself. My health, already tenuous, crashed. I stopped eating, lost weight, and my resting pain level approached intolerability. I had been prescribed non-narcotic analgesics, and I upped the dose beyond what was recommended; but they were of no help, and I ran out, not wanting to ask for another prescription for fear of being labeled a drug-seeker.

When I did leave my room, every person with features even faintly resembling my accuser set off anxiety. I overheard rumors of her being in an abusive relationship and discovered, much to my surprise, that she had acquired a boyfriend. He was a cheerful philosophy major and hippie who liked rock climbing, but also a notorious drinker with the approximate physique of a miniature Incredible Hulk. He frequented my dorm and, for someone who was ostensibly convicted of threatening his girlfriend, I attracted no unusual treatment from him. And while no one else seemed to be aware of the secret reality I was living in and no new information emerged, I constantly feared what he, she, the school, or the police might do to me. I was a successful student enrolled in an elite liberal arts college, but it felt as if I was in a war zone.

The semester approached its end and, finally, I ran out of patience. After running into my ostensible accuser on a footpath, I walked by quietly, but then once again found the courage to change course, furiously crunching the gravel as I caught up to her again. She stared at me with a sort of clueless worry as I explained the discipline I was under. But when she again claimed ignorance of the matter, I refused to buy it, and asked her to accompany me to the Public Safety office the next day to undo what had happened to me. She agreed as if it was nothing, and took a step and reached out towards me as if offering a hug, but I recoiled.

Months of pent up fear and anger bubbled dangerously close to the surface. She asked what was wrong, and just for a moment, I snapped, saying I would be fine if she wasn't such a "vicious bitch." She jumped a bit, and for the first time, it felt as if I actually had threatened her in some way. Perhaps, if I was aggrieved, she offered, it might be better if I contacted her in writing. I agreed, and we walked our separate ways.

And that was it. I wrote for her a detailed account of how I'd been treated by the school along with my request for her help and a profuse apology for snapping. And I was, indeed, wracked with guilt for a short time before and after sending that email, until the reply came back with a single line telling me never to contact her again. Given her promise the previous day, I finally accepted that there was no way she could be telling the truth, and I realized I'd been had. But it was far too late.

I went without food or water for well over twenty-four hours, refusing to leave my room. Eventually, hunger won out, and I stumbled into the cafeteria at the end of lunch when I deemed her unlikely to be present. And yet, she followed me in a moment later. My hands went numb. I could feel the panic attack coming, but I calmly walked for the exit before deciding I wouldn't make it. I stopped to ask another classmate for help, and very likely traumatized the poor girl for life as I collapsed to the ground writhing in pain. I said, to no one in particular, "Does it matter?" An ambulance came, but I rejected their ministrations once I regained my feet. My accuser, and everyone else, was gone. I stumbled out having eaten no more than the corner of a lettuce leaf. It was, after all, exam time, and I went straight to my Psychology final.

When I emerged, I walked through the neighboring parkland as if I were savoring my last meal. And when I returned to my dorm, Public Safety was there waiting. I rode with them to the office, and when the subordinates left, the remaining officer asked me to close the door. In doing so, I turned my back. An elbow rammed into my ribs, and I collapsed, paralyzed again. A series of derisive kicks to my midsection followed and with each one I cried out, silently for lack of breath. "Help me," I mouthed, "crazy girl."

The expulsion that followed led to a lawsuit, and while my parents were skeptical of my innocence, a few minutes of listening to the school officials talk quickly convinced them. Our requests for records yielded minimal evidence, only two damning documents dating to before the whole mess had started, each a complaint painting me as a stranger who showed up too frequently, neither with any tangible details or specific allegations. It was a worst case scenario. She had lied, though it wasn't clear why. It still isn't.

Fortunately, the school's incompetence lent itself to a successful lawsuit. My record was cleared and I moved on to another school. I did not associate the events that had occurred with feminism, politics, or anything other than sheer madness. The whole thing seemed a bad dream, and I wanted nothing more than to wake up.

My second false accusation came years later. Having decided to use my experience to help others through difficult times, I pursued medical school, but the road was difficult (and the role of my disciplinary history uncertain but ominous), so I did a graduate degree to help my chances. I got to know the small and cohesive class very well, and I started to relate to people. I even started to talk about what had happened, in veiled terms as a response to others' personal disclosures. But when I took the brave step of giving a hug to a classmate undergoing emotional distress, the hammer dropped, and I found that I was the third member of our class to face a sexual harassment claim for such an act. Fortunately, I wasn't a recluse anymore, and the friends I had made helped me through it and witnessed for my character. The charge was dropped, and this time, the trauma only cost me a few weeks of terror.

This being said, I started to think deeply about the issue. After changing schools, I had aggressively pursued women's studies classes, almost adding a minor to my existing (and lengthy) academic resume before graduating. I had become an expert on the research on sexual violence, harassment, and everything in between. Much of it was astonishingly distorted, as if established social scientists were reporting back from some fantasy world where women lived as perpetual victims. I felt quite alone. No one else talked about it, and to discuss these issues in polite circles seemed heretical.

Then something changed. The news media caught hold of the issue of sexual assaults on campus and evident falsehoods started to emerge. I heard stories of young men going through experiences eerily similar to mine, and when a credible organization of their families emerged, I was no longer alone. What had seemed a nightmare started to make sense. A horrifying narrative of politics, money, and lies emerged, and it became clear that what had happened to me was no accident. I accepted the reality and moved on, going so far as to speak about the issue in Capitol Hill offices before finally leaving the country to find a medical school that would take me.

All of which takes us back to the beginning. I'm thirty years old, technically a man, but unfulfilled as such. I live in fear, and no therapy can convince me that this fear is irrational. Blatant falsehoods about sex crimes and false accusations thereof are peddled as scientific fact, helping no one, victims included. Principles of justice are being thrown to the wind to support a grievance-fueled bureaucracy to fix a sex crime epidemic that doesn't exist.

Can all of this be blamed on feminism? Surely not. My accuser was an adult. She made a choice. To this day I don't know why, but I am under no duty to explain why she did what she did. The school employees are likewise responsible for their actions. So are the bureaucrats setting policy and the researchers and reporters cranking out lies.

But I think all of it traces back to a basic human impulse: that overwhelming protective instinct that men have towards women, the organizing principle of all of human society. The problem is that there isn't enough real danger left, so we're making things up to fulfill our biologically ordained roles as protector and protected. Call that feminism or not, it doesn't matter. It's wrong.

I feel quite driven to be close to women. And in many ways, I am. In healthcare, I've worked with more women than men by far, many of them attractive and a few of them intelligent and personable enough to be genuinely appealing. I like to think I'd have a lot to offer one of them, and that a relationship with one would make me a better person as well, make me whole. I'm smart, I'm funny, and I cook pretty decent vegetarian food.

But every time the possibility of romance presents itself, I flash back to the floor of my college Public Safety office, even as my encounter with that floor is almost a decade past. I feel the guilt of my one moment of anger towards a woman, mitigating context be damned. Pain still flows through me, a silent judgment as much as a neurological disease.

I realize bad things happen to good people. I don't think my struggles are the worst of anyone's, not by a long shot. I don't expect the government to cater to my needs, the media to embrace my story, or academia to study my plight. I don't think that anyone owes me a happy life, sexual fulfillment, or even civility, no matter how nice I am. But between the myth of universal female victimhood, the sickening reality of male suffering, and my torrid encounter with the insanity of gender politics, I think it fair to say: I deserve better than this.

Chapter 8 – A Fateful Chance Encounter

Anonymous

The author unpacks the long-term effects of cultural misandry on his life choices

My story regarding feminism is a minor one compared to the horrors that many men worldwide have endured over the course of their lives. In many ways, my experiences with feminism are more like *collateral damage* with respect to the full range of what feminists are capable of doing to anyone who opposes them. I've never had my physical safety threatened by a feminist mob, nor have I been falsely accused of raping a woman, nor have I faced the threat of job loss or the ruin of my reputation simply for expressing a principled disagreement with anything that a feminist says or does in the public or private sphere. I've never allowed myself to be put in dangerous situations where I could face such horrific outcomes that other men have encountered.

While the state of affairs is such that I now feel compelled to end my silence about the evils of feminism as I know them, my knowledge of feminist retribution against men like me leads me to make very certain that whatever comments I'm compelled to share are done anonymously. Therefore, if you happen to be a feminist reading my story right now, then you need to understand why I must keep myself hidden from the likes of you.

Although I could write a detailed account about some disturbing dating experiences I had that could have resulted in situations similar to the horror stories described in this book, in all frankness they aren't compelling enough to justify being shared here. As a private man by nature, I don't have any interest in explaining details of my personal life involving these women; and I respect their personal dignity as a matter of forgiveness based upon my belief in God and my desire to conduct my life honorably as a man of faith. Furthermore, I don't want to take space away from the genuine disasters described in this book.

Instead, my own story regarding feminism concerns a chance encounter in a public setting over two decades ago. Despite this brief and deceptively trivial experience that literally took only seconds to transpire, its cumulative impact upon my life over the course of decades has been profound. The impression it made on me is so strong that I can still recall every detail.

My story took place while I was attending a prominent university in North America. This university was already well known for having a particularly strong feminist presence on campus, one that remains so to this day. Like all the incoming students at the time, I was subject to the condescending lectures from various support groups about the dangers of date rape, knowing the rules for establishing consent, and being subjected to the logically absurd feminist lie that *"one in four women will be raped on campus."* Of course, these messages were always grounded in the loaded rhetoric about men as the overwhelming perpetrators of violence against women—this despite all of the public pronouncements made by feminist advocates that they believe in *gender equality*.

At the time of what I now regard as the coercive indoctrination of all students by feminists, I generally accepted at face-value much of what I was told back then, even though for several years prior I had already developed some suspicions about many feminist claims such as the mythical gender pay gap, to name just one. Following my first formal introduction to campus feminism, I had already gained more than enough indirect experience observing the conduct of feminists in public to know what they were really like, and so I made every effort to stay well away from them, knowing that any entanglements wouldn't go well for me.

The specific incident happened during the spring of my final semester on campus, just a few weeks before final exams. At the time, I was walking inside the main university building towards the exit to leave for home off-campus. The exit in question was comprised of two glass doors with a push-bar to open outwards. As I was approaching the exit, I saw a reasonably attractive white woman—a brunette about my age with not-quite shoulder-length hair wearing a white blouse and dark colored pants—heading towards me to enter the building.

Because I'm someone whose natural instinct is to hold the door open for anyone who crosses my path, I made the effort to push open the door closest to me with my right hand and prop it open, while angling my body towards the wall to give her enough clearance to pass through comfortably. Even though I did notice her physical attractiveness, I honestly had no expectation of anything romantic to happen for holding open the door, except maybe to receive a simple thank you.

What I failed to anticipate at the time was that this woman was a rabid feminist, since her response to my kind gesture was the polar opposite of what I would expect from a *normal woman*. The fact is that as soon as this woman saw me holding the door open, her demeanor *completely changed.* Instead of walking calmly towards me as before, she immediately stiffened and marched at double speed towards the other door, to then violently wrench it open and angrily march past.

I was so taken aback by her reaction to what I had done for her—simply by holding a door open—that I felt myself as if frozen in space, speechless. Time seemed to stand still while I stood there looking like a fool, with my arm propped against the open door for exactly no one to pass through while watching her sail by through the other opening she had created for herself.

Despite my stunned reaction, I had enough foresight to catch a glimpse of her face looking straight ahead while she marched past, after which I followed her with my eyes when her back was turned as she headed further away. The look I saw on her face is one that I will never forget. The lines on her face were twisted and contorted with rage. Her eyes were narrowed tightly into a sharp scowl and filled with fury. Her nostrils were flared open and her lips were tightly pressed together, as if she was trying to stop herself from screaming insults at me. Through her facial expression and her overall body language, this woman conveyed the attitude that I was not worthy of her attention and that my very existence as a human being—let alone the fact that I had dared to hold open a door for her—was an offense so unforgivable that I should be treated like the worst person to have ever lived.

My own reaction after she left my space was to shake my head in bemusement at the absurdity of her response to what was a simple and benign expression of kindness towards another human being. While immersed in the experience, I did feel the urge to gently confront her to ask exactly what I did to justify being treated so harshly. However, that look on her face told me *immediately* that I was better off to keep my mouth shut and let her walk away from me as quickly as possible.

Had I opted to speak, I would have told her that my holding the door open wasn't some clumsy attempt at chivalry on my part to create some romantic encounter. I would have done exactly the same thing if the person approaching me were a gay man or an elderly person, a child, someone disabled, or literally anyone else. I saw her simply as a human being for whom I wanted to do something nice for its own sake, and in exchange for my effort I was treated as something worse than dirt. Did I really deserve that?

What's more, the most disheartening thing about that whole experience was that she *never even bothered to look at me* once she made up her mind that I had offended her so horribly. It was as if my mere existence as a man was sufficient to justify spitting on my effort—small as it was.

Immediately after she disappeared from view and I walked towards home, it became clear that this woman was not only a hard-core feminist, she was most likely also a student of Women's Studies. By her treatment of me in that moment, she became the embodiment of such a student who seamlessly absorbed every feminist lie taught to her by all of her instructors, who wrote assignment papers based on obtuse feminist ideas that aren't worth the paper they're written on, to ultimately obtain an advanced degree in public stupidity.

I could easily imagine this woman looking at every awkward situation she encountered and finding some way to tie it in with her innermost beliefs about the supposed evils of all men—irrespective of any evidence to the contrary— reinforced and supported by all of her feminist friends. In fact, I could imagine her meeting up with her feminist friends on campus afterwards to say: "*Do you know what just happened to me? Some ugly, evil, patriarchal man actually dared to hold open a door for me! Can you believe that?*"

Her feminist friends would then reply: "I know! Who does he think he is, that stupid male oppressor? How dare he stare-rape you like that and get away with it! What a horrible, sexist, misogynist pig to think that you need a man to open a door for you!"

And so on.

Everything about my encounter with that woman— someone whom I had never seen before and will never see again—speaks volumes about everything that's wrong with feminism in the world today and why it's a pernicious evil that must be opposed.

Irrespective of what feminists would like people to believe about this ideology and its claims about gender equality, the unvarnished truth about feminism was conveyed in that split second chance encounter that I can never erase from my memory, no matter how hard I try. That look of white-hot hatred, betrayed in her face and in her eyes as she stormed past a perfect stranger, was so intense that it still sends chills up my spine whenever I think about it.

In the two decades since that meeting, I have had occasion to wonder periodically about how that woman's life has evolved since then and what she might be like today. Would she even remember that some male stranger over two decades ago bothered to hold open a door for her, only to be rebuffed? Somehow, I doubt it. If she could be so hostile to an unknown man simply for being nice to her, what type of reaction would she give to some man who might—God forbid—actually be *attracted to her* and want to know her better? If a perfect stranger can elicit such hostility that can take her from a *normal state of mind* to becoming consumed with *rage* in a matter of *seconds*, what is it about her view of the world that could generate such an outcome?

If I ever had the opportunity to come into contact with this woman again, I would like to inquire about the quality of her personal life and the state of her family relationships. Would she have married some man and had children with him? Would they still be together? If she had sons, what type of upbringing would they receive from her according to feminist doctrine? If she had daughters, would she instill in them the same type of hatred for men that she flashed towards me? Would she be a happy and emotionally fulfilled human being, or would she be miserable with the current state of her life, and—most importantly—would she choose to blame men as the cause of her misery?

Obviously, I won't ever get any answers for these questions—at least in this lifetime—but they're questions that continue to weigh on my mind. Whoever reads this account, especially the feminists who think and behave like this woman behaved towards me, I ask that you *think very carefully* about what sort of world you want to have for yourselves and how men like me are supposed to function within it. For example, are we even allowed—let alone welcomed—to speak honestly about serious issues that affect men's lives due to the pervasive abuses of feminism in this world?

There's something grotesque and evil within the core of feminism, to generate such a volcanic eruption for an act of courtesy. More than anything, I feel sorry for her that she's been fed a load of lies about men like myself that bear no resemblance to the realities men experience on a daily basis or the values that they carry within themselves. What could be the cause of such hatred of all men on the part of feminists that *they can't even see the goodness that men provide to the world?* Do feminists today feel so entitled that they claim men's labor and resources for themselves, only to stomp on them whenever they feel like it? Are men not human beings deserving of kindness and respect?

With the benefit of hindsight, I now know that I had unwittingly committed the cardinal feminist-defined sin of *benevolent sexism*, or the act of doing something charitable for a woman as a mere pretense to exert some claim of *male superiority.* Of course, no feminist bothers to explain how some man like myself is ever able to recognize on sight who's a feminist and who's not. Had I been able to know in advance, I would never have bothered to make the effort, thus avoiding the hostile reaction.

Of course, there's no way that I could have known that I'd encounter a man-hating feminist on campus, and while I wasn't particularly traumatized by the whole experience, I do get very angry whenever I hear women complaining about why men today supposedly don't do nice things for them anymore, such as hold open the door, or buy them flowers, or other social niceties that men had been happy to do for women in the past as courtship rituals. The whole concept of benevolent sexism is patent nonsense that only serves to sow seeds of discord between men and women.

These days, if a man approaches a single woman on the street to wish her good morning or say that she looks nice because he might like to know her better or simply to be nice to her, he's risking being accused of street harassment or something to that effect. What then happens to his personal self-esteem or his willingness to be complimentary to some other woman who might actually *want him to approach her?* How is he supposed to succeed if the risks are too great to be worth the effort, only to be confronted with the constant moaning of single women frustrated by their inability to attract men, who ask, *"Where have all the good men gone?"*

For all the women out there who still haven't figured this one out, the good men in this world are literally *everywhere,* but feminists like the one I met have forced them to go into *perpetual hiding.* This is because they don't dare try to be nice to women out of fear that they may get themselves arrested or abused for their trouble. They often take the safest course of action and choose not to even bother—and the world is worse off for their doing so.

I suspect that feminists don't actually want men to take the initiative to approach women because they despise the idea of men freely expressing themselves in the world; they prefer to force men to second-guess every move they make, to accept increasingly onerous restrictions on their own forms of self-expression—even when no women are involved. The accusation of benevolent sexism is particularly effective in instilling that sense of mistrust in men, since feminists don't want men to be comfortable while in the presence of *any woman*, regardless of whether the woman may actually appreciate the effort.

In addition, two other noteworthy feminist rhetorical concepts, *mansplaining* and *manspreading*, are clearly designed to impose further restrictions on how men interact in public, especially when women are present. By using the word *"man"* only in a pejorative sense, while simultaneously using the term "person" for any discussion of positive conduct that is almost exclusively male, feminists further marginalize men.

While it's bad enough that feminist women make use of these hateful concepts to advance their beliefs, it's much worse, in my opinion, when feminist men debase themselves by adopting them in a misguided attempt to redress the fictional wrongs of men. Even more infuriating to me is the presence of sell-out feminist men in academia like Michael Kimmel from Stony Brook University in New York, who build entire careers on the destruction of men in the guise of education by advancing concepts like toxic masculinity to be force-fed to his students and the public at large. While I vehemently reject such a concept, if it's to become part of the social discourse today, then I believe the best example of toxic masculinity is none other than Michael Kimmel himself.

Feminists detest the idea of men and women actually *liking each other*, since that would undermine their narrative that all men are *"oppressors of all women"* and that women are all victims of men's aggression, irrespective of the thoughts and actions of individual men and women towards one another. As someone who believes in God and strives every day to regard all people as deserving of love and respect at some essential level, I'm deeply disheartened by what I've seen of the rise and growth of feminism. Do we want to live in a world where men and women are deliberately pitted against each other by ideologues who don't care about the catastrophic damage they inflict upon society as a whole?

When I think about this woman that I came across, along with others I've seen who display equally disturbing behaviors and attitudes, I'm compelled to challenge all of the leading feminists over the past 50 years on what gives them the right to malign literally half of the human race. Who are they to create a false narrative about the nature of men and women throughout human history? Yes, there are individual men who have done very destructive and evil things in this world, but there are also incredibly kind and caring men who have brought forward very good things, often for the benefit of women they cared about. Conversely, individual women are fully capable of doing overwhelmingly evil things, just as much as any man, and yet you won't find that acknowledged *anywhere* within the feminist movement.

For example, I seriously doubt that any Women's or Gender Studies student would be taught the fact that tens of thousands of women in Nazi Germany were full participants in the murder and brutality of the Holocaust, as described in chilling detail by historian Wendy Lower in her 2013 book *Hitler's Furies: German Women in the Nazi Killing Fields*. In this book, Lower recounts the story of *"The Beautiful Beast,"* Irma Grese, a particularly vicious SS guard at the Auschwitz and Belsen concentration camps, who took pleasure in savagely beating prisoners, releasing attack dogs to maul them, and shooting them at random. When the war finally ended, she at age 22 was tried for war crimes and, upon conviction, was executed by hanging. Besides Grese, there were the wives of SS officers like Lisel Willhaus and Liselotte Meier who took pleasure in the sport shooting of prisoners, along with Johanna Altvater who joyfully took small children imprisoned by the Nazis and tossed them over the balcony of a three-storey building. In addition to that, she was known to lure children with candy in order to shoot them in the mouth with a small pistol she kept nearby.

There are countless others like them who comprise this horror story of Nazi Germany, along with the role of women who brutalized African slaves during the pre-Civil War era of the United States, or were members of the Ku Klux Klan and other hate groups. Despite what feminists might suggest, these women were never *victims of male oppression* but fully responsible for their own depravity and deserving of the full condemnation of the world's people for their acts of evil.

It's time for us to be honest and forthright about the true nature of feminism, in that it's never been about gender equality, but is rather a hate movement intended to consolidate power for a few feminists.

For whoever reads this account, I have the following messages. If you're a young man who feels rejected, alienated, and despondent in what seems like an uncaring world, especially due to feminist abuses of which you may not even be aware, I want you to know that you have intrinsic value and self-worth, even if the outside world doesn't care about how you feel. You are a valued creation of God who loves you immensely and who predestined your existence for reasons that you cannot even begin to imagine. I lament the countless men and boys who end their lives every year who were unable to see their own value.

I have a message for men in general who have decided they want nothing to do with women because of the very real dangers that exist for them in sexual involvement, marriage, or child rearing. I believe in the value of marriage as an essential institution that needs to be strengthened if humankind is to survive and flourish. That said, until fundamental changes are made in how marriage, divorce, child custody, and a whole list of other grievances are handled in law, you absolutely have the right to avoid marriage entirely. Personally, I think that an immediate end to no-fault divorce is a necessary first step towards making marriage a safe institution for men and for the raising of happy and emotionally secure children.

I have a message for women of good will, particularly those who describe themselves as feminists and/or people of faith. Please understand that feminism is a toxic brand that has *never* represented your interests. I fully believe in gender equality, but I will *never* call myself a feminist. The simple reality is that feminists want only to use you as cover to satisfy their own agendas, built on their hatred of humankind—not just of men and boys, but also of women like yourselves who don't think as they do. All they can offer to you is a culture of death and perpetual misery.

Feminists don't care who they use or who they hurt in pursuit of their materialistic desires, while creating a vision for the future that leads directly to George Orwell's 1949 dystopian novel *Nineteen Eighty-Four*. You not only need to disabuse yourself of the label *feminist* right now, you need to make the effort not to ever let any feminists try to push you into living a life of perpetual victimhood, which is what they need to justify their relevance. Furthermore, you need to find every way you can to defend men and oppose feminism wherever you see it, since it represents an existential threat to everyone, and taking the choice not to counter this threat amounts to being complicit in its abusiveness.

This warning also applies to any self-described male feminists and other men who have been fortunate to avoid feminist rage—at least for now. *All men*—no matter who they are or how rich and powerful they may be—are potential targets of feminist abuse, and so long as this hateful ideology remains present in this world, that reality will *never change.*

I have a very special message for all other feminists as described in this account, both prominent and otherwise. Men and women are sick and tired of your abuse! I guarantee you that—one way or another—*it will come to an end, and you will be the worse for it if you don't change your ways.* For the feminists who are particularly responsible for introducing to the world what I regard as the most hateful of all the feminist slurs in existence, *"All men are potential rapists,"* you need to issue a public apology to every man and boy living throughout the world for forcing them to wear an invisible sign that says to all women *"I am a potential rapist! Stay away from me!"* By the way, that formal apology must also include every male feminist who was brainwashed into adopting feminism with good intentions, along with the loser sell-outs of men's interests like Michael Kimmel, since you accused him of being a potential rapist, too.

How would you like it if men were to unfairly make the pronouncement: *"All women are potential gold-diggers"* and force *all women* to wear a similar invisible sign that tells all men *"I am a potential gold-digger! Stay away from me!"* based on the wrong actions of a few women who *are* gold-diggers? That would be obscene and rightly so. Therefore, if you don't want to be regarded as hypocrites who deserve to be shunned by everyone, it would be in your interest to make amends for your abusive and evil conduct, if not for the sake of men and the women who disagree with you, then at least for the well-being of your souls that are subject to the full judgment of God after your death, whether you like it or not.

Finally, I have a message for that woman I encountered over twenty years ago, who revealed to me her inner self through her scorching hatred. I'm neither angry with you nor hurt by what happened then, and I forgave you a long time ago. Perhaps the best way to put the experience in perspective is to quote from Jesus Christ on the Cross: *"Father, forgive them for they know not what they do."* My hope is that you were able to overcome your hatred of men and become a happy and fulfilled human being, and avoid the course of life followed by these feminists who told you lies about the true nature of men and women who live in this world together. With that said, I wish you well.

SECTION THREE – MEN IN FEMINIST INSTITUTIONS

Chapter 1 – Feminist Warriors in Astronomy

An Astronomer

The author discusses the invasion of the academic discipline of astronomy by feminist and social justice politics.

I embarked on an academic career in astronomy almost two decades ago. At the time, I was convinced that space sciences, based on factual observations and physical modeling of the vast universe, would always be immune from the obsessive navel-gazing and politics of hurt feelings of Women's Studies and related departments. Things have changed a great deal since then, and not for the better.

Social justice warriors (SJWs) and feminist activists have penetrated astronomy departments almost as much as the humanities. The influential *Women in Astronomy* blog (womeninastronomy.blogspot.com), whose juvenile rants are foisted upon us at major conferences as if they were divine revelation, contains very little astronomy and a lot of political campaigning on leftist issues and victim-group grievances.

There are, in my opinion, two main reasons why even astronomy has succumbed to this disease. The first is that astronomers are one of the most politicized subgroups of scientists, and the most susceptible to peer-pressure in an overwhelmingly leftist campus environment. The second is that there are more men than women in astronomy (http://www.iau.org/administration/membership/individual/distribution/). This indisputable fact is simplistically interpreted as self-evident, mathematical proof that women are discriminated against in their careers. I shall now discuss both arguments in more detail.

Political Bias

An average astronomy career develops almost entirely within the narrow boundaries of academia (more than other applied sciences). Most astronomers have a very limited knowledge and understanding of the social and economic structure of the real world. Their worldviews are shaped by the green-left activism of their student days and are strongly affected by the ideological social-justice movements sweeping western campuses today with a fervor reminiscent of Mao's Cultural Revolution. Moreover, success or failure in astronomy (again, more than in applied sciences or engineering) depends substantially on the opinion of our peers. Grant and fellowship applications, requests to use the over-subscribed major telescopes, and invitations to speak at international conferences are all determined by small panels of colleagues in the same field, based essentially on how much they trust the applicant's ability as a scientist.

In the highly competitive field of astronomical research, it usually takes only one particularly unfavorable assessment to sink a good telescope time application. Job applications require recommendation letters from several colleagues who have the task of extolling our personal qualities and explaining how well we would fit in with the group and the institution. It would be nice to believe that such judgment is founded entirely on the applicant's research results, regardless of personal friendships, social connections, and political opinions, but we know that is not the case; collaborations and connections are often informally created at BBQs, Christmas (sorry, end-of-year) parties and social events. In these circumstances, the safest (perhaps the only possible) strategy for a young astronomer to survive is to "fit in" and follow the dominant political ideology of the group.

Visibly and loudly endorsing the latest fashionable leftist causes (especially feminist and identity politics) with colleagues at lunchtime and around the water cooler can be a matter of academic survival, especially when leftist colleagues outnumber conservatives by a ratio of 20 to 1, as is the case at the Harvard-Smithsonian Center for Astrophysics in Boston (the largest astronomy institution in the USA). Being leftist becomes a positional good, a signal of superior morality. There is no escaping the moral gaze of SJWs in astronomy; they seem to spend an egregious amount of taxpayer-funded working hours every day hooked on Twitter, Facebook, and whatever leftist blog is in vogue, scourging the unenlightened and looking for signs of ideological dissent.

Gender Imbalance

This is the second main reason why feminist politics has gained significant traction in astronomy. There is an appalling lack of women in STEM fields, we hear from feminist astronomers every day. Many job and grant applications include questions about one's commitment to and track record on bringing more women into astronomy in a way that makes it clear that any dissenting opinions, doubts and questions are not welcome. And yet, there are many pertinent questions on the issue that I would not be afraid to ask if universities were more open to free speech. A lack of women with respect to what? Is it a problem worth spending time on? If and only if it is a problem, what are its true causes and most practical solutions?

The fact that women occupy less than 50% of senior positions in astronomy, or are conferred less than 50% of astronomy PhD degrees, is not evidence either of a problem or of a social injustice. The statistical imbalance in favor of men in math and physical sciences is mirrored by a symmetrical imbalance in favor of women in education, arts & humanities, health, and biological sciences. This is mathematically inevitable, since women now represent a majority of college graduates in the Western world. Perhaps, instead of spending so much time and money to get women into STEM, we could try pushing women out of education and humanities, with aggressive targets for a minimum number of men or a maximum number of women in those careers. But if society benefits from more women moving to STEM fields because of the new talent they bring, will it also suffer from the loss of a corresponding number of women and talent from education and health? Has anyone tried to do a cost-benefit analysis? Or do SJWs believe that gender balance should be aggressively imposed only in fields where women are currently the minority while not touching the female advantage in the other fields?

Such questions are rarely discussed because the drive to shift women into STEM has mostly ideological rather than practical justifications. Two unrelated but equally obnoxious ideologies are clearly apparent in the minds of STEM SJWs. The first driver is the profound feminist dislike of free choice. Women have the right to choose whatever lifestyle they want, provided they choose the one approved by their leftist minders. A young woman who chooses to study English literature or work in education rather than pursue an astronomy research career is somehow being unconsciously oppressed by the patriarchy, even though she erroneously believes that it was her own choice based on her personal preferences. This is analogous to the feminist distaste for women who choose to leave their careers and raise a family at home.

The second ideological driver is the self-belief of almost all STEM practitioners (astronomers above all), male and female, that their field of knowledge is superior to every other. Because we model "important" things like stars, galaxies, black holes and the universe, most of us truly believe that we are also expert in politics, economics and social matters. Plato's Republic remains the ideal state structure in the minds of so many of my colleagues, who dream of imposing their superior knowledge and tidy mathematical order onto the unenlightened, hopeless plebs for the common good (which the masses cannot discern on their own). Maths and physics represent the only true knowledge and power: social justice requires that more women be elevated from the muddy fields of humanities, health and education to the Elysian Fields of astronomy, whether they like it or not.

The ideological motivations driving feminist initiatives in our field would not matter much if more women in astronomy really meant more competence and more scientific progress, as claimed by our SJWs. As the Royal Society of Edinburgh stated, in a 2012 report chaired by astronomy professor Jocelyn Bell Burnell, "The country cannot afford this wastage of talent. We need to tap all our talents." The problem with this argument is that the number of astronomy jobs is limited: society already has all the astronomers it needs, universities already hire more astronomers than they can fund, and the few major telescopes and satellites (essential tools for our research) are routinely oversubscribed by a factor of five. Doubling the number of astronomy jobs is unrealistic and would be a waste of taxpayers' money. So, in practice, "tapping all our talents" translates into replacing a large number of male researchers with female researchers in order to achieve parity. This can be justified as a political goal, but not as a scientific one: there is no evidence that enforced parity is leading to better research outcomes. In fact, the opposite is happening. In practice, half of the astronomy jobs will be available to a large pool of male applicants; the other half will be reserved for a smaller pool of female applicants. Already today, to obtain a good job, a male astronomer needs to be in the top 10% of male applicants, while a female astronomer only needs to be average. If we were really concerned about the science outcome, instead of tapping all our talents, we should try tapping the very *best* talents: and that requires a free competition on the job market with no quotas or targets and no attention to gender balance.

Having dismissed free choice as the main reason for gender imbalance in astronomy, SJWs need to come up with different, politically correct explanations that put the blame squarely on the patriarchy. Two of the most quoted reasons are selection bias and the culture of sexual harassment.

Selection Bias

As a male astronomer, I am apparently unable to assess fairly the quality of scientific research done by female colleagues due to my unconscious bias against people who are different from me. Similarly, as a person of non-color, I am told I am biased against people of color. As a straight, cis-gender male, I am biased against LGBTQWERTY astronomers. And so on. I am also told that any attempt to deny my bias is further proof of how dangerously strong my bias is. (This argument is never applied to political bias: insulting people on the conservative side of politics, saying that they should not be allowed at university, or their funding should be cut, or that they are knuckle-dragging idiots, is perfectly acceptable, as I have experienced many times.)

Most astronomy departments have succumbed to political pressure and have decided they have to do something to "correct" the effects of this alleged bias. They do so in at least three ways. The first is to create jobs and fellowships specifically reserved for female candidates. Such appointments are usually described in terms of "creating role models," a politically correct term more palatable than quotas or targets. Apparently, young girls need to see someone who "looks like them" in a position of academic power to become interested in astronomy. And of course, people of color need their role models, genderqueers need theirs, and so on. This is a complete betrayal of a fundamental principle of astronomy: that the universe can be modeled with physical laws independent of the observer; the motion of a planet, the evolution of a galaxy are not open to interpretation according to our age, sex, gender orientation, race, religion, or veteran status.

The second re-education technique is to leave job ads open to male and female applicants, but include clauses that clearly favor a certain type of political activism. For example, astronomy job ads at the University of California routinely include the request for a "statement of contributions to diversity addressing contributions to diversity through research, teaching, and/or service." The assumption here is that my astronomy discoveries are more valuable if they contribute to diversity and other leftist causes. That apparently innocuous statement contains the same dangerous idea that science should be used to promote a certain ideology, just like physicists in Nazi Germany had to show their commitment to race theories, and Soviet scientists had to explain how their research promoted socialism. Personally, as an old-fashioned libertarian, I still believe that the purpose of astronomy is astronomy itself. None of the great discoveries in the history of astronomy were made by scientists with particular interest in diversity policies. Newton would not have been able to fill out a job application form at the University of California.

The third method used by astronomy institutions to correct for alleged unconscious gender bias is to introduce an even stronger, conscious bias in the opposite direction (the idea of using "good" discrimination to offset "bad" discrimination). Before telescope-time or grant application meetings, we are now commonly subjected to patronizing speeches by diversity figureheads, who remind us how important it is to be fair to female applicants, how we should think twice before rejecting their applications, and how we should be mindful of gender balance and role models in our selection. It is a low-level form of brainwashing. We know that if we select too many male applicants (even if we do it on merit) our choice and motives will be scrutinized, monitored, criticized. Instead, if we select a few more female applicants (even if not all on merit), we will be praised and left in peace. Most astronomers unsurprisingly choose the path of least resistance.

Sexual Harassment

If you believe the hype of astro-feminists, our departments are rife with sexual assaults, bullying and violence. The gender imbalance in astronomy is the result of young women being too scared to venture into this ugly, violent, testosterone-dominated environment.

This is a nice, simple theory that gets parroted by every astronomer eager to show their progressive credentials, but is it consistent with the empirical data? Feminists in every faculty claim that (loosely defined) sexual assaults are rife in their own faculty; indeed, campuses as a whole are said to be in the grip of a rape culture. So, why would that (alleged) widespread violence deter women from doing astronomy but not other fields of studies where they are the majority? Moreover, "sexist" comments and workplace flirting are more tolerated in Latin cultures than in the Anglosphere, and yet the fraction of women in astronomy is higher in Italy, Spain and Argentina than in the more diversity-obsessed Canada, USA, Australia, and Sweden.

I am not saying that sexual harassment never happens in astronomy. There have been a few highly publicized cases of famous male professors flirting or having inappropriate relations with young post-docs or students, and such professors have been duly shamed and harshly punished. I have seen other senior male astronomers having similar relations and getting away with it. I have also seen female students and post-docs who have been happy to flirt with senior male professors and whose careers have benefited from such interactions (but I would be lynched if I said that in public). And I know of senior female professors who entered into relationships with younger male post-docs while nobody complained. In short, inappropriate sexual relations and unwanted flirting do happen sometimes, creating stress in the work environment, but it is not a crisis, it is not worse than in any other human field, and it is not the reason why there are fewer women than men in astronomy. It has been manufactured into a crisis by special interest groups who try to depict women as perennial helpless victims to be protected and compensated, and men as perennial creepy aggressors to be shamed and punished. The Women in Astronomy blog (widely re-tweeted and shared through social media) has become similar to the Red Guards' *Dazebaos* during the Cultural Revolution. As a male, I could be anonymously accused of sexual harassment on that blog without a shred of evidence, and my career would be over in a frenzy of online lynching before I had a chance to defend myself. No wonder we all choose to toe the line in public.

Other Reasons for Gender Imbalance

If, as I have argued, sexual harassment is not the reason for a relative scarcity of women in astronomy, what are the true causes? One possibility we need at least to consider is that male brains are better at the higher levels of theoretical physics and math. I saw first-hand what happened to Harvard University president Lawrence Summers when he suggested such a possibility (I was there at the time), and it was not pretty. In fact, I do not believe that a gap in innate intelligence is the main reason for the gender imbalance. Most types of astronomical research do not require special intelligence or mathematical skills higher than, for example, in biological or health sciences. I suspect the main factor is the hard lifestyle required for a professional career in astronomy. It is often a lonely research pursuit, with a lot of online work in front of a terminal rather than verbal inter-personal communication. It requires working long hours, evenings and weekends. Post-docs have to relocate and move around different countries for a decade (while in their 30s) before they can start competing for tenure-track jobs. More guys than girls enjoy or reluctantly come to accept this lifestyle; it is particularly hard for women who want to have children. The willingness to work longer hours or weekends on short notice is also the main reason behind the so-called "gender pay gap" in other sectors of the economy.

Is It Fair?

My colleagues and I were recently pressured to attend a rather patronizing lecture on work-life balance at our University. The speaker was a young female astronomer hired into a women-only fellowship for which she was the only applicant. She argued that in order to narrow the gender balance, astronomy departments should not schedule meetings and seminars after 4pm or before 10am, because such times would be particularly inconvenient for women with children. There should also be restrictions on working long hours and weekends, and in any case people (mostly women) who choose to work shorter hours should not be penalized on the job market compared to those (mostly men) who work longer hours. What I would have liked to reply to her (if I had a suicidal wish) is that it is easy to say so when you have protected jobs with more positions available than applicants. But as a male astronomer, I have to compete with ten other equally desperate people to get a job, and I have to work unsociable hours to survive.

Is it fair that more astronomy jobs and perhaps higher salaries go to people who work longer hours and make more sacrifices in their private lives (which statistically happen to be mostly men)? By analogy, is it fair that all the players selected for our national football team are people who train several hours a day every day rather than people who only have a kick-around on a Sunday morning? Has anyone realized that by selecting only workaholics, our team is missing out on the experience of a diverse group of people and lifestyles and is not representative of the general population? Surely, our team would be twice as good if half of the players were selected based on football skills and the other half on diversity criteria.

Check Your Privilege

Shaming guys for their "privilege" has become an obsession of SJWs in astronomy, who are aping similar trends in the humanities. At an important astronomy conference, we were lectured by a "senior diversity officer" of the host university, who gave the opening plenary speech on what he called the "white heterosexual Anglo-Christian cis-gender male privilege in astronomy." After reminding us how we male astronomers cannot even begin to understand the constant state of fear felt by women and people of color in astronomy departments every day, the diversity officer instructed the audience to pair up in male-female couples. Each couple was told to read, acknowledge and discuss a list of "29 white male privileges." A few male astronomers randomly picked from the audience were then asked to stand up and publicly confess instances of their privilege. It all looked straight out of a Maoist textbook. And yet, some male astronomers enjoyed being shamed like that. Nothing gives more pleasure to committed leftist academics than to openly proclaim their shame for their own gender, social class, religion, skin color and nationality, because feeling ashamed is a sign of moral superiority, in the same way that whipping themselves and wearing hair shirts make some ascetic monks feel closer to God.

Conclusions

There are now clearly two streams of astronomy careers. The first stream is based on hard work, and leads to merit-based appointments for whoever (male or female) is prepared to accept the asocial research lifestyle. Luck and chance factors play a big part, of course, in determining the outcome of job applications, but usually not deliberate discrimination. The second stream leads to fast-track tenured positions with much less competition for those who are willing and able to play the grievance card on behalf of their officially recognized victim group. Some astronomers still spend most of their time researching and monitoring the sky; others instead spend most of their time researching and monitoring gender balance within astronomy departments, setting up equity-and-diversity committees, writing 200-page reports on discrimination, conferring awards to themselves for their social-justice work, making up new types of privileges, and running blogs full of political propaganda. Unfortunately, funding is shrinking for the former class of astronomers like me, and is ever-expanding for the latter. We can predict with Newtonian certainty that the outcome of every diversity committee, the recommendation of every inclusion report, is that discrimination is "worse than we thought," the new women-only jobs or initiatives are "only a first step," and "Much more has to be done."

Facing the corruption of a profession I love, an old-fashioned astronomer like me can only do small acts of passive resistance. I am not in a career position where I can express open dissent with the Women-in-Astronomy gang and their socio-political theories. I have seen illustrious scientists (remember comet explorer Matt Taylor and Nobel Prize winner Tim Hunt) being brought down by a frenzy of online bullying without any intervention in their defence from their own department or faculty. Kill one to warn one hundred, as Mao said; it is ugly, but of course it works. There is no easy solution; in the current situation, leftist views totally dominate the campus discourse. Things will only get worse for merit-based rewards and for free speech in general unless political diversity is pursued in our campuses with the same determination as gender and ethnic diversity.

Chapter 2 – The Invisible and Lethal Lace Curtain

Tom Golden

The author narrates the mysterious disappearance of a series of health commission reports, and what the experience of following the reports' trail taught him.

This chapter will tell the story of radical feminism spinning out of control and attempting to subvert the efforts of an official Maryland Commission of experts on men's health. The first section will tell the story of what happened. The second section offers my observations and guesses about the how and the why of the efforts of this group. And the third section will examine the underlying societal factors that allowed this sort of thing to transpire.

***

I began working as a therapist for grieving men in the late 1970s. In the 1990s I started going public with what I had learned and began giving workshops to mental health professionals on the unique ways I had seen men heal. A part of those workshops provided ideas for therapists on ways they could support and aid men in their loss.

The majority of men and women were very appreciative of what I offered. The women would usually come up afterwards to ask why they had never heard about this before, saying they couldn't wait to go back and "try it out" on their husbands. They were happy to celebrate the many differences between men and women. These women loved the men in their lives and wanted to understand them on a deeper level.

There was a small minority in these workshops, however, who had no such desire and weren't so happy with the training—in fact, they were bitter. They would try to derail the training with negative comments about men. Their underlying and unspoken message seemed to be that there was something wrong with men and that they did not deserve special treatment. It took me a while to figure out that they were radical feminists who were certain that men were the sole problem of the world, and thus were undeserving of compassion.

They seemed to believe that what men deserved was only condemnation. I realized that these folks were operating under the assumption that to provide special treatment for men was like admitting the rights of a hated enemy. I had to develop ways not to let their anger ruin the training for the other 95-99% of the attendees. This was my first introduction to what is widely called gender feminism.

What I didn't realize at the time but have since begun to understand is that talking about the needs of men is a dangerous thing. By our cultural mandate, men are not supposed to be needy. They are supposed to be strong and to provide for others.

I continued working with men and teaching mental health professionals. Eventually I wrote a book on the topic, *Swallowed by a Snake: The Gift of the Masculine Side of Healing*. In 2007 I was selected to be a part of the Maryland Commission for Men's Health. I was excited that the Maryland government had seen fit to create such a commission, which included a number of well-known MDs, politicians, researchers, lawyers, and others, and during the first meetings, I was elected Vice-Chair. Eventually I took responsibility for three reports, one a general report on the health of men in Maryland, and the other two on male victims of domestic violence and male victims of suicide.

In writing the first report, I wanted to do an audit of the health programs in Maryland that served the health needs of women compared to the programs that served the health needs of men. The commission mandate stated clearly that our support staff would be available to help us in our fact finding and any in-house research. I asked our support person for assistance with this task of surveying sex-typed services. It would be an understatement to say that she seemed less than interested. Her response to requests was slow and non-committal. When I continued to press her, she would help a bit, but it was obvious that she didn't have her heart in it. I wondered at that point if maybe she was like the feminists in my workshops 15 years before who were reluctant to accept anything male-positive. In the end, I had to do most of the research on my own.

What I found in the short time I researched these issues gave me a possible clue about staff reluctance. The State of Maryland sponsored many programs for women's health, but very few for men.

As the date of our last meeting approached, the support person who was responsible for materials for our meetings sent out the one report written by the Commission Chairman for the commissioners to review at our last meeting. She was supposed to have sent all four reports. I wrote to her and asked about the other reports. After a few emails and phone calls, she sent the other three reports to the Commission where we voted unanimously to send all four reports to the Governor.

All seemed well and the work was done. Almost.

Later that fall of 2010, I found myself wanting to check to be sure that the files had made their way to the Governor and to our legislators, and I discovered that only one of the files had been submitted — the one by the Commission Chair. Somehow the three reports I had written didn't make it. I got in touch with the Chair and he said he would check with the person who was supposed to have filed them. With some urging on my part, he instructed her to file the other three reports. She sent an email to us in December of 2010 stating that she had now indeed filed them.

I didn't trust her. That winter I decided to check on the files again. Still, the only file that had been submitted was the Chair's report. I got in touch with him and the support person. At this point the support person said that the files must have been lost in the system. I asked her to track them down; she suggested that I call a certain Health Department employee who would know more. I made that call and found the employee totally unhelpful. She said, "Oh, it's in the system, we just need to wait to see if it gets to the next level." When I went back to the support person, she sent me to someone else. Same deal. This next person sent me on yet again. The process lasted several months, with each person not calling back, being scarce, and finally once contacted telling me to be patient: "It just needs to get to the next level."

Finally I must have reached the end of their string of players and was told that I needed to talk to the Deputy Secretary of the Health Department. It was now May, nearly a year after the reports had been approved by the Commission. She admitted that the files needed to be submitted. She also apologized to me for not including me on a previous email a month before about these three files. Here's what she sent to me on May 18 and what she had said to the Chair a month previously.

"Hi Tom, I apologize for the confusion and not including you on the email sent to [the Chair] back on April 22nd, which you can see below. We felt it would be most appropriate for the addendum to come directly from [the Chair] vs. the department since the original report had already been submitted. Hopefully this will clear up any misunderstanding.

Thanks for contacting my office."

So after months of being put through a wild goose chase to track down the whereabouts of these reports "within the system," the landscape suddenly shifted. The Deputy Secretary claimed that the reports simply needed to be submitted by the Commission Chairman. This was a surprise, but nowhere near the surprise of learning what she had told the Chairman the month before (but never admitted to me): the reason *he* needed to submit the files was due to the Maryland Health Department's not wanting to appear to "approve" of the reports. Here's the note to the Chair in April.

4/22/2011 11:00 AM

"Hello [name of the Chair],

Attached is a copy of your addendum including a cover page for the MD Commission for Men's Health Report. I have reviewed and we will not be submitting from the Department of Health and Mental Hygiene as we feel submission from our agency would indicate our approval. The addendum should be submitted directly from yourself as Chair of the Commission. Please feel free to contact me with any questions at [telephone number].

Sincerely,

[Name and credentials], Deputy Secretary."

This was the first I had heard of the approval aspect. Pretty strange stuff.

Note also that the Department was now calling these reports the "addendum," as if they were some sort of add-on and not part of the original work of the Commission.

At any rate, they were at least admitting that the reports needed to be filed and were laying out a plan to get them sent in. I am sure that at this point if they had had any arguments against the reports being submitted they would have used them. They seemed to be going to great lengths to subvert the reports, but had no overt reasons to offer.

All I needed to do now would be to contact the Chair and have him send in the reports himself. I called and got no return call. I emailed him and got no response. He had been slow to respond in the past, so I gave it a week or two and tried again. Nothing. He was definitely in town and was even meeting with some folks I knew. Yet he simply would not respond to me though we had had a very good relationship up until this point. It was starting to look as if the Chair was a player in stopping the reports from being submitted, but I didn't know for sure if that was the case (I still don't know). All I knew was that without the Chair, the reports were dead in the water. Considering that he had made no efforts in a month to submit the files as the Deputy Secretary had requested, it seemed likely that he wasn't planning on taking that action. So I gave up trying to reach him.

At that point I decided to work backwards. Rather than seek out the Health Department to do their job and to steward the reports to their proper place, I decided to call the Legislative Library directly and talk with them about what they required to get the reports submitted. I realized that, as the Secretary had suggested, the Chair needed to file the reports as the Chair of the Commission. It dawned on me that, in his absence, the Vice-Chair could step in to get the job done.

I contacted the librarian, who quickly put me in touch with the person who receives files and processes them. She was wonderful. As soon as I escaped the clutches of the Health Department, people started telling the truth and offering helpful suggestions. I explained that these reports had not been filed but were a part of the Commission's full report. The librarian gave me the details on how the files were to be submitted to the Library and also how they were to go to the Governor and other officials. I followed her directions and within a few weeks the reports were where they should have been nearly a year before. Success!

If you have been with me this far, you must be assuming that after all of this effort to keep the reports from being filed, the reports must have said very condemnatory things. Not so. What they said, loudly and clearly, is that our men are in need and are being ignored. This is the message that the Health Department didn't want to say they were approving: men need services. If you would like to see the reports, you can find them at http://dlslibrary.state.md.us/publications/Exec/DHMH/HG1 3-2407_2010(add).pdf as appendix B, C, and D: or in a more readable format at http://menaregood.com/wordpress/ maryland-reports/

***

Looking back, it is clear that from the beginning, the support staff didn't like the idea of a Commission that looked into the needs of men.

The first huge red flag was when the support person sent only the one report written by the Chair for approval at our final meeting. That report was a tame, politically correct look into male health statistics in Maryland. It made no mention of the bias in the services provided. That final meeting was to complete our work and vote on the four reports. Sending out only one report was a telegraphed strategy; likely she was hoping to make that the only file that was voted on, allowing the other reports to be permanently overlooked. But her attempt was foiled, as she was forced to send out all four and the Commission reviewed and approved them unanimously.

But if she couldn't foil things by failing to send the three files for the meeting, the next strategy was simply to file only the one report, saying nothing about the others. The Commission had had its last meeting, there would be no more communications between the members, and it was a good bet that simply by omitting those files, no one would ever notice.

But she was found out in that maneuver, and so in December she simply said, oops, I made a mistake, now I *really* sent them!

But she didn't really send them. She never did. She was found out yet again and her strategy changed again. Now the claim was that the reports were lost in the system and she solicited a half dozen other health department employees to take part in her ruse. At this point we can see how the strategy went beyond the support person. She had a good deal of support. In fact, although it is possible that she had a radical agenda of her own, it seems more likely that her superiors were giving her direction.

After it was discovered that only one of the reports was filed, the Health Department went into full lace curtain mode and did all of the distracting and obfuscating they possibly could. What is remarkable is that these reports were not particularly damning towards the Health Department. They simply told the truth about men in need.

I suppose that was enough to warrant blocking them. All of the folks I talked to during the wild goose chase likely knew that the files were not lost in the system; they likely intentionally misled me and fostered a fruitless path to nowhere hoping that the reports would never see the light of day.

The support person's strategy of claiming the files were lost in the system lasted months, but I was persistent. I am guessing that she and her confederates expected me to simply give up, and when I didn't, they likely had a meeting and chose to have the Secretary basically admit the ruse and also refuse to file the reports with the approval of the Health Department. It seems that the message was that if we can't keep the reports from being published, we can at least say we don't like them. This was a critical admission, strongly indicating that not filing the reports and then creating the wild goose chase were acts of deceit. It's also worth noting that the Secretary never said anything to me about the reports not meeting their approval either when we spoke via the phone or via email. Was she afraid of what might happen if she admitted the truth to the author of the reports? I guess so.

My response to all of this was shock and disbelief. The extent that my government representatives went to mislead me and stop the publication of the reports profoundly weakened my faith in our system. That Health Department employees would fabricate a tall tale and speak it repeatedly made a strong statement about their integrity. But my personal reaction is not as important as the larger picture. In part three we will look at the societal and psychological forces that allow such obstruction to occur.

***

The more important part of this story has to do with why a Commission such as this could be subverted and how this dynamic may play out on a much wider scale. What made this sort of arrogant and imperious action possible?

It's hard to imagine what it would take to presume you have the right to alter the work of a group of experts. Imagine if a secretary for a law firm filed only one of the four legal reports that her employers had drafted and asked her to submit. I'm sure if she was found out, she would be fired immediately. How could a group of non-experts have the power to suppress reports and to believe their wrongdoing was acceptable?

The first answer to this question is that we live in a culture that focuses on the needs of women and ignores the needs of men. This structure, called gynocentrism,[2] has operated invisibly for thousands of years and is based on the necessity to protect women from harm in order to ensure community survival. Women are valuable, men are disposable.

Men are expected to provide and protect. Think about how much women and the culture dislike needy men. While needy women are a call to action, needy men cause both women and men to look away. While some men may indeed have economic and social power, they use that power, by and large, to serve and protect women.

A quick look at American legislation will show a multitude of bills focusing on the safety and needs of women. The US has seven national offices for women's health, and none for men. The Violence Against Women Act protects women from violence while ignoring the men who are more often victims of violence and nearly as often victims of domestic violence. This is not to say that women have never faced discrimination. They have faced discrimination in the workplace, in our educational system, in financial systems, and more. But most of the discrimination has been due

---

[2] For more information on gynocentrism you can go to an excellent web site on the topic: gynocentrism.com.

primarily to their being valued highly, put on a pedestal and protected, not hated and oppressed.

Gynocentrism is just one factor in our current situation. Enter feminism, especially radical feminism, and the powerful energy of gynocentrism becomes a hammer in not only serving women but in denying men and boys their share of compassion and care. Keep in mind that in a gynocentric world, the complaints and cries for help of women get immediate attention while the same cries from men will be ignored. Feminism took advantage of this sexism to attain its ends. Women's cries for help got traction and action from our legislators.

Radical feminists created a mantra that our society has accepted as truth: men are bad, men are the problem, men are selfish and are oppressing women. Feminists successfully spread this message to the general public in such a thorough fashion that most on the street would agree with the basic idea. If you take an already gynocentric culture that is focused on keeping women safe and avoiding the needs of men, and combine that with a media mantra that women are oppressed and men are the problem, you create an environment in which disdain for men increases and most people will fret over the needs of women and girls while scoffing at the needs of men.

The lie that men have oppressed women has been particularly difficult for men. Both women and men of the past faced discrimination under rigid gynocentric sex roles. But now women are taught that they were uniquely oppressed while the discrimination that men faced (death in war, etc.) is ignored. Rather than being respected as the traditional protectors and providers, men are now vilified as oppressors and seen as the enemy. Admiration and respect are the fuel for masculinity; without it, men limp along. Some men try to get the respect and admiration our culture now denies them by condemning other men as misogynists, agreeing with the misandry of radical feminists. However, this tactic is futile and will never produce a mature man.

More than two generations have grown up with this bias. You can see our young girls feeling as though they have been shortchanged by boys. The typical attitude is, "You had it all for a long time and now it is my turn." It drives the girls even more in the gynocentric direction of feeling perfectly justified in focusing only on the needs of women and girls, and not really caring about boys and men.

A great deal has been said about male violence and the importance of stopping it. Whether it is domestic violence, bullying, or some other issue, men's violence is rightfully called out as needing to be contained for the well-being of all. I really don't have a problem with most of that, but I do have a problem with the way our culture turns a blind eye to women's violence, and especially to their relational violence, which is often the feminine form of violence. In the feminine version, rather than be physically violent, one gossips, shames, misdirects, or refuses to take some needed action. This form of violence is nearly as lethal as male violence but not nearly as known, seen, or condemned. Much of what was done by the support staff in suppressing the reports is a type of relational violence—passive but hurtful.

When you combine gynocentrism, feminism, and relational violence, this is what you get: A person with a great deal of interest in the needs of women and girls, a strong sense of blame towards men as oppressors, and a proclivity to use passive means to negate male-positive outcomes while feeling justified in doing so. We can see this clearly in our media and schools, and of course, in this chapter's example, our bureaucracies. Failing to file the reports was a passive act expressing a willful disregard for men and boys. It took someone who can write off boys and men without blinking. If the perpetrator really buys into the feminist narrative of men being oppressors, they may even feel as though they are doing everyone a service.

Remember the feminists in my workshops at the beginning of this chapter? They were spouting the 'men are bad' mantra, and wanted to be sure that men did not get any special treatment. Those women have now been integrated into our bureaucracies.

This was just one commission in one state. Imagine how hundreds of thousands and maybe millions of people who have this mindset—of men not needing services or care—could be planted in all of our bureaucracies. Our educational system is pumping out people who have been flooded with a hateful ideology, and these folks have been filling up jobs in education, public policy, human resources, office assistance, middle management, and many other spots. If that is not bad enough, imagine that they are not only in the bureaucracies but are also in our media, our courts, and our government. Look at the impact this small group in the Maryland Department of Health had in nearly stopping any message that might be pro male, and multiply that by a zillion across the country. Notice that their power is mainly through passive violence. The hallmark of relational violence is that even if it is found out, it can be denied that it was meant to be harmful. The support person could easily say that she had just made a mistake: why is everyone getting so upset? This is the nature of relational violence.

Ultimately, then, this chapter is not about one commission and a small group of women who tried to sabotage its message. It is about one instance of sabotage that was miraculously exposed and gives us a sober look into the possibility that this sort of malfeasance is commonplace in our culture, leaving us with a system that caters to the needs of women and avoids the needs of men. Think about the media portrayal of women's needs versus men's needs. All of our systems are now flooded with this hateful ideology. It's easy to see the filters that work to keep women's issues prominent and men's hidden. We are in deep trouble.

Chapter 3 – Goddess Worship in the Church

Simon Dennerly

In the Catholic Church and in the schools it runs, the author explores how feminist goddess worship has invaded even a literal patriarchy.

I know that feminism is not about equality, or even justice, as feminists are the people who tried to ruin my life. My crime was trying to expose theirs.

When anti-feminists like Milo Yiannopoulos say "Feminism is cancer," it's not a baseless accusation. Feminism corrupts everything it gets its hands on. And make no mistake, there is no area of human thought or activity that feminism does not have a position on: it is a totalitarian ideology.

Let's take science, a discipline looking at the workings of the natural world. Various feminist scholars have made a number of claims such as that $E=MC^2$ is a "sexed equation" and that "chemistry is sexist." Don't even get me started on the article "Glaciers, gender, and science: A feminist glaciology framework for global environmental change research." Perhaps nowhere is the anti-science mindset of feminism more pronounced than the denial of all the science that shows the clear biological foundations for gender. It matters not what any scientist says and can prove: to feminism everything is a social construct that can be re-imagined.

Many commentators reflecting on the totalitarian mindset of feminism have likened it to a religion, but what is always overlooked in our increasingly secular societies is the role feminism has played in the downfall of Christianity in the West. Before the assault of its Third Wave, feminists had infiltrated and practically broken the back of its major rival: Christianity. In its hubris, feminism believes it can re-imagine God as a goddess.

The following is not just a case study of this phenomenon: it's my story.

I have no intention of giving a faith testimonial, only outlining the facts of the matter. Despite my family not being particularly religious, I always had faith, and at age 15 I decided to do something about it. After much research, I joined a Catholic youth group though I did not formally join the Church until eight years later. The reason for this was my awareness of a certain disconnect between the way Rome laid out how the Church should conduct itself and how the Catholic Church in New Zealand conducted itself, often disregarding Church teaching. As a teenager I thought we were just slack, but as I got older and looked more deeply, I realized that I was witnessing a decades-long agenda to supplant Catholic orthodoxy with Cultural Marxism, the largest faction of this movement being feminism.

On Sundays, I attended Mass at the Cathedral. One day, however, the Cathedral closed for renovations. After that I went to a neighboring parish, and there I witnessed an event that ultimately changed my life. Some friends and I had accidentally shown up for what could be termed the Social Justice Warrior service, which was so wacky and off the wall that it was held in the basement of the church, away from public view. A lay person gave the homily and used it to attack the Church to the point of outright despising it (and got applause for it). He also referenced the big council that had just finished in Rome at the time. The very next day one of my friends came across an article quoting comments on the council by various Catholic groups, including a notorious international one that was Catholic in name only, which promoted abortion, homosexuality, contraception, and woman priests, and their statement contained many identical statements to the homily at the local SJW service.

I found the international group's online forum and confirmed that the New Zealand SJW service did have links to it. Then I found an email that had been posted to the forum. It advertised an upcoming feminist symposium; the woman who posted it was most excited about the keynote speaker, "Carol Christ in NZ!" The sender was the chair of the diocesan council (a diocese being a region a bishop oversees), and the recipients on the list were all well-known feminists and comprised about 20% of the diocesan staff. Having no idea who Carol Christ was, I did a quick Google search and discovered that she was considered the founder of the modern goddess movement. According to Christ, it was necessary to reject the male god of Judaism and Christianity. Women were to find the divine within themselves and celebrate their sacred connection to the earth, discarding the idea of a male savior or religious leader.

Then I looked into another keynote speaker, Sister Elaine Wainwright, an Australian nun who had been lecturing at a Catholic seminary in Australia. Her religious vision was heavily indebted to paganism and goddess worship. She referred to the divine as "Sophia." Sophia is the Greek word for Wisdom, and in the Old Testament, wisdom is often gendered feminine. Feminists such as Wainwright employ Sophia as a female version of God, with a vague justification in Scripture, in order to replace the Christian trinity. Wainwright even quoted another radical feminist scholar, Elisabeth Schussler Fiorenza, who called Sophia "the nemesis of God."

Wainwright eventually became Professor of the Auckland University School of Theology which put under one banner the majority of Christian theological schools in Auckland, New Zealand. The main reason she got this role was that she was sponsored by the Catholic Institute of Theology (CIT) an organization made up largely of feminist nuns. Wainwright's main interest as a feminist theologian was to bring pagan images, influences, and beliefs into the Catholic tradition. She spoke against the destructiveness of what she called an androcentric bias in the Catholic Church and the need to reinterpret Scripture to emphasize female goddess wisdom. She even re-interpreted Christ as Christa (feminine) and was wont to show images at her lectures of nude women on the cross in place of Jesus.

As I delved more deeply in the months to come, I found the scale of the betrayal to be greater and greater. I discovered nuns who became ordained Reiki masters (a Buddhist energy massage practice), with their centers running "dream interpretation" workshops, the text books for which talked about past-life experiences, telepathy, and clairvoyance. They embraced something called the New Cosmology, which is pantheistic in nature. Pantheism is the belief that everything is God, which is the polar opposite of Christianity's core belief in a transcendent deity. In pantheism, creation is "birthed" from an earth mother. The celebration of the female connection to the fecundity of the earth is central to this ideology.

To non-Catholics, such ideas may seem relatively benign. Why shouldn't people celebrate nature if they want to, or explore the spiritual traditions of Eastern theologies? Fair enough. But when they do so as practicing Catholics, pretending that what they are promoting is part of Catholic doctrine—rather than an outright rejection of and undermining of Catholic doctrine—they are attempting to destroy the foundation of the Church they represent. Moreover, through Catholic schools and universities under their control, they are creating armies of Social Justice Warriors to transform the wider society: whether you are Catholic or not, this does affect you.

The whole thing was madness of the highest order, and as I came to understand the extent of the corruption, I made the decision to oppose and expose it—a decision that cost me dearly in terms of years, money, status, relationships, and career. But the worst of it was that most of it was already known and tolerated.

The phenomenon, as I discovered, is called the Goddess Cult, and feminism is literally its orthodoxy. At its heart were orders of nuns that had become cults. The Catholic Church had been hit by the perfect storm in the 1970s with not only the cultural revolution in society at large but also the mass confusion that followed the Second Vatican Council, as leftist reformers, including proponents of Marxist "Liberation Theology," ran rampant, challenging core Catholic principles and practices. In countless orders of nuns, feminist reformers held meetings to plan "reforms," used intimidation and brought powerful psychological techniques (as used in cults) to bear, forcing out those who wanted to be actual nuns. In this way they also procured millions of dollars in finances and property, and control of institutions like Catholic schools to further the feminist crusade to remake the Catholic Church from within. A more thorough explication can be found in Donna Steichen's ground-breaking book on the issue, published in 1991, called *Ungodly Rage: The Hidden Face of Catholic Feminism*.

Of course, while it is widely known that not too long ago homosexual men sought to enter the Catholic priesthood to hide that they were gay, very little focus has been put on lesbians entering the convent. While some of them, no doubt, were propelled by sincere religious devotion, others had a political and ideological motive, seeking to live without men and to change the Church so that the role and value of men within it would be profoundly altered. Indeed, orders of feminist nuns are perhaps the only genuine working models of the political lesbianism some feminists promote.

I read books on feminist theology and found that in every case their concerns were almost the exact inversion of core Catholic concerns. Not once did I come across reference to life after death. The only concept of sin is the Marxist injunction against social injustice—or sin against the environment. I found it most striking how a number of feminist theologians made the claim that they had more in common with feminists of other faith traditions (either other Christian, Jewish, Muslim, Hindu, etc.) than they had in common with people in their own tradition. Just as globalists seek to undermine the state, Catholic feminists seek to undermine the notion of Catholicism as "the one true faith."

What really got to me then, as it does now, is the fact that "they know." The feminists know that if they let their true beliefs and motives be known—if they openly declared themselves non-Christian—they would be rejected not just by the Church as an institution, but by the common people whom they lead and teach. They know everyone they have driven out of jobs in the Church or committees, or prevented from getting such roles, because those people insisted on Catholic orthodoxy and had every right to do so. They know that in the teaching positions they so eagerly sought (and almost gained a monopoly over), they were paid to teach the Church's beliefs but taught their own countering and dissident views instead. They know that millions upon millions of dollars and support would not have come to them in terms of donations from the faithful, wills, government grants, courses, etc. They know they are frauds and liars, and they know they can (and do) severely punish those in the Church who try to stand against them.

These discoveries were happening at a time when I decided to get my life on track. After finishing university, I decided to get into teaching, as I loved learning and imparting what I learned to others. I wanted to teach History and Classics (two subjects that kept me going through school) and being a Catholic man I wanted to teach religious education in Catholic schools as well.

My career goal also gave me an opportunity to see what things were like in Catholic schools. Feminists had written the Religious Education (RE) curriculum and ran the centralized education offices. I wanted to know in an intimate way what was being taught to young Catholics.

I was accepted into teachers' college and my first placement was at an all-boys' Catholic school. This one was atypical: they had rejected the feminist religious education curriculum and written their own, a more traditional framework of studying philosophy for the first half of the year and theology for the second half. Although the staff members were of a liberal bent, the all-male environment allowed for a stand to be taken. A standard was set that staff in the department had to have either a Master's or PhD in Theology or Philosophy. The department used university essay formats, which the students brought into other subject areas as well. It was a model for excellence. But what was most telling is that the teacher who came up with the system was so persecuted by the feminists who ran the Auckland regional Catholic schools office that he ended up leaving the country for a year to get away from them.

During this time I took the opportunity to look at *Faith Central*, the national resource website for the Religious Education curriculum that every Catholic student was meant to consult for course work. It was thoroughly feminist. There were multiple articles directly attacking the Church's teachings on various subjects such as woman priests and birth control (without actually presenting the

Church's position), links to pages promoting Pantheism, links to the Jesus Seminar, a group of dissident Biblical scholars who upheld the Gnostic Gospel of Thomas and dismissed the Gospel of John. One link was to a feminist theorist who claimed that men's spirituality led to "heart attacks and Hiroshima" (and this was to be read by every male student doing that course unit). To put it simply, it was full of material that would be at best confusing, at worst perilous, to a young person's faith.

Using the alias Dirk Van Holland, I sent a report on this teaching website to every Catholic authority I could find. The next day, the website was taken off-line. A couple of days after that, a very rough new website was launched. I got a letter from the bishop in charge of education saying that when he went to look into my claims, it just happened that a new website was being launched and all the objectionable material was gone. Case closed. I replied to him, and to the hundred-plus on the email list, saying that half of the material was still up. I got no reply, but immediately that material disappeared as well. I continued writing mini-reports exposing the goings on, but it was clear there was no will within the Catholic hierarchy to root out the anti-Catholic teachings or to discipline the many individuals involved in promoting them.

My second placement was at a Catholic girls' school run by the order of nuns who were the biggest exponents of the Goddess Cult, the Sisters of Mercy. If I had known what was to come I would not have looked forward to it. By the end of the whole affair they had twice tried to stop me registering as a teacher.

As an all girls' school, it was not a surprise that it was a feminist stronghold. Indeed the symbol that the Goddess Cult uses—a Spiral—was everywhere in the school. I did have one ally, a female teacher who was a faithful Catholic and not a feminist, whom the other religious education teachers referred to, quite openly and contemptuously, as "the Fundamentalist"; other non-Catholic staff innocently asked her what fundamentalism entailed. As a side note, in the Religious Education Curriculum there was a section on "Fundamentalism," which stated that fundamentalists in the Catholic Church were considered those people who *"interpret documents of the Church in a literalistic manner,"* with the clear message that such people were narrow-minded and ignorant. The implication was that by virtue of their qualification, feminists could tell you what the Church documents "really" meant.

Three of my classes were in religious education, and there was a stark contrast between the intellectual level of my group and the boys' school I had been at before. At one point, I tried to have a standard discussion that I had had at my former school and was told that it was over the heads of the girls, indeed over the heads of any student at the secondary school level—which I had seen was not true and was an insult to the intelligence of the girls. They were simply not being taught to a high intellectual level.

I got off side soon after this with my primary teaching associate. She said something in a class that was blatantly wrong, and after class I sought to respectfully discuss the matter with her, explaining what the actual case was. She was immediately angry and resentful. I brought the matter up with my friend in the school, and she told me to watch my back: my teaching associate had already complained about my action to her, saying I was "too young, too arrogant, and too male to be a teacher." "They do not like men who stand up to them," she said, reminding me of a mutual associate of ours, a man, who had been driven out of his position as a head of department at the school.

The next week, I finished my five week placement and a month later was meant to go back for a final two week period, but was informed that the school was not going to pass me.

While waiting for my final placement, I wrote up and released a full report on what I had discovered about the state of feminist undermining of Catholicism in my diocese, citing numerous sources, eye witness accounts, leaked internal documents, and extensive quotations from various teaching resources to show the malignant influence of feminist theory in all areas. It came to 70 pages in all and can be seen here, as "A Report on the Crisis in the Catholic Church in New Zealand" published at Catholic Culture.org (https://www.catholicculture.org /culture/library/view.cfm? recnum=7620).

It was completely ignored by the powers that be. Some clergy contacts told me that it stopped some people from getting key appointments and stopped some dodgy projects from going ahead, but no one was fired or disciplined. Apparently there were some token investigations, but I was never contacted about any of it. My bishop refused to see me (probably as I was tugging on threads that would lead to his downfall) and decried me as a madman. My report was heavily discussed and attacked on a New Zealand Catholic online forum, but when people asked for details and evidence of errors in the 70 page report, none were put forward. Leaders of some Catholic groups contacted me personally to praise my good work, but declined my invitation to make a public stand alongside me.

I had bled, had risked my desired career path, risked my reputation to fight the corruption of the feminists, and no one would stand with me: that is a betrayal I still feel to this day. I kept fighting for years afterwards, writing exposes, and I got verbal support and even cash donations from many, but no one took any action. I came to realize the heart breaking truth, what the bishops and feminist nuns already knew: no one wanted to end up an outcast like me.

Towards salvaging what was left of my teaching career, I started my final placement, which was at an Auckland Boys' Grammar School, one of the best schools in the country. Initially, my confidence was shaken, but I was assessed twice, and passed both times with flying colors.

I was meant to get my certificate after finishing my second assessment, but a few days afterwards I was called into a meeting with the three top officials at the teachers college. I learned that the Sister of Mercy school that had refused to pass me had now launched an official complaint to stop me from graduating. They cited unprofessional conduct, owing to the fact that in my report I had mentioned some of my experiences at a teachers' college, Sisters of Mercy, although there are a dozen such schools in the diocese, and I gave no specific details that could identify them; but that did not deter them. They did not dispute the facts of what I had said, just that I had brought the school into disrepute. The officials told me that this was a very serious matter that would likely result in my being denied my teaching post-graduate diploma.

I asked to bring support people to the next meeting: two respectable looking older gentlemen in suits who "accidentally" gave the impression of being lawyers and who stated very forcefully that if I were not allowed to graduate, there would be serious consequences. The officials were taken aback. What had been "a very serious matter" was downgraded to "just having some questions." I was able to get my diploma.

I had dodged a bullet, but there was more than one: a couple of my Catholic teaching sources informed me that an email from a diocesan office had gone out to Catholic schools warning them not to hire me. I thought of suing the diocese for damages—if for no other reason than to bring to light what was going on—but neither of my colleagues would give me a copy of the email, explaining that they had their families to think of and worrying that they could lose their jobs.

I personally cannot believe that people think feminists actually support tolerance and inclusivity. Whether it is in churches, universities, schools, or government, they create a 'Culture of Fear' wherever they go.

I spent some time as a relief teacher in a girls' state school, which was safer by far, but still not without incident. At one school they actually had a philosophy class, and as the only relief teacher with a philosophy background, I was the one who filled in. One day, we were reading a passage on the euthanasia debate and the text mentioned how in some US hospitals, babies born after failed abortion attempts were left to die. I made some comment regarding how the abortion and euthanasia debates were linked; one of the girls said "abortion is murder," to which many of the other girls looked confused, so I asked them if they knew why, to which they replied they did not. So I gave a very short and basic run down on the position and related it back to euthanasia and continued with the text.

Soon after this incident, I was told by the coordinator of relief teachers, with whom I was friendly, that the philosophy teacher came angrily into her office to exclaim that "that MAN is never to take my class again" (I was told the emphasis as it was in a raised voice that took my friend aback). This teacher also headed the Amnesty International group at the school, which at the time was pushing "abortion rights" internationally.

I will never understand how feminists who crave, seek, and obtain powerful institutional positions see themselves as oppressed freedom fighters, while using institutional power against others in a manner they claim is being used on them. Within Catholic diocese, this power is intense indeed.

You would be forgiven for wondering how, in the Catholic Church—a literal Patriarchy—feminists could get away with such relentless subversion of Catholic teaching and practice. The only thing that can be said for sure is that wherever feminists infiltrate, corruption and a code of silence follow. While feminists claim to be "resisting" oppressive institutions, they have been remarkably successful in persecuting anyone who tries to maintain the core beliefs of the Church.

At this time, I am making another attempt to expose the corruption in the Church and plan to head overseas to regroup soon. I have led a very church-centered life, but the local environment has become toxic for me. It's not just the corruption: it's how precious few will stand up to it. The Culture of Fear trades silence for safety, integrity for peace. It's hard not to lose respect for people when you can't tell whether they are exercising prudence or cowardice. People profess a great love for the faith and the Church, yet when they turn a blind eye to such outrageous heresy it makes their professions seem quite hollow. I can't be a part of the lie anymore. I am heading off into the unknown, though not to find peace: I have not finished fighting feminism yet.

Chapter 4 – Witch Hunt at Oxford University

Jeffrey Ketland

The author tells of his persecution by feminist zealots following the suicide of a mentally ill woman whom he had tried to help.

I was witch-hunted at the University of Oxford in 2013-14 by a group of feminist vigilantes. Their misconduct was appeased and enabled by the University of Oxford in order to hide its own liability for welfare failings leading to a student death. This witch hunt destroyed my career and my reputation and ruined my life. The saga itself was long and complicated, and occurred over roughly six years.

I was the victim of a violent stalker, Charlotte Coursier, whom I'd known for many years. She was a student, originally, when I was a lecturer at the University of Edinburgh. I met her in 2008. She made several suicide attempts and hundreds of telephone calls to me, including "countless suicide threats" as my wife later put it. I helped her and prevented the suicide attempts, as she acknowledged repeatedly—for example, writing in one of her love letters to me in June 2011, "You are still the person that saved my life and my degree." Her crisis occurred over a period of about six months, November 2008 - May 2009. It caused major problems in my marriage, and led eventually to that breaking down two years later.

Charlotte and I were close for a subsequent two years; a judge later described it as a "quasi-matrimonial relationship." In late 2010, after I had separated from my wife for a time, Charlotte and I had a short consensual relationship. However, she became violent and abusive. Those with medical expertise who looked at the evidence all agree that this was Borderline Personality Disorder. Charlotte had been detained by the police once, earlier in 2010, after she confronted my wife at our home. Later, she sexually assaulted me in November 2010, and the police were called. At this point, I distanced myself and broke off contact; she then sent me harassing, abusive, and threatening messages for months afterwards, and stalked me obsessively for a subsequent two and a half years up to June 2013.

She followed me to my new academic position in 2012 in Oxford. There, she stalked my wife and son for months, until they left town in distress; she eventually began stalking me at my seminars in May 2013, turning up pretending not to know me. After I had told her to leave me alone, she was encouraged by feminist friends around her to make false accusations against me to the university and to the police, who "believed" her: they outrageously gave me a PIN ("Police Information Notice," often called a "harassment warning": no evidence is required, the accused is not consulted, and my stalker refused to provide a statement). But their view changed when I told them about her history of abuse and violence against me and her suicide attempts.

I notified others of Charlotte's mental instability and the Faculty of Philosophy was notified, but all of these notifications were ignored. A few days later, Charlotte contacted the police and retracted her false accusations and I again explained to them her past behavior and expressed my serious concerns about her mental state, something later confirmed by the Oxfordshire Coroner, Mr. Darren Salter.

A month later, in June 2013, Charlotte's boyfriend broke up with her in London. She threatened suicide but he ignored the threats; she returned to Oxford and committed suicide about three hours later. As I learned much later, their relationship was filled with turbulence and problems; her boyfriend had earlier persuaded her to have an abortion in March 2013 which apparently upset her a great deal, making her think that she had "murdered her child." The fact that their relationship was breaking up was precisely the reason she had begun contacting me again in May 2013. But I did not know this.

In May 2013, several people around Charlotte, including her flatmate, had cajoled her into making a series of false accusations against me, accusing me of "harassing" her even though I was the long-term victim of stalking and violence, and at that time did nothing wrong: I merely told her to stop contacting me and I notified others of my serious concerns about her mental state.

The agitators were American feminists. The academic profession of philosophy has been convulsed in the last five years by feminist activists running campaigns against male academics whom they — often falsely — accuse of "harassment." Many such campaigns have occurred and these have had devastating consequences for the victims of their false accusations. In Oxford, the cajolement of Charlotte by feminist activists prevented her from receiving psychiatric attention which might have saved her life. Her welfare crisis was ignored because feminist fanatics decided to "believe" a mentally unwell stalker and to persecute her (male) victim.

After Charlotte's suicide, I was subjected to a witch hunt set up by the flatmate who recruited other feminist vigilantes. I was slandered, smeared, intimidated, and cyber-harassed; I was driven out of my teaching; eventually my family was driven out of our home. The police advised us to leave after we reported cyber-harassment: I was anonymously sent messages calling me a "murderer."

The vigilantes distributed their false accusations on Twitter, Facebook, and blogs over a period of eight months up to Feb 2014, including "feminist philosophy" blogs, where I was accused of being a "sexual harasser," a "blackmailer," and even a "stalker" responsible for someone's death. They got their story into a Coroner's court at the inquest into Charlotte's death (I was not consulted about this or allowed to reply) and into the national press in February 2014 (I was not consulted or allowed to reply). They then authored an apoplectic "Open Letter" filled with smears and demands for my punishment.

Cowardly university administrators then fired me, giving the activist mob what they demanded; they also covered up the facts, including their negligence of Charlotte's welfare. They portrayed a stalker with a police record of violence as the "victim" (they held a conference in her honour and placed a memorial bench outside the Philosophy Faculty in Oxford) and they portrayed not just me but also my family who were actual victims of a long-term stalker as "guilty." In fact, we had suffered appalling harm, including PTSD.

After this, I appealed through a legal process (without legal representation), which was emotionally gruelling, but I was vindicated and I won. I was reinstated.

It was the most horrific experience of my life: a witch hunt driven by feminist vigilantes, and it destroyed everything in my life and career. I was left penniless and homeless in August 2014. Although I was reinstated, since then I have been made a pariah in my academic profession and quietly forced out of my job. I have been blacklisted and prevented from publishing and from attending academic events.

Chapter 5 – Accused of Sexual Harassment

David

The author analyzes the series of baseless allegations that led to his firing.

My personal hell in my workplace began when 'Ruth' initiated a conversation with me. I thought she was very pretty, and one day asked if she was married. I was separated from my wife at the time and headed for divorce.

"Yes," she replied.

"Oh, you just broke my heart," I said in a joking manner.

I immediately apologized, to which she said, "No Problem." (I later described this to an employment attorney, who said it would not warrant corrective action because there was no pattern of vexatious behavior.)

We went on to have a friendly, platonic work relationship for several more months with no issues. At no time did I hit on her or invite her to anything.

On my birthday, she yelled out my name and waved me over to talk. (Doing so implied she was comfortable with me, I think.) I obliged. She asked if I was going to the Christmas Party the next day, and said she thought I should go. She asked how I had liked my work birthday gift (an inexpensive, fun, gag gift) and remarked, "It must be nice to be so popular."

I told her I wasn't going to the party. (Wouldn't you think I'd make sure to go if I was 'obsessed' with her?) I wished her a great time and left.

The next work day, she was diametrically different to any other occasion I had interacted with her. She wasn't mean—just quiet, cool, and aloof. It even crossed my mind that she might be high. She was acting so strangely that I asked, "Is anything wrong?"

"You stand too close," she said.

I was shocked. I had expected she might say she was tired due to the shift-change, maybe suffering from a headache or something. I didn't stand any closer to her than anyone else in the plant, and I was rattled by her words.

To make a long story short, I wrote her a note and said I was sorry if I had made her feel uncomfortable. I went on to explain that I had always been quiet around her because I thought she was pretty. I ended the note by saying I didn't think we should talk anymore.

I know. Dumb to write the note. And I know management probably interpreted the "pretty" comment as inappropriate. But the fact is, it wasn't a new revelation to her. She already knew I found her pretty and was fine with it for months. I was trying to be kind, agreeable, and accommodating—to end things nicely. However, from that moment on I was in her crosshairs. She began a double-pronged campaign of gossip and dirty glares every week.

"She thinks you're going to stalk her," a co-worker said, though it had been only days earlier that she was waving me over to talk, encouraging me to attend the Christmas Party.

I asked the person to please tell her that I'd never hurt her or stalk her. "You know what, I don't want to get involved," she said.

I left it alone for approximately a week. But I didn't want Ruth to feel that way, to be afraid of me. So I approached her, solely to convey that she had no worries, that I'd never stalk her.

Her face went beet-red. I continued: "You misunderstand; you're wrong about me." "I don't care!" Ruth replied. I left and never had a conversation with her again.

Another co-worker was asked, "Is that the guy who's harassing the woman on Floor 2?" The chatter sure didn't come from me.

Ten months later, after the glares and gossip, she went to HR and complained, marking the beginning of a tedious and humiliating investigation. I was never told any of the allegations. However, I was told post-investigation and off-the-record that Ruth had left the impression she was "deathly afraid" of me.

One rainy morning, five-months into the corrective action, I decided to walk to my work area through the plant. As I was walking a very long, straight aisle, Ruth popped out from the right-side and began walking towards me on the opposite side. We were about 120 feet apart.

When the distance closed, she crossed over to my side of the aisle and cut right in front of me. She was so close she had to turn her hips and shoulders to get around me. We didn't say a thing to one another. It didn't seem like the behavior of a deathly afraid woman.

I think I was nothing but a game to her.

I immediately informed management of the incident, harboring some concerns she might accuse me of something. Predictably, management and HR didn't think a deathly-afraid women behaving in such a manner was of any consequence. I couldn't help thinking of what would've happened to me if I'd done the same thing to her.

Some months later, my tow-motor was stuck behind traffic close to Ruth's area. (I worked in Materials delivering parts to the assembly lines.) I heard a woman say, "Buddy, you shouldn't even stop here; you should just keep on moving."

"Are you speaking to me?" I asked. "You should…" She replied.

"Do you even know me?" I asked.

She turned to a woman beside Ruth and said, "Samantha, is this the man you're talking about?" Samantha turned away—in embarrassment, it seemed.

"Are you talking about me to people?" I asked Samantha. She claimed not to know what I was referring to.

Again, I told management what had happened, but the gossip didn't stop.

During the 18-month period between Ruth's allegation and my termination, two more women made allegations about me.

The second woman to complain was Melissa. I had known her two weeks; she was new to Materials but an employee for ten years. Our conversations were few but pleasant; we'd always wave when passing one another. The waves soon ceased. She wasn't open and friendly like before.

"Are you okay; is anything wrong?" I asked. "No, I'm just learning a new job and have to focus on it." At break she went to management to tell them she didn't want me ever to speak to her again.

After the break, a co-worker said, "Dave, what's goin' on, man?" "I don't know. What's going on?"

"I hear that Miller (Group Leader) was hauling all the women into a room and asking if they're being bothered or harassed by you," he said. I was furious. I unhooked my train and went looking for Miller. I found my manager instead. In a meeting room, he informed me of the latest complaint and I asked about the questioning of my female co-workers. "There's a perception about you out on the floor," he replied. I imagine speaking to all my female co-workers wouldn't help with that, would it?

I told him the gossip was originating from Assembly 2 (Ruth's line). Things got a little heated and I said, "I will not be treated like a criminal!" and stormed off. I went home in tears. It was wrong of me to leave.

A meeting was set for the following week. I feared for my job and was feeling intensely stressed. I decided to call my friend Gina, to tell her I wouldn't be at work for a few days. (A while back when I'd returned from short-term-disability, she had said, "I missed you" and "I didn't know where you went.")

 So I decided to phone her. We talked for about an hour and a half. In the course of our conversation, she politely excused herself to speak with the water softener repairman a few times. She also went upstairs to say something to her husband; I could hear a male voice other than the repairman. She said it was her husband. We laughed, joked and had a great conversation. She was in no hurry to end the call; I ended it.

I then called a male co-worker and talked with him for 15-minutes. I just wanted to talk to someone, anyone—for comfort.

Approximately 30 minutes later, I received a call from the regional police informing me that "The household" (Gina's) didn't want me to call them. At first I thought it was a joke because Gina is a practical joker. I asked the officer if it was Gina or her husband making the request.

"The Household…" was the reply.

I called Gina. I thought it had to be her husband upset we talked so long. We spoke for ten seconds. I said I was sorry "if I got you into trouble with your husband." "No Dave. Don't worry." She said.

I know. Dumb. I own it.

I called again the next day because I was in disbelief: we had just had a great conversation, and then I was supposed to believe she thought, "Oh, gee, I'd better call the cops on Dave now!" If I had known it was Gina behind it, I never would have phoned. This time the police showed up at my door. My parents were there, too. I knew now it was indeed Gina making the request. The constable explained that "Gina considers you a work friend; the conversation was very civil, polite and there was no animosity in the calls. But she doesn't want you to call her at home."

I never called her again. In retrospect, I believe Gina called the police because of something I had said in our phone conversation. I had told her that there was no good reason for Melissa to complain about me, that someone had to have told her about the harassment complaint by Ruth. Well, I am now certain that person was Gina. Melissa and Gina were/are good friends, but I didn't put it together then. Gina knew that calling the cops would be the final nail in my coffin at work. It would mean that she would never have to explain why she had been gossiping about me.

It's the only context in which calling the police makes any sense. Gina was too comfortable and knew me too well to legitimately fear me. She had to have had an ulterior motive. But whatever her motivations, her action just might be the most destructive thing ever done to me.

I was terminated two days later, told only that I had "failed to cease the harassing activities."

After applying for unemployment insurance, I was asked a few questions about my termination. At that point, I was able to learn more from the unemployment officers than from my own management. I learned that I was fired because of the Gina incident. Gina claimed she was alone with her children when I called (she was not). It was one of the things that bothered me so much about the whole process—that she could allege anything, entirely unchallenged. The company had no serious investigation process. My guilt was determined based on the unverified words of three accusers.

I know that I could have done some things better, and that my actions were at times unwise. But I did not harass anyone.

My accusers could have done things better also—yet they didn't pay any price for their false accusations.

Only one person pays.

**

Among the painful thoughts that linger is that I was honest throughout the whole affair. I trusted my employer and assumed management would conduct a professional, fair, ethical investigation. Consider how ridiculous my case would have been if a man accused a woman of my actions; he'd be laughed out of the room.

I think of my life in two sections: pre-and-post allegation. My life changed absolutely. My opinion of the world and of people changed. My ex-wife would tell you that I was happy, positive, and consistent every day before my firing. Depression was foreign to me. Now we're very well acquainted.

Of course, I realize that my situation is not unique. A teacher I know was recently accused of looking down the top (I think that's what it was) of a 16-year-old girl, a girl who was failing in her classes and very troubled. As a result of the accusation, the teacher had to go off work on a stress leave and have a stent put into his heart. He is ruined. I, too, had to go off due to stress.

A woman I've known most of my life works for the police. She told me about two officers who had a brief fling. After the relationship ended (he broke up with her), the woman began claiming sexual harassment, vandalism, and more. She claimed he was putting notes on her car, at her home and vandalizing the same. He was put on corrective action, of course. The complaints didn't stop. So the boys just happened to have video cameras around when notes and other things were put into her mailbox/on her car. BY HER!

She was fired. My friend described her as very attractive, great at her job, and on the fast track to promotion. These people often don't present as "freaks." They are believed.

Chapter 6 – Surviving the Tsunami of Second-Wave Feminism

Matt Ryan

The author outlines the effects of second-wave feminist assumptions and policies in the workplace and in intimate relationships, with a particular focus on sexual harassment versus sexual exploitation.

I was the first male feminist I knew.

University

It was the early 70s and I was in first year university in the Arts program. I was a bit of a shy guy and although I played rough sports and had an edge to my humor, I was on the gentle side. Accordingly, when I showed up for first year Arts and was introduced to feminism, which was just getting going, I agreed with a lot of what I perceived as its main points. I, too, found some guys too macho, too loud and too unwilling to admit a mistake. I agreed that women were not necessarily the best parent, and that some women were well suited for the workplace in traditionally male jobs. I was on board.

I went along with all this for about two years. Then some aspects of feminism became clearer. One big feminist push was for the right to make post-conception reproductive choices. There was also a push for men to perform half the housework and half the "parenting," the word then in vogue to replace mothering.

I waited in anticipation for feminists to articulate the principle of equality in reproductive choice and child custody and to enthusiastically fight for it. Forty-five years later, I'm still waiting. Instead, feminists fought for post-conception choice for the female sex only. On custodial equality, they were dead silent. It was, at best, an asymmetrical application of the equality concept.

Also disturbing was the extremely negative emotion coming from women's groups and many individual women, aimed at men. Even early on, the animus was so strong that any fair minded person would have had to describe it as hatred.

Workplace Harassment and Exploitation

Later in life, in the workplace, things were also asymmetrical. There was a push for rules against sexual harassment. That started out okay, if limited. The "okay" part was that bosses shouldn't extort sex from women who worked under them in exchange for a promotion or just to keep their jobs: no one could quarrel with that. However, the bad behavior I witnessed in my office wasn't primarily "sexual harassment," something for which a male boss would be to blame and the woman his unwilling victim, but rather "sexual exploitation," the use of sexuality for work-related personal gain, something typically driven by female employees (but for which the male boss is also at least partly responsible). I routinely saw more exploitation than harassment where I worked.

There are two reasons why exploitation is more common than harassment. First, one of the most natural things in the world is for young women to be attracted to men who have power and can do things for them. Back in the day when women working in an office would almost always be secretaries and almost never professionals, the goal of female flirtation would be to get a date or find a husband. Any favouritism shown by a male boss for a particular secretary would typically be short-lived and cause minimal harm. The relationship would either end altogether or result in marriage, which would lead the woman to leave the workplace in due course.

It is just as natural for men to be attracted to, well, attractive, fertile (young) women. This mutual attraction has helped humanity reach seven billion people and is not inherently bad.

However, in the context of the modern workplace, where a professional woman competing with other professionals can flirt, be highly feminine, or make other sexual displays in order to obtain a promotion rather than merely to get a date or a husband, something that is natural becomes problematic. When a woman uses her sexual attractiveness to advance professionally and to gain advantage over her colleagues, integrity and fairness are seriously damaged. In addition, an organization ends up with an unethical, often less capable person moving into decision-making positions.

The second reason why there is likely more—but let's settle for "at least as much" or even "some substantial amount of"—sexual exploitation *by* women than sexual harassment *of* women (by men), is that in the case of sexual exploitation, nobody directly involved in the exchange is likely going to complain about it. If a man harasses a particular woman, she is unhappy about it. On the other hand, if a woman exploits her sexuality with a particular man, he is likely to be pleased or even thrilled. Obviously she, as the main driver of the bad behavior, can't complain about her own bad behavior. And *he* is not going to complain. Often, it has seemed to me, men don't even quite realize what is going on.

There are a myriad of ways in which women can and some do exploit their sexuality. Any display of female vulnerability, from seeming helpless to expressing fear, will get a man on a woman's side. Being smiley and displaying feminine body language can be exploitative before the woman even begins to flirt through speech. I have been astonished to walk into a room full of women I know well when a powerful man was present: their faces were so soft with big smiles and their body language so feminine that at first glance I hardly recognized them. It's clear that sexual exploitation by women or girls doesn't necessarily require sexual intimacy, though that is not uncommon.

Therefore, one would expect more sexual exploitation than harassment because the former is based on the entirely natural mutual attraction of the sexes, particularly fertile young women and powerful older men, and because with sexual exploitation, unlike sexual harassment, both of the people involved enjoy the experience. Neither party to the transaction wants to complain. Both are to blame, although it is typically initiated by the woman.

However, to the best of my knowledge, no policy against sexual exploitation has ever been adopted, developed, or even contemplated. As a result, the greater workplace problem goes unaddressed. While this double standard (no formal prohibition against sex-related bad behavior driven by women) is, of course, problematic in its own right, the current focus on sexual harassment leaves the false impression that *only* men engage in inappropriate behavior related to sexuality in the office. That perception opens the door to stricter and stricter rules against typically male behavior and greater exemptions for female misconduct.

Specifically, the concept of "sexual harassment" has been expanded to include such things as a man without power (not a boss) asking a female co-worker for a date, or saying something of a sexual nature that may not even have been directed at the woman but that she happened to overhear. The effect on men is to make the workplace an often uncomfortable, even professionally dangerous, place.

Personal Experience

I've run into the over-application of the idea of sexual harassment more than once. As mentioned, I have an edgy sense of humor. At one point there was a secretary at my workplace who seemed to particularly enjoy engaging in banter with me that was unquestionably "over the top." One day a senior boss said to me, after he overheard one such exchange, "I worry about you two." I took his point: while he could tell that our exchange was mutual and light hearted, the friendly dynamic could change in a heartbeat and cause a problem for him as well as for someone like me.

I thought then that I should tone it down with her, so I did. A few weeks later she stopped by my office to ask why I had stopped bugging, bantering with, and teasing her. When I repeated the comment made by the big boss she replied, "Aw, I'll sign a waiver." So I figured I was on pretty safe ground, and we did have a ton of fun saying outrageous things to each other. Eventually, however, I managed to say something that did offend her. Unfortunately, instead of just telling me that I had finally gone too far, the imaginary "waiver" was revoked and she was building up a head of steam to report me. Fortunately, I have in general a reputation for being good to get along with, so someone intervened on my behalf and got her to drop the complaint before it got formal. I am certain it would have been no defence if I had said "Sure, the comment was over the top, but everything I said to her was over the top, and she had said she'd "sign a waiver.""

This incident destroyed my trust in her. In fairness, I admit that the particular comment was further over the line than usual, so calling me on it would have been fine, entirely reasonable. But with our history and rapport and her offer, you'd like to think that the first reaction would have been a warning, with no consideration of a formal complaint. Even to consider a formal complaint in such a situation, when she had explicitly encouraged me to engage in the banter, was unreasonable

And now I had a problem. I didn't really want to joke around with her anymore because the joy was gone now that I couldn't trust her. You'd think something that could or would amount to "harassment" under the expanded definition would have an expiry date for complaint. But instead, it was like murder: no statute of limitations. So now I had to find a way to stay on good terms with her without joking around. I'd built myself an ongoing task related solely to workplace survival. A smart guy would learn the obvious lesson and stay away from anything "jokey" with office females.

While it didn't relate to that particular incident, one of the secretaries went ballistic about how strict the harassment rules were against men. She was quite male-friendly and seemed to find most of the male professionals easier to work with than most of the women. She said— unfortunately only to us male line level (professional but not managerial) workers—"What are you guys supposed to do? Walk on eggshells around all the females, carrying a flip chart showing which of us will or will not be offended by this type or that type of comment?" She continued by saying that "These policies are making men uncomfortable around me, and that takes something from me. I don't like it." Hers seemed to be a minority opinion, however.

The "flip chart" comment brings another memory to mind. I was in the office working after hours and saw that one other fellow was still in the office. We were the only two single males there at the time. So I asked him, "Are you seeing anyone these days?" When he replied "No," I then asked "Are you at least in close contact with any females?" It was an allusion to sex, but it was in no way crude. Sadly, his answer again was "No." Just as we were discussing the second question and answer, a female co-worker walked around the corner. So, my male co-worker and I weren't the last two in the office after all. I instinctively and immediately stopped talking, lest she be offended by the topic. She walked past us, then turned back and said, "Your discussion doesn't offend me. Stopping it because of me, however, does offend me." So now men are in a classic double bind: there is no safe way to play it. I believe this woman was as male-friendly as she presented, but that doesn't alleviate the fact that some women will be offended by one thing and other women offended by the opposite thing—and that both might be called harassment or be "offensive."

I had an experience even milder than that, but again showing men's general difficulty in the modern office. A while ago, I worked with a secretary for a year while my regular secretary was away on maternity leave. The replacement secretary was in her late 20s, maybe early 30s. We got along well. She had naturally red hair with a complexion to match. After my secretary returned, my temporary secretary was now on the opposite side of the office. Consequently, I saw her surprisingly infrequently. A short while ago, I was walking toward the front desk and saw her talking to someone. Something caught my eye, so I looked at her a little closer. I was picking up that she looked different; she had died her hair blond. At this point I saw that she saw me looking at her. While my look wasn't a "stare," it was definitely longer than a "glance," so, in today's climate, I felt I had to explain myself lest she feel I was examining her in some inappropriate, however mild and fleeting, manner.

So I said, "You've dyed your hair." As soon as the words were out of my mouth I realized that I knew enough about most women not to make an observation like that and leave it at that, so I added, "Looks good." Well, the look of anger and offence that crossed her face was a sight to behold. I could see her thinking, "What right do *you* have to notice, much less comment on, how *I* look." To her credit, the anger lasted only a couple of moments and then passed from her face. She didn't say a word. I have no doubt she was thinking that she and I had worked in close contact for a year and got along fine, so she'd "let this one go."

We can see that having anything to do with women outside of work-related subjects can be a real trap for men. The only reason I looked at her beyond a glance is that my subconscious mind automatically focused on something different about her. So I looked a little longer. Feeling somehow "caught" looking, I then felt obliged to explain myself, which in turn led me to feel (with only a split second for decision making) that having noticed "change" and saying so, I simply *had* to make a positive comment about the change. The one funny part about the whole thing is that in a sense I lied: the change didn't look that good. She is a natural redhead whose complexion looks best by far with her natural red hair. While I've gone on about this incident, I want to convey the complexity and potential peril in *any* interaction with a female colleague. What should be a casual comment for which no thought is required can, in a heartbeat, morph into a minefield with serious consequences for the man.

On another occasion, I had one completely fabricated, more or less, actual complaint. I worked with a secretary who never seemed to get much done. She was almost universally loathed by the other secretaries for behaving like a "princess." Another male professional who worked with her described her as "not built for heavy typing." At one point she was underperforming so markedly that I simply had to say something to her, as it was affecting my productivity excessively. It happened that I had a colleague who would buy and read general circulation men's magazines, and often would then pass them on to me. Immediately after I commented on her lack of productivity, she complained to our director about the magazines in my office. It appeared to be blatant payback. I then had to get the colleague who gave them to me to go to our director and explain there was nothing untoward, they were general circulation magazines marketed to men.

But her larger point wasn't lost on me. I consulted with a male colleague who was assigned the same secretary. I described what had happened and asked for his analysis. He advised, "This is a warning shot. If you criticize her work again, she will escalate with a stronger complaint." I knew he was right.

I can't imagine any of the above events happening without feminism.

In addition, I have a close female friend and a close male friend who were unintentionally involved in a case of female sexual exploitation.

Male Friend Meets Sexual Exploitation

A number of years ago now, but in the age when there were already quite a few women in non-traditional positions, a friend of mine was a manager in a large corporation. He had to hire a new employee and settled on a young woman who looked good on paper and who presented adequately in the interview. Fortunately for him, the position being filled didn't directly report to him. Over the next four years or so, amazing things happened. She ended up in a "relationship" with each boss she worked with or sometimes with her boss's boss. Sometimes the men were single, sometimes married. She hopped across branches and even departments. Shortly after arriving in each new position, she began a sexual relationship with the most powerful (and willing) man around, and shortly after that she would receive a promotion. She was skyrocketing up the corporation. My friend said to me "She *will* make it to the top. It *will* be on her back. And I'm the fool who hired her."

Female Encounters Sexual Exploitation

More recently, a female friend I'll call Jane was pretty much fired, or at least let go, over her complaints about sexual exploitation by another woman in the workplace. She worked for a fairly large corporation where everyone, other than clerical staff, had a professional designation—with one rather dramatic exception. My friend and a co-worker of hers had to meet with two senior bosses, one of whom was a woman in the position of Assistant Vice President (AVP) of a division of the company. In the meeting the female boss, an attractive single woman in her late thirties or early forties, seemed to find reasons to touch the (married) male boss (who was also her boss) repeatedly during the meeting. Both Jane and her co-worker later commented to each other on how unprofessional it all was and how uncomfortable it was for them as unwilling observers. Jane asked her co-worker, "What did you think about that?" "That they should get a room," replied the co-worker, adding "or that they think they've already got one." While nearly all line workers were professionals, this woman had made AVP with a Grade 12 education. It was obvious what was going on. And most people, including people in positions of power, knew it.

This company had a policy of annual reviews of all employees and confidential annual reviews of the company by all employees. One year, Jane took the opportunity of the annual review to make the observation that "in a company full of professionals, one would think one would need more than a grade 12 education to become an AVP." The next year Jane's evaluation of the company was that "in this day and age when women have every opportunity to advance based on merit, it shouldn't be possible for a woman to sleep her way to the top." Unfortunately for Jane, that year brought a downsizing exercise, and Jane was let go. While she attributed her dismissal to her evaluation, she said to me "But those evaluations are *confidential*." Not *that* confidential, it would seem.

Sexual Exploitation in My Workplace

In my own area of work, a married woman who was good, solid, and competent as a line professional worker had an affair with a powerful man, also married, in the same organization. After they both left their spouses and became a couple, the woman received several, in fact an entire series, of somewhat surprising promotions until she landed near the very top of the organization. In the case of the first promotion, the position could reasonably have gone to her or to one or two other people. She was certainly an understandable choice, perhaps even the best choice. For the second promotion, she barely met the minimum qualifications, and there was at least one other candidate, pretty much universally viewed by secretaries and by other professionals, male and female alike, as head and shoulders above her. For the third promotion, it was difficult to see how she met minimum qualifications; for the fourth, impossible.

Sexual Harassment Claim Abuse

I have seen a woman abuse her sexual harassment complaint power. One such woman in my office was working with a man from another organization. When he told her that they needed to advance their work, intimating that he felt she was the one slowing things down, she complained about this "harassment." I have worked with this guy, and I don't like him—he's a jerk. However, a sexual harasser he is definitely not. And I note that my female colleague very carefully complained about "harassment," not "sexual harassment." The only thing "sexual" is the fact that he is of the opposite sex. When I worked with him he was unpleasant, too, but that's not a ground for a complaint about "harassment." What was really going on is that senior people in his organization were pressuring him to "get it done" and when he passed that pressure on to her, she reached for the weapon at hand. There was a big hullabaloo. Senior people from both organizations had to get involved, delaying the project even further. Yet somehow all this was an informal complaint, because my female colleague complained to me that the female sexual harassment investigator eventually said to her "Do you *really* want to make this a formal complaint?"

Could any of the described events happen without feminism?

True harassment, extorted sex, exists. We are all against it. Sexual exploitation also exists, and we should all be against it, too.

Personal Relationships

While the workplace issues are problematic enough, most men can't escape from feminism's influence even (or especially) at home.

I have in my family of origin one hotly feminist sister whose beliefs seem not to require facts and whose voice apparently isn't heard unless she shouts. She never stops talking and never listens, a fact that makes many family gatherings unpleasant. Currently, she seems to have bought into the "everything is rape" mantra—well, not really "everything," of course, just everything heterosexual and male. And while holding such extreme anti-male views, she has two sons and two grandsons—no daughters or granddaughters. Shouldn't she have at least a little understanding of and empathy for males? If there is no understanding in a woman in *her* position, what are the chances of finding broad-based reasonableness and fair-mindedness from women in the larger society who may not have sons or grandsons?

Still, one can avoid family-of-origin contact to some extent. But what about intimate relationships? Do they offer any escape from feminism?

Intimate Relationships

One need only look at the divorce rate of 40% in Canada and 50% in the US, with 70% of divorces initiated by wives and with mothers nearly always being awarded the kids, the house, and associated maintenance, to come to a conclusion about the wisdom of a man choosing marriage.

I can talk about my experiences.

A girlfriend in my university years, I'll call her Leslie, appeared to be a sweetheart, a "beautiful person inside and out," as one friend observed. It turned out not to be the case.

While we were at school, an article came out in the student newspaper about sex between professors and students. One interviewee complained that a professor had offered to raise her grades in exchange for sex: bad stuff, we all agreed. However, another co-ed indicated that often the female students were eagerly involved in such transactions, with the implication that they were approaching some professors with an offer of sex for higher grades. She said the insider lingo in the female student world was "a lay for an A." When my girlfriend and I discussed the article, I found it odd that she seemed to think the catch-phrase was cool. To make a long story short, I eventually discovered that she had indeed slept with a professor, a married man, with the intention of getting an A. However, she never did get the A from him. I was on good terms with a female professor in the same department and when I approached her to see if she could shed light on what had happened, she told me that the professor involved had something of a "reputation" for sleeping with female students, but also had a reputation for being "ethical" in the sense of not offering or providing grades in exchange for sex. So my then-girlfriend just *thought* she'd laid an A. As awful as it was to find myself in the situation of having a girlfriend who was not only unfaithful but who was willing to prostitute herself for academic advancement, I confess to feeling a certain satisfaction in knowing she had been "cheated" out of her A.

Later in life, my girlfriend Alice discovered that she was pregnant, and I learned what it was to be the man involved with an unplanned pregnancy.

First, I endured a roller-coaster ride about the abortion—one day she was keeping the child, the next day she was going to abort—which took a massive emotional toll on me. Of course, I had no say, no equal right to choose the destiny of our unborn child, because of being a man. When Alice got back from seeing her doctor the first time, with information on an abortion referral, she told me the doctor had told her that she'd have to wait a certain number of weeks before it would be advisable to have the abortion. She and I both understood this to mean that the fetus needed to get bigger for the abortion doctor to be certain to "get" all of it during the abortion. (This information was consistent with a terrible story told to me by a female friend who'd had an abortion—first an unsuccessful one, in which the abortion took only half of the fetus, requiring a second visit to finish it off.)

Both Alice and I felt angst about the being needing to grow bigger, to be more human, in order to ensure it could be effectively killed. After going back and forth almost daily, it seemed, with her indecision about whether or not to have the abortion, she finally decided to go through with it. However, she had left it so long that now the only option for the abortion was a Morgentaler clinic. I refused to participate in the abortion and didn't drive her to her appointment, which she then missed. Accordingly, I ended up with a wonder baby boy whom I'll call Mike.

Second, upon learning that she was pregnant, Alice's attitude changed almost instantly—for the worse. She became verbally abusive. On average, she was abusive at least once every day or two, sometimes several times a day. I won't bore the reader with the gory details, but I'll give an example that is on the milder end of what I received. I got reading glasses when I was 17, which is not uncommon. I never required them for driving but as I got older, I needed them to read small print. Every time I reached for my glasses or stood under a light, Alice would make a comment along the lines of what a "decrepit old man" I was. Anything I did might result in a demeaning comment.

This went on for the entire pregnancy and continued until Mike was two, at which point Alice moved out. She had used proximity to abuse me when we were together; now she used distance to abuse me when we were apart. Although I took a day off work to help her move, what she did next was to get an unlisted phone number and to move into an apartment block where the buzzer code was one's phone number—so I could neither call to see Mike nor show up and buzz her apartment. I didn't want to sneak into her apartment building, because custody of Mike was at issue at this point, and I didn't want to read "broke into the apartment block" in an affidavit. But I was beside myself, not seeing Mike. When I called my mother for advice, she counseled me, "Don't worry. This woman is too lazy to raise a child on her own. She'll come to you". And that is exactly what happened. I had been seeing Mike every day and now I didn't see him for two whole weeks. But after the two weeks, she called and wanted me to see Mike. While she did throw up other impediments to access over the years, for the most part I was able to see my son more regularly.

The worst part, though, was when she was moving out, when Mike was two. She knew that I thought I was a better parent than she was and would want custody of Mike. She dealt with that by telling me that if I sought custody of Mike, she would allege I'd molested him. I said to her "You know that's not true. I can't imagine what you would even say?" She replied "I'd say that when you stepped out of the shower and would go into the bedroom to dress, if Mike saw you go into the bedroom, he would walk in after you." She continued, "All it takes to destroy a man these days is an allegation—especially a man in your position."

One of the ironies of this is that just around the time this personal horror was unfolding, family law lawyers in Canada were commenting that a claim of sexual abuse was becoming "the weapon of choice" in child custody disputes. Feminists, however, were claiming that it was sexist to say that women were making false allegations: for feminists, the allegation of false allegations must itself be false, for no other reason than that the people allegedly making the false allegations were overwhelmingly women. In the feminist mind, being equals doesn't mean that males and females can do things equally vile as well as equally good. Instead women must always be seen as innocent victims and men as monsters.

After Mike turned 18 and she was no longer able to collect maintenance for him (unless he had sought higher education), his mother let him come live with me. Before that, as we were breaking up, I went to three family law lawyers to get advice on the chances of getting custody of Mike. They all gave the same advice: "You have no real chance because you are the dad." One who practiced exclusively in the family law area told me "Listen, you little idiot, don't even think about going for custody. If you do you will be her enemy instantly and her enemy forever. I don't want to tell you about the terrible things mothers often do to dads in those cases, because they're too awful.

Just know that if you try this, she will do terrible things to you and the system will do nothing to help you."

I also went to an expert in family conflict to see what his experience was in family court. Basically, he said the lawyers were *understating* the case. This expert said that dads almost never got custody unless the mom was so defective that her bad behavior put the child at "immediate risk of serious physical harm." Let's parse that statement, because he chose his words carefully. Serious emotional harm wouldn't be enough. Probable immediate minor physical harm wouldn't be enough. Foreseeable, but not immediate, serious physical harm wouldn't be enough. It had to be immediate risk of serious physical harm.

Conclusion

Most people would agree that women faced some real problems in the workplace, particularly in the early years when they moved into traditionally male jobs, and that it was right to address those problems. One could say that feminism insisted on these problems being addressed.

However, we've "over-solved" some issues (see sexual harassment, above), while down-playing or ignoring other issues caused by women in the workplace (see sexual exploitation above). That is to say, even in the workplace, men are not the only problem; women too can engage in bad behavior.

After doing a bit of good, feminism quickly went off the rails, vastly expanding the scope of sexual harassment while ignoring sexual exploitation by women.

A second problem, however, is that the workplace, traditionally a place where men's rights dominated, isn't the only place of gender inequality. In the home and family, traditionally a place where women's rights dominated, men's rights need a major upgrade, at minimum in areas of reproductive choice and child custody. Again, feminism missed the mark, calling for men to "take responsibility" for half the housework and parenting, while ignoring reproductive and custodial equality for men.

In this story, I've changed everyone's name, including mine, for two reasons. First, I don't want my son to know what his mother has done lest it affect his relationship with her. Second, I work in a particularly politically correct environment, and therefore need to keep my own identity under cover. A wise old male colleague counseled me long ago; "When it comes to equality issues, trust our female colleagues and co-workers not at all, our managers only slightly more."

Recall the boss I mentioned, the one who said "I worry about you two"? He was a politically correct guy with a hotly feminist wife, but he made a more general, more telling comment one time. Several of us, all male, were going down the elevator at work, heading to the main floor. On the way down, the elevator stopped and one woman got on. She got off before we reached the main floor. After she got off, he commented, "These days, just riding down the elevator, you don't want to see a woman get on." Even he could see it.

Did I mention: I am the first *former* male feminist I know. Contrary to the feminist slogan, I say, "*No one* should be a feminist."

Chapter 7 – A Conspiracy of Silence

Marginalizing Male Victims of Domestic Violence

Mal Maguire

The author explains how, as a man who was abused by his partner, his attempts to set up counselling and other support services for male victims of domestic violence were deliberately thwarted

It was a single, soul-crushing moment of disappointment.

The woman I'd been pouring my heart out to over an entire weekend was a domestic violence counselor. I was lucky to have met her not two weeks after leaving my girlfriend. Having endured a year of psychological, emotional and physical abuse, I was shaky, confused and in need of healing. So I went to a weekend Qi Gong retreat. On the first day we introduced ourselves; as soon as I heard her say that she was a DV counselor, I knew I had to talk to her.

She was very kind. Over the entire weekend, after the sessions were over, she spent hours listening to me, advising me, clarifying things for me and eventually telling me that after the intensity of what I'd been through, this was just the beginning of my healing journey and that it could be rough.

On the last day, I was so grateful, I must have thanked her half a dozen times and said I couldn't wait to come to her office and start my counseling. She suddenly looked at me as though she was about to tell me my puppy had been run over by a car.

"You can't," she said. "Though we're the only office that offers free counseling for victims of domestic violence, we only offer it to women and we rehabilitate men who use violence. I'm sorry. I'm afraid we have a lot of work to do to reach out to men like you."

I was shattered. I left her, feeling abandoned and hopeless.

Two months from then I had my first panic attack. I was haunted by nightmares, eviscerating pangs of sorrow, melancholy and intense anxiety. A tooth my girlfriend broke that was still in my mouth became infected and I had to have it pulled to stop a life-threatening case of sepsis. I fell into a depression and lost my will to live.

I was too ill to work and had run out of my savings. The only option I had to access the mental health system was to get a referral from Community Services. In order to do that, I had to have no fixed address, so I went into a homeless shelter and began the counseling process roiling in shame and feeling at the lowest point of my life.

If domestic violence counseling had been available for all victims of domestic violence, or if I had merely been born female, I would have received the counseling and support I needed at the time when the intervention was so acutely pressing.

Yet things started to come together. I did get assessed with PTSD, severe anxiety, depression and complicated grief. I was spending my nights sleeping among a roomful of drug addicts and men recently out of prison—a stressful experience. I was destitute and homeless. But I was on my way and determined to sort things out.

That's when I ran into Robert. Being homeless, you spend a lot of your day walking around the city, often hungry, so one day I walked into a local library and saw a huge spread of sandwiches and fruit in a conference room with people milling about. I surreptitiously entered and had a coffee—real coffee—which was like nectar. And as I was standing there with a piece of brie and a grape, a man came over.

"Hi, I'm Robert," he said with a huge smile. "Are you here for the group?" It turned out that he was leading a support group for male victims of sexual violence. I asked him if he would consider starting a group for male victims of domestic violence and he handed me his card. "Meet me next week and we'll talk about it."

As we began to discuss things, he said it had taken him ten years to get a sexual violence group on the go because the women who run the shelters for women were not amenable to the idea that male victims needed services, and there was a concern that any funding from the pool available would take away from the needs of women.

He cautioned that my idea would take a long time to materialize, and it did. For two years he spoke with his peers in social work, eventually had a conference with them, and then told me the time was right. We wrote a grant proposal to the Nova Scotia Mental Health Foundation in conjunction with a wonderful woman who was the director of a community house. Robert proposed that he would supply the counseling and the community house would provide the space. We had letters of support from various people in the community. To our utter joy, we received a grant of $6500 to start an education platform for human services providers and to begin the support group.

I had a feeling I can't describe. It was closure, I guess. I had turned a painful episode in my life into a positive change in society. After a traumatic experience and loss, you have to reconstruct meaning in your life. I had done so, and it felt great.

The director of the community house was moving on and passing the reins to another woman pretty much as soon as the grant came through. A couple of months went by, so I called to ask how things were going. The new director said I wasn't going to like what she had to say: that she didn't share the same vision as her predecessor and would not be following through with the support group. The cheque had been delivered to her organization, and she was hoping to use it for a community kitchen.

I couldn't talk her out of it. I tried to tell her how important the support group was and how much it was needed, and she just said it wasn't part of her interest and mandate. I felt as if a Napoleonic-era ship had just broadsided me. After all that work and all the people who put so much effort into it, one single individual who didn't feel she wanted to support male victims of domestic violence had killed our plan.

I don't know if the people who run the counseling service are feminists, and I don't know if this particular director was. But their policies reflected an almost psychopathic disregard for male people in pain. Here in this city of three hundred thousand, thirty four percent of all the calls Victim Services get about domestic violence are from men. That amounts to almost twelve hundred men a year. I thought back to the counselor at the retreat telling me that she couldn't help me. I couldn't stand the thought of another man going through that experience, being told there was nowhere for him to turn—and worse, knowing that there are people in our society who will actively destroy an effort to help men. I'm almost afraid to write this essay because I want to offer hope.

Reeling from the disappointment, I got in touch with a friend of mine who's also a counselor and he agreed to start a peer support group from the ground up. He got hold of a healing center to provide space.

But again there was a roadblock: the center got a complaint. Someone called and said they were uncomfortable with the idea of a support group for men because of the potential that it could be a hate group. Somewhere in that conversation there was, I am certain, talk of having a safe space for women. This is a center that hosts yoga and meditation groups. No one is safe from yoga.

I never imagined that feminists would be so violently opposed to the healing of men. If I ever had the chance to talk to any of these people, I'd tell them it's really not a good idea to have a bunch of wounded men in your town. Let them heal, support their healing and they'll be more peaceful, better contributors to society. They'll be better fathers, brothers, sons and boyfriends. No one, no matter who they are—male, female, gay, straight, transgender or gender fluid or whatever—is exempt from violence, and everyone has both the right and the need to heal.

More importantly, society as a whole must actively send the message that we all benefit from healthy citizens. We already have a damaging cultural narrative that men are the root cause of violence; it is unproductive, to say the least, to marginalize and potentially further damage the psyches of already deeply wounded men.

I cannot comprehend how any person who has ever felt marginalized could fail to empathize with any other suffering person. I can tell you from personal experience that men don't hold a monopoly on being violent. Nor do they hold a monopoly on perfidy and malevolence. I often wonder if there isn't some veracity to the idea a therapist friend of mine expressed about gender roles. Here it is: Men in the workplace, in social gatherings, etc., are subject to the expectation to fulfill a masculine role. Besides thousands of years of evolutionary conditioning, there's the exacerbating influence of pop culture images of the rugged individualist. Yet, have you ever heard a man pick up the phone and talk to his wife, girlfriend or daughter? All of a sudden his voice changes; it's softer, he'll be more expressive emotionally. Now picture that man at home, after a long day at work fulfilling that masculine role: often he is tender and cuddly, nurturing and loving. Why? Because he is a human being with all of these attributes and the need to express them in a safe place, free from criticism.

My friend's point was directed to women who commit domestic violence. In her daily public life, the woman usually fulfills a feminine role. She is kind, a good listener, gentle and non-violent. Where does she get the chance to express her more aggressive side, as a human being with all these attributes? Behind closed doors.

I believe there is some truth to this. It is often assumed that the vast majority of domestic violence is directed by men at women; however that is not the case. The truth, if you simply call a Victim Service office, is that the balance is closer to even. I can't tell you how many women I've talked to who have confessed to me that they've been emotionally or physically abusive.

Conversations between men and women are a huge factor in making change. I envision getting men and women who have experienced domestic violence together in a support group. But there are people who want to keep us separate, as though they are afraid something along the lines of empathy might develop. I also want to reach out to women who have expressed violence. There are almost no services available for them.

The vilification, shame and lack of services lead men to stay in violent intimate relationships longer than they would if there were services such as a helpline, a support group, and a shelter. The lack of these basic services leads directly to men suffering longer periods of exposure to psychological and physical violence.

If it wasn't for a transgender friend of mine who saw what was happening to me, came over to the house to keep me safe, and eventually got me out of my abusive relationship, I'd most likely be dead now. That one compassionate person became my helpline and my shelter. I was lucky. We've often talked about whether he'd have intervened earlier if I was female bodied and what would happen to him if he was in a violent relationship. Would he be welcome at a women's shelter? There are no shelters for men, but if there were, would he be welcome there?

I keep running into taboos. One day, when I was talking to a friend, a man who had experienced sexual violence, I told him that part of my healing was deeply moved forward when I began to explore forgiveness and my own agency in the relationship. He cautioned me that, according to the doctrine around dealing with domestic violence, there is no room for forgiveness or agency, as that would re-victimize the victim. However, a lot of research shows that forgiveness not only to oneself but to those who hurt you has a significant impact on mental and physical well-being. And self-awareness about one's participation in intimate partner violence can lead to change for the better.

The counselor I referred to at the beginning of this story told me that my healing would be rough, and she was right. Eighty four percent of all people in Canada who begin a therapeutic journey give up by session four. They may feel a short term sense of accomplishment and relief, but once the layers of hurt begin to surface, it becomes too much to bear and they give up. We really need to encourage men, who are generally reticent to express emotions, to engage in healing. I was lucky. The woman, Tamsyn, who wrote the grant with Robert, gave me free counseling for a year and a half, and that made a world of difference, but she's one in a million.

So I've decided to try to keep on making a difference.

I am working with a group of friends to make a documentary on the subject. These friends were with me throughout my journey. No one has ever done a full length documentary on the subject of male victims of domestic violence. I asked Robert if he thought it could make a difference and he said "What's the state of the conversation around male victims of domestic violence in Canada? Almost nil. When the pond is that still, that documentary will be like throwing a pebble into it. It could make a lot of ripples."

So that's the next part of the journey. Support has been minimal. There are no grants available for it, and three videographers have bailed on the project because they are afraid that if people in the arts community, which is heavily feminist, find out about the project, their careers will be ruined.

Yet I still have hope. Change comes slowly, but I focus on being persistent, not vilifying anyone, deconstructing the narratives of male and female victims, leveling the playing field and, most importantly, demonstrating that men and women can work together to solve the problem of domestic violence. I want to talk to experts in the fields around gender roles, psychology, neuroscience and sociology because there are so many questions to answer. Dr. Jeff Karabanow of Dalhousie's Social Work department studies fragility, vulnerability and luck in his work with transient, homeless youth and adults. One of the most profound things he said to me was, "It doesn't matter who we are or where we come from; all of us, every one of us, are a hair's breadth away from our lives falling apart given the wrong circumstances." But he also speaks of resilience and the power of someone being there for you in a crisis.

I want all of us to know that there are many people out there who don't have anyone or anything for them in their crises. It's common knowledge that men trying to fulfill a masculine role while being victimized by a woman will be quickly feminized by other men, disbelieved by many women, and potentially arrested even if they are the victims of a violent assault. We need to come together and help these people, and nothing in an ideology should get in the way of that. I would go so far as to say that the woman who derailed the work of both the social workers and myself is complicit in extending the pain and suffering of those who needed that help.

We can't solve this societal problem if we're only looking at one part of it and ignoring those who are suffering in silence.

Before it's violent, it's domestic. People need to remember that.

Chapter 8 – Militant Feminism in the Forces

A Military Officer

The author explains his concerns about the weakening of the armed forces by the perceived need to showcase women's achievements and welcome significant numbers of women into the military.

I am currently serving in the military with a 19 year career specializing in security and ground defense. I hold the rank of Sergeant. I am married with three sons and have served my country on operations overseas on many occasions. For the last seven years I have primarily been involved in the instruction of new recruits and officer cadet training. The skills and experience I gained throughout my career have made me an ideal candidate for this position, and I have seen countless recruits transformed under my guidance from civilians into well-drilled servicemen and servicewomen who have moved into life-long careers in the defense forces.

I was originally tasked with the goal of strengthening our recruit training unit. It had been observed by higher ranks that the current team needed an experienced supervisor willing to lead and coach the junior trainers. The junior trainers were to be coached to demonstrate greater commitment to the recruits and to bring the level of training up to a very high standard. I worked closely with six junior instructors at the rank of Corporal, three of whom were female.

When I first started, I observed that the level of enthusiasm and energy in the training unit was low. I also identified a need to improve the skills of the instructional staff in most areas of training. I put great effort into encouraging the team to produce an all-round higher professional environment and better quality of trainee. I received positive feedback from command for my efforts.

My dealings with subordinates have always been measured and professional. However, part way through my third year of leading the training unit, I observed that two of the three female instructors had become less receptive to my leadership. They were less inclined to communicate with me than formerly, and seemed to withdraw in general conversation. Although I never took their behaviors and attitudes personally, I regularly discussed these concerns with my superiors, fully expecting support, potentially leading to an open discussion with the two female Corporals at some stage to "clear the air" and move on.

Eventually, I was summoned to a meeting with my Officer Commanding (OC) and told that he was removing me from my role, effective immediately. He stated that his decision was based on personal complaints about me from the Corporals under my command by way of the chaplain. I later discovered that it was the two female Corporals who had complained. The specific details of their complaints were never revealed to me so that I could address their concerns in a restorative meeting, something I requested but was denied. I was stunned by the actions of my OC in being willing to let junior-ranked staff sideswipe me, especially since I had a proven track record of being transparent and professional in my duties. Other personnel around the base commented to me that they were also dismayed about the decision to remove me from my position, and that they felt bewildered by the steps my OC had taken. It is no exaggeration to say that what happened to me had a ripple effect throughout my peers, who expressed apprehension in dealing with their own subordinates in the future for fear of having similar complaints raised about them.

Later, it was revealed to me by some of my colleagues that the two Corporals had been overheard discussing how they could get rid of me. My role of supervising and setting a professional military training standard was causing them stress. They preferred to work in a more casual way with fewer obligations to the role in order to keep friendlier social hours and return to a more relaxed style of training.

It was also made clear by my OC that my damaged integrity and feelings of injustice were irrelevant to him, even as I appealed for disclosure in order for clarity. He felt compelled to treat the complaints as "the evidence," ever mindful of a cultural environment that is reluctant, in many instances, to hold female staff accountable for fear of accusations of insensitive leadership and discrimination. Such accusations can have serious consequences for one's military career.

Immediately following the accusations, I voluntarily took a two-week leave at home, spending most of the time depressed and disillusioned with the politics of the military. This became a particularly low point in my life as my self-esteem and confidence were shattered to the point that my personal relationships were adversely affected. However, after much soul searching and encouragement from friends and family, I returned to work, having been reassigned to training officer cadets, a role that kept me from coming into contact with the two female Corporals. This was my choice. Although I was expected to improve my leadership style, nothing more was discussed regarding the complaints and to this day I still have no idea what the details were. I was encouraged to shrug it off and carry on, showing up to work each day well aware that I had been the victim of female spite and, although innocent, had to continue my duties with a cloud of shame hanging over me.

At a meeting with the OC some time later, he praised me for "turning my situation around" and actually admitted (off the record) that he felt a high level of guilt over the irrational haste of his decision and acknowledged the unfair treatment. Despite this, I noticed that both Corporals were soon after promoted to Sergeant, which spoke volumes to me about the direction our defense force is taking under pro-female policies.

On a more recent occasion, during a routine inspection, when I instructed a female recruit to clean her dirty pack and boots, I was summoned for a dress-down meeting as my assertive tone had apparently upset the feelings of a recruit who decided to use her father's official role in the military to activate a complaint on her behalf. Normally this type of petty complaint would be ignored, as any experienced professional would be given "the benefit of the doubt" due to the nature of the role. Although I wasn't disciplined, I was nevertheless left with feelings of trepidation as to how I should behave in future with female recruits. My leadership style has never been a loudly barking Sergeant-major type (often portrayed in the movies) but rather a calm and rational coach and mentor who is firm but fair. I pride myself on treating every recruit equally. On this occasion, however, one of them felt that I had singled her out, even though I had given feedback to several of the female recruits during the same inspection. It was as if she felt that I had no right to point out her shortcomings within a communal living environment where efficient housekeeping is an absolute necessity for the effective running of a unit. I have observed over the years that this "sense of entitlement" to special treatment has been on the increase.

Having spoken to a number of male colleagues, I am aware of a growing trend that has male trainers and leaders feeling as if we are constantly walking on egg shells with regards to how we communicate with female personnel. There is an ever growing concern of being misunderstood, viewed as controlling or oppressive by those under our tutelage, who perhaps set out to undermine our authority due to the pressure we put on them to bring them up to a reasonable standard for military service. At other times, flirting and pity-pleading are used to test our boundaries, for which we have to take extra care in how we conduct ourselves, mindful of our total vulnerability to any accusation of harassment regardless of facts.

In a recent survey on bullying and harassment in the military, I was interviewed by an independent civilian researcher. I was asked if I felt there was any unfair bias or sexism in the forces. When I explained some of my own concerns and experiences, she openly laughed and mumbled "Cry me a river." She was literally only interested in bias/discrimination against women, not caused by women.

Very early in my career, it became evident that the policy of increasing female numbers in the military was a matter of high priority along with strongly enforced feminist ideals. I was once told by a female warrant officer that it was good to have young females joining the military, as it reflected women's ability to be equal to men in all areas.

Although not bothered by this remark at the time, I did point out the significantly reduced physical requirements and expectations for female recruits (55% fewer push-ups and extended time given to complete fully kitted marches). I also pointed out that when performing physical group tasks such as building sandbag reinforcing or erecting barbed wire fences, male personnel are expected to apply chivalry and take on the bulk of the manual labor, often carrying more than twice the weight of female personnel in order to ensure group success in a minimal time frame.

She then informed me that it was women's superior emotional intelligence that was unique and added value to our military. This remark became an absurd "truism" which also seems to be echoed by higher ranks, as we are often told by our commanders that the military needs to attract more women as our female numbers are too low and that women provide a unique skill set that we need to value. This view fits well with my own observations of female personnel who had actually shown less ability and aptitude in most areas during training being promoted ahead of and at a faster rate than more fully qualified male personnel.

Over the years, the military has adjusted to create a more comfortable environment for women at the expense, in my opinion, of combat effectiveness. It has indeed fully recognized them for their "higher emotional intelligence" and in turn catered to their demands at every opportunity. Some further examples follow.

More flexible hours granted. A career in the military requires commitment and is often demanding of personal time for which flexibility is essential to meet all obligations, yet there is an obvious trend with some female personnel to obtain an exemption because they are either unprepared or unwilling to meet the requirements. Where this would not normally be tolerated, a special dispensation such as reduced hours is given along with insulation from any future negative implications or repercussions further down the career track. Whilst the same opportunity is also provided for males, it is the females who take most advantage of these provisions.

Less restrained grooming requirements than men. Whereas it is essential for males to have short neat hair and clean shaven chin, women are given the freedom to choose long hair (half way down the back). Women may wear modest make up, color their hair and wear earrings. Males cannot.

Specially designed uniforms that cost more and cater to femininity, such as skirts and gender specific head dress, handbags, stockings, high heeled shoes and sandals.

Extra bathrooms, toilet buildings, and facilities specifically designed around female needs and to minimize privacy issues.

When on overseas deployments, personal feminine hygiene products now provided for by the Defence Force due to recent requests (It is noted that similar requests for basic disposable shaving gear for men while on deployment were denied and not considered the Defence Forces' responsibility to provide).

A team of people in full-time employment by the Defence Force to oversee gender equity, specifically focused on discrimination against women and to ensure that the feminist version of equality is adopted by all and adhered to at all times.

Frequent and ongoing compulsory training for all staff that teaches and promotes the female victim narrative and helps all males recognize their privilege while shaming males for the rape culture we have apparently created. (The use of supposedly "unbiased" statistics is often produced to hammer this message home.)

An exclusive women's development forum has been established where female personnel can collaborate, celebrate and discuss women's issues in the military in a secure non-threatening environment. (In contrast, no forum exists for the "less emotionally intelligent" gender as this would be deemed sexist.)

Women's service in the military is apparently cause for annual celebration. The military bestows a special anniversary to give credit to women's unique contributions throughout history—contributions, however, that are difficult to identify as unique and pale in comparison to the contributions of men who lost their lives by the thousands while showing outstanding leadership, bravery, and personal sacrifice. Women's contribution to warfare has been elevated to the same status as those in direct combat, again to appease the feminist agenda that demands a sense of equality to be portrayed.

Women are specifically selected for roles that place them in the media spotlight so as to push the Defence Force's diverse and inclusive image. Command positions on parades are given specifically to women for this purpose, and articles are regularly placed in our monthly magazine detailing the positive contributions made by women. As an example, on a recent trip to France where the Defence Force was parading units to commemorate WWII battles, certain key positions were only available to females, ironically given that no combat positions whatsoever were given to female soldiers during the Second World War.

In sum, society has encouraged young women to believe they can do anything. Young women regularly sign up for a military career with the mindset that they are special and have unique abilities that make them equal, if not superior, to men. In reality, many women fall short of meeting even the most basic requirements. From the obvious physical demands and in many cases the technical skills required to the overall commitment and self-discipline needed to become a true asset in the Defence Force, women's obvious shortcomings are frequently overlooked as we continue to usher them in using lopsided feminist-driven policies. We use scarce military resources to pander to their special needs and in most cases fail to hold them to the same standards as the men who serve, thus creating a false equality. What is happening is an application of the principle of equality of outcome rather than of equality of opportunity.

A recent example of special treatment given to women in the Defence Force occurred when I was required to train a flag bearer for an upcoming high profile parade. The bearer, who was selected by command, was a slightly built female officer. Due to the weight of the pike and flag, she was unable to carry out the drills during practice. I suggested that she spend some time practicing to build up the necessary muscle strength for the drills. She assured me she would do this; however, she became sick the next day and a male officer took over as flag bearer. I trained him for nearly two weeks and he performed very well in front of about 500 attendees and parade participants, receiving many accolades for his efforts. At the conclusion of the parade a superior asked me to start training another female officer who would be representing our service as flag bearer (for the same flag) in France for WW2 commemorations. I asked why the male officer could not serve in the role and was told that the position of flag bearer in France had to be female. I questioned why and was told that we need to represent the female population within our organization. Although I didn't say so, I thought to myself, why then aren't we representing diverse ethnicities, religions, and sexual orientations in the role also, as our military has quite the diverse population? It was clear to me that gender politics was alive and well.

At the beginning of this year, I was a member of a team of instructors for a six week Officer Induction course. There were over 100 students on the course, 31 of whom were female. There was nothing out of the ordinary about the course; we encountered the usual issues such as injuries, welfare, and disciplinary problems. About a week after the course ended, the latest issue of our monthly Defence Force magazine was published with a full page article titled "Women leading the way on #### Course." The article showcased the exploits of a number of the women on the course. From a professional standpoint, there was nothing noteworthy about their exploits. In a nutshell, 31 women had attended the course (a record number, in fact) and received top-notch training. There were plenty of quotes from the women expressing their reactions to the training. I was not alone in feeling rather bewildered about the headline. I and many of my colleagues felt that an agenda was being pushed that simply did not match reality. The reality was that the women on the course did not outperform, lead, or even stand out as any better or worse than the men. Reading the headline again, I could not help but interpret the subtext: "Look, boys, we are natural leaders who deserve special recognition." The article was yet another example of the drive for women to be placed at the forefront of our organization and to have their career path swept and weeded by the men who lay the foundation of the organization's very existence.

My fear is that when I retire in the near future, I am leaving a Defence Force that, although it has the responsibility of protecting our nation, is so concerned with being politically correct that it overlooks its specific function, a function that is not designed to be equally representative of the groups that live in our country but rather should represent only the strongest, fittest, and most skilled men and women we can produce through a totally level playing field. These men and women must have, above all, the distinct ability to defend the nation effectively should the need arise.

Appendix – Recommended Reading

Stephen Baskerville. *Taken into Custody: The War Against Fathers, Marriage, and the Family*. Nashville: Cumberland House, 2007.

Roy F. Baumeister. *Is There Anything Good About Men? How Cultures Flourish By Exploiting Men*. Oxford: Oxford University Press, 2010.

John Davis. *False Accusations of Rape: Lynching in the 21st Century*. Old Town Publishing, 2015.

Warren Farrell. *The Myth of Male Power: Why Men Are the Disposable Sex*. New York: Berkley Books, 1993.

Warren Farrell. *Why Men Earn More: The Startling Truth Behind the Pay Gap—and What Women Can Do About It*. New York: Amacom, 2005.

Tim Goldich. *Loving Men, Respecting Women: The Future of Gender Politics*. Chicago: Anima-Animus Publishing, 2011. Revised 2014.

Tom Golden. *Helping Mothers Be Closer to Their Sons: Understanding the Unique World of Boys*. Gaithersberg, MD: G.H. Publishing, 2016.

Christina Hoff Sommers. *The War Against Boys: How Misguided Policies Are Harming our Young Men*. New York: Simon & Schuster, 2000. Revised 2013.

Christina Hoff Sommers. *Who Stole Feminism? How Women Have Betrayed Women*. New York: Simon & Schuster, 1994.

Peter Lloyd. *Stand By Your Manhood: A Game-Changer for Modern Men*. London: Biteback Publishing, 2014.

Wendy McElroy. *Rape Culture Hysteria: Fixing the Damage Done to Men and Women*. Vulgus Press, 2016.

Paul Nathanson and Katherine K. Young. *Legalizing Misandry: From Public Shame to Systemic Discrimination Against Men*. Montreal & Kingston: McGill-Queen's University Press, 2006.

Daphne Patai. *Heterophobia: Sexual Harassment and the Future of Feminism*. Lanham, MD. Rowman and Littlefield Publishers, 1998.

Herbert Purdy. *Their Angry Creed: The Shocking History of Feminism, and How It Is Destroying Our Way of Life*. Ips Publishing, 2016.

Steven E. Rhoads. *Taking Sex Differences Seriously*. New York: Encounter Books, 2004.

David Shackleton. *The Hand That Rocks the World: An Inquiry into Truth, Power, and Gender*. Ottawa: Take2Now, 2015.

Helen Smith. *Men on Strike: Why Men Are Boycotting Marriage, Fatherhood, and the American Dream—and Why It Matters*. New York: Encounter Books, 2013.

David Thomas. *Not Guilty: The Case in Defense of Men.* New York: W. Morrow, 1993.

Author Bio

Janice Fiamengo, creator of the *Fiamengo File* YouTube series at Studio Brulé, is a writer, professor of English, and advocate for men's issues and free speech. She teaches literature at the University of Ottawa and is the author of *The Woman's Page* (2007), a study of early Canadian female journalists, as well as of numerous periodical essays and edited books. She has also published online articles criticizing feminism and political correctness in magazines such as *PJ Media* and *FrontPage*. She lives in the Thousand Islands region of Ontario with her husband; poet and songwriter David Solway.

Printed in Poland
by Amazon Fulfillment
Poland Sp. z o.o., Wrocław

84783126R00181